FOOD IN VOGUE

FOOD IN
VOGUE

FROM BOULESTIN
TO BOXER

Edited by Barbara Tims
Introduction by Arabella Boxer

PYRAMID BOOKS

Acknowledgments

Page 1: Tessa Traeger 1986
Page 2: Tessa Traeger 1987
Page 6: Tessa Traeger 1988
Page 8: Max Beerbohm 1905
Page 9: Charlie Stebbings 1984

Project Editor: Penny Summers
Art Editor: Jo Tapper
Production Controller:
Audrey Johnston
Designer: Behram Kapadia

First published 1988 by Pyramid Books
an imprint of the
Octopus Publishing Group
Michelin House
81 Fulham Road
London SW3 6RB

ISBN 1 871307 27 9

Printed in the United Kingdom
by Butler & Tanner Ltd,
Frome and London

NOTES ON METRICATION

In this book quantities are given in Imperial measures. Exact conversion from Imperial to metric measures does not usually give very convenient working quantities and it is therefore advisable to round off metric measures to units of 25 grams. The tables below give recommended equivalents.

Weights

Ounces/ Pounds	Approx grams to nearest whole figure	Recommended conversion
1 oz	28 g	25 g
2 oz	57 g	50 g
3 oz	85 g	75 g
4 oz	113 g	100 g
5 oz	142 g	150 g
6 oz	170 g	175 g
7 oz	198 g	200 g
8 oz	227 g	225 g
9 oz	255 g	250 g
10 oz	283 g	275 g
11 oz	312 g	300 g
12 oz	340 g	350 g
13 oz	368 g	375 g
14 oz	396 g	400 g
15 oz	425 g	425 g
1 lb	454 g	450 g
1¼ lb	567 g	575 g
1½ lb	680 g	675 g
1¾ lb	794 g	800 g
2 lb	907 g	900 g
2¼ lb	1 kg	1 kg

Note: When converting quantities over 2¼ lb, first add the appropriate figures in the centre column, then adjust to the nearest unit of 25.

This method of conversion gives good results in nearly all cases, although in certain cake recipes a more accurate conversion is necessary to produce a balanced recipe.

Liquid and volume measures

Millilitres/Litres	Fluid Ounces/Pints
1 teaspoon (5 ml)	1 teaspoon
1 tablespoon (15 ml)	1 tablespoon
1½ tablespoons	1½ tablespoons (1 fl oz)
2 tablespoons	2 tablespoons
3 tablespoons	3 tablespoons (2 fl oz)
4 tablespoons	4 tablespoons
5 tablespoons	5 tablespoons (3 fl oz)
6 tablespoons	6 tablespoons
120 ml	4 fl oz
150 ml	¼ pint (5 fl oz)
175 ml	6 fl oz
200 ml	⅓ pint
250 ml (¼ litre)	8 fl oz
300 ml	½ pint
325 ml	11 fl oz
350 ml	12 fl oz
400 ml	14 fl oz
450 ml	¾ pint
500 ml (½ litre)	18 fl oz
600 ml	1 pint (20 fl oz)
750 ml (¾ litre)	1¼ pints
900 ml	1½ pints
1 litre	1¾ pints
1.2 litres	2 pints

Oven temperature guide

	ELECTRICITY °C	°F	GAS MARK
VERY COOL	110	225	¼
	120	250	½
COOL	140	275	1
	150	300	2
MODERATE	160	325	3
	180	350	4
MODERATELY HOT	190	375	5
	200	400	6
HOT	220	425	7
	230	450	8
VERY HOT	240	475	9

CONTENTS

FOREWORD 7

INTRODUCTION 8

SOUPS 10

EGGS AND CHEESE 24

PÂTÉS AND PIES 38

FISH 50

MEAT 72

POULTRY AND GAME 94

SAUCES AND STUFFINGS 110

SALADS 122

VEGETABLES 138

PUDDINGS AND DESSERTS 160

CAKES, BISCUITS AND BREADS 174

INDEX 190

FOREWORD

In 1916 when British *Vogue* was first published there were four emperors and 15 kings reigning; Ottoman was an empire and the Czar enthroned in Russia. Neither penicillin nor antibiotics, neither computers nor organ replacement surgery had been envisaged. One soldier was dying every minute at the Front and the atom bomb had yet to be conceived.

A *Vogue* writer complained about the scarcity of servants and the dearth of coal, while confessing that it was a comfort not to have to keep up appearances. Dinner at Simpsons in the Strand cost 3s 6d (17½p) and included Sheep's Head Broth and Pupton of Pigeon.

Mr Iva S. V.-Patcévitch, Chairman and President of Condé Nast for 30 years, said of *Vogue*, 'It holds up a mirror to its time: a small mirror perhaps, but a singularly clear, brilliant and revealing one. Its purpose is not to reflect a vast panorama, an epoch or even a year, but a smaller segment of time.' In the 70 odd years that British *Vogue* has been published, many people, some professional and some amateur, some famous and some anonymous, have contributed words and pictures and ideas that have mirrored the life of the times. It would be impossible to acknowledge them all but apart from the cookery writers – most of whom Arabella Boxer pays tribute to in her introduction overleaf – it was the photographers and illustrators who put the visual icing on the well-prepared cake: the artists of the twenties from the *Gazette du Bon Ton* like Lepape, Marty and Brissaud; famous illustrators like Eric who used food as a fashion accessory; McKnight-Kauffer, whose posters for the London Underground are now collectors' items; Denton Welch and John Minton who illustrated *Vogue*'s Portfolio of Wartime Economies. There were also contributions by great artists: Picasso's plate, which appears on page 53; drawings by Toulouse-Lautrec, which were used in 1961 to coincide with his exhibition at the Tate Gallery; Erté's stylish vegetable costume designs for the theatre; and Alan Cracknell's witty contemporary drawings that illustrated Arabella Boxer's early cookery features. The photographers who approached food with such originality included Lester Bookbinder, whose surrealist attitude played with the laws of gravity, Tessa Traeger whose imagination took food into a new dimension, and Daniel Jouanneau of French *Vogue* who viewed cookery from a new angle, resulting in enhanced reality.

Both illustrations and recipes are reprinted as they first appeared in *Vogue* and readers may have to adapt some of the cooking times and quantities given in the recipes to suit their own needs. Metric conversion tables are included on page 4 to assist readers who are unfamiliar with Imperial measures.

BARBARA TIMS

INTRODUCTION

If I had been told, aged 17, that I should one day write for *Vogue*, I would have been totally amazed, and thrilled beyond my wildest dreams. Each year I entered their Talent Contest, but without success. It was not until I was over 30 that *Vogue* Editor Beatrix Miller asked me to take over from Robert Carrier as their regular food writer. Two years later I ran out of ideas and resigned, to be succeeded by Veronica Maclean. Then, seven years on, over lunch in San Lorenzo, Beatrix persuaded me to return to *Vogue* and I agreed, on condition that I could work with Tessa Traeger, who was already a *Vogue* photographer, and whose work I much admired. Today, 14 years later, Tessa and I still work together to produce the food pages each month, and occasional travel pieces.

Although I have been a faithful reader of *Vogue* since my mid-teens, I can't of course remember the very early days, or even the first food pages which started in 1923. This is my loss, for their first regular food writer was X. Marcel Boulestin, who I admire more than any other. He was a perfect choice to act as guide for the English housewife at that time, struggling to come to terms with post-war Britain, for his own experience of life was wide. It covered his French provincial background, literary life as a young man in Paris, and a career – albeit unsuccessful – as a decorator in fashionable London just before the outbreak of the First World War. He also understood about economy, for he had been at times on the verge of bankruptcy, before his culinary career took off in 1923 with the publication of his first cookbook. He was a regular contributor to *Vogue* from 1923 to 1929. It is hard to imagine now what the impact of those pieces must have been, with their nicely judged mixture of modesty, charm, and commonsense. Even now, his pieces remain as full of good things as a duck's egg – unlike the curate's egg, which was only good in parts.

After Boulestin came another food writer I admire, although few people seem to remember her name today. This was the American June Platt, who wrote regularly for *Vogue* from 1935 to 1940. The English had much to learn from the Americans at this time, for they had already adapted to such things as life without domestic help, and eating simpler meals – things we were not to learn for another ten or 15 years.

X. Marcel Boulestin

The war years inevitably cast their shadow over the food pages. Instead of recipes, we find photographs of society ladies 'down on the farm': Lady Diana Cooper feeding her pigs and Mrs John Betjeman milking her goat. With the end of the war in 1945, Doris Lytton-Toye took over as regular food writer. Mrs Lytton-Toye had run a cookery school with Marcel Boulestin before the war, and was well qualified to cope with the difficult post-war years: food rationing went on until 1954. She urged her readers to concentrate on simple dishes, and to discover for themselves the advantages of modern conveniences, from frozen food to pressure cookers.

For keen cooks like myself, the great event of the fifties was the coming of Elizabeth David to *Vogue* in 1956. This was perfect timing, in that two years after the end of rationing readers were longing to try their wings. For me, it also coincided with the year I got married, and started to cook *au serieux*. Elizabeth David had already published four books before coming to *Vogue*; her fifth, *French Provincial Cooking*, arose out of a series in *Vogue*, and was published in 1960. I still have a large cloth-bound book, made specially for the purpose, in which I kept all her pages: Food at its Best in January, etc., French Provincial Food, Italian Food, and French Food Markets, admirably photographed for the most part by Anthony Denney. Much has been written of Elizabeth David's writing, and her influence on her readers was enormous. Not only did she teach us how to cook, she also taught us how to live: to be courageous, and to set our aims high; to be demanding, and to refuse to be satisfied with anything less than the best.

Arabella Boxer

Sadly for us, Mrs David left in 1961, but her place was taken by the ebullient Robert Carrier, whose infectious enthusiasm for the good things of life also had its effect.

Together with Veronica Maclean, Pamela Harlech, and myself, these names make up the sum of regular *Vogue* food writers since *Vogue* began, but these have of course been supplemented by a host of talented and amusing characters. These include such sophisticated figures as Lady Colefax in the thirties, Mapie de Toulouse-Lautrec in the sixties, and Nathalie Hambro in the seventies. All had something to contribute, from Gentleman's Pudding (Lady Colefax) to Poulet Bamako (Nathalie Hambro).

For diverse reasons, this book has a special significance for me, in that it represents the sum of my ambitions, and acts as a record of many working friendships. To be included in an anthology with Boulestin, and to find my name linked with his in the title, is in itself a source of deep satisfaction. Then again, I find in the book a fragmented record of my partnership with Tessa Traeger, many of whose unique photographs have been included. The book itself has been scrupulously edited by Barbara Tims who, as Assistant Editor of the magazine, was for many years my own editor. It's true to say that *Vogue* has played a central role throughout my working life, and this I owe largely to my ex-husband Mark, who persuaded me to start writing in the first place, and who, as Editor-in-Chief of *Vogue*, became again my editor shortly before he died.

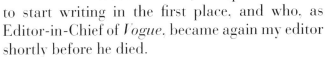

ARABELLA BOXER

SOUPS

'Soup is to a dinner what an overture is to an opera. It is not only the commencement of the feast, but should give an idea of what is to follow.' The famous chef Carême was able to concoct 300 different soups. Few can boast any such repertoire today, but there's still a wonderful variety, as the recipes in this chapter illustrate.

Soup is all too often the Cinderella of our meals, but, treated with a little more respect, it can be transformed into something special. Warm weather brings us iced consommé and chilled cucumber; then, with the first sharp air of autumn, soups become hotter and thicker, returning to the soil for their ingredients – onion soup and carrot soup.

Lord Curzon claimed that 'no gentleman has soup at luncheon' and Lady Astor refused to found her dinner 'on a lake'. It was left to the Mock Turtle to extol the virtues of 'Beautiful Soup, so rich and green, Waiting in a hot tureen'. Some hundred years later, Stephen Sondheim – admittedly describing airways food – wrote: 'The shiny stuff is tomatoes. The salad lies in a group. The curly stuff is potatoes. The stuff that moves is soup.'

Above: Douglas 1933
Opposite: von Alvensleben 1984

In the twenties, serious dinner parties started with a thick soup and a clear soup, followed by fish, an entrée, a roast, game or chicken, a sweet, a savoury, and finally a fruit. But by 1945 soups were viewed in a different light: 'such an admirable beginning to a meal; if it be Scotch Broth or Minestrone it may even be a meal in itself.'

As *Vogue* said in the early months of World War II: 'Canned foods are sure to play a big part in this winter's menus. It's well worth learning how to doll them up to the best advantage . . . a dash of something fresh, a flavouring of cream, or wine, may turn a pleasant dish into an exciting one. It's a shock to recognize at an elegant dinner-table the flavour one has so often turned out of the tin at home. Give your canned soups a cachet of your own. Add a spoonful of cream to tomato or asparagus soup – a dash of sherry to consommé. Stir an egg yolk and a little cream into smooth vegetable soup, and serve with grated cheese.'

Of course, tinned soups are still with us, but there is nothing to compare with the flavour of a delicious home-made soup – a hearty broth, fish chowder or creamy vegetable purée.

WATERCRESS AND POTATO SOUP

3lb potatoes
4 pts water
salt and pepper
2 bunches watercress
4 oz butter
2 egg yolks
1 cup cream

Peel and wash the potatoes and cut them up finely. Boil the water, add salt and the potatoes and cook until soft. In the meantime wash the cress, carefully cutting off the thick stems. Chop the leaves and add them to the potatoes with half the butter. Cook for 10 minutes and put through a sieve. Put the egg yolks in the bottom of a soup tureen and beat them well with a fork. Add the cream and pour slowly into this the hot potato and cress soup. Season to taste. Add the rest of the butter, stir and send to the table at once. Serves 8.

JUNE PLATT 1934

TOMATO SOUP

Melt 1 ounce of butter in a pan and, when it is hot, fry 1 ounce of lean ham, 1 large carrot and 1 onion in it for a few minutes. Add 1 pound of tomato pulp and pour in 1½ pints of medium veal stock. Cook until the vegetables are tender. Rub through a sieve and return to the pan. Season with salt and pepper and add a little sugar. Throw in 1 dessertspoon of pearl tapioca which has been soaked in water. Cook until the tapioca is clear and serve with fried snippets of bread.

ELEANOR BROUGHAM 1939

PEA SOUP

Boil 2 pounds of fresh peas and half their pods, together with some chopped cucumber, in 1 pint of beef stock. Season with ½ teaspoon each of salt and of

Douglas 1933

sugar and some sprigs of mint. When the pods are soft, pass the soup through a sieve. Reheat, if necessary, then stir in a little whipped cream and serve at once.

ELEANOR BROUGHAM 1939

APPLE SOUP

Take 6 or 8 large apples, peeled, cored and minced. Boil them to a mash in enough water to cover, with an equal amount of breadcrumbs, a sprinkling of cinnamon, a few drops of lemon juice (squash or essence may be substituted), 3 cloves and 3 or 4 peppercorns. Rub through a sieve and add 1 dessertspoon of white wine (cider or vinegar may be substituted). Sweeten slightly and add an extra cup of liquid if the soup is too thick; potato water, blended with a little cornflour, gives a rounded consistency. Return the soup to the pan and boil it up. Serve with chopped parsley, sippets, and grated cheese.
Note: Sippets or 'little sops' are small pieces of toasted or fried bread.

NELL HEATON 1943

BISQUE OF TOMATO AND GREEN PEA

Blend 1 tin of green pea soup and 1 of tomato soup in a saucepan; thin out to the consistency you like with scalded milk. Reheat gently. Season with freshly milled pepper, salt if necessary, and a good pinch of sugar. Beat in a nut of margarine. In each bowl, put 1 teaspoon of sherry and 1 teaspoon of top of the milk. Pour on the boiling soup and serve without stirring.

DORIS LYTTON-TOYE 1948

FRESH TOMATO BOUILLON

In 1 ounce of butter fry 1 medium carrot and 1 small onion, both diced, until golden; add 12 ounces of quartered tomatoes. Cook together gently until they fall to a pulp. Add 1 pint of white stock and ½ pint of tomato juice, a little salt, a few peppercorns, a pinch of sugar and a bouquet garni (parsley, thyme and half a bay leaf with half a clove of crushed garlic). Boil slowly for 10 minutes or so. Next, put in 1½ level tablespoons of the finest tapioca, which has been washed in a strainer under the cold water tap. Continue simmering for about 20 minutes, when the tapioca should have melted and also lightly thickened the bouillon. Pass through a fine strainer. Reheat and serve in cups (glass if you have them), garnished with a sprig of chervil. For 4 persons.

DORIS LYTTON-TOYE 1951

PUMPKIN SOUP

2 lb pumpkin
2 tomatoes
1 onion
2 pts hot milk, or good stock
knob of butter
salt and pepper

Peel the pumpkin, and cut it up small, with the tomatoes and onion, in a large saucepan. Do not add any liquid. Cook in a very slow oven for about 2 hours. When cooked, sieve the vegetables, add the milk or stock, butter and salt and pepper. Serve with small *croûtons*.

SHEILA DE BURLET 1956

BLENDER SPINACH SOUP

2 lb fresh spinach leaves, stalks removed
4 tbsp butter
salt and freshly ground black pepper
½ pt double cream
½ pt chicken stock

Wash the spinach leaves well in several changes of water and drain them well.

Put them in a thick-bottomed saucepan with butter, salt and black pepper to taste, and simmer, stirring, until tender.

Whisk the spinach in the blender or put it through a sieve. Adjust the seasoning if necessary. Combine the purée with the cream and chicken stock; heat and serve. Serves 4.

ROBERT CARRIER 1966

PEA AND CUCUMBER SOUP

1 small packet frozen peas
2 pts chicken consommé
4 tbsp butter
½ cucumber, peeled and seeded
2 egg yolks
¼ pt double cream
salt and freshly ground black pepper

Defrost the peas and simmer them in 2 tablespoons each of chicken consommé and butter until they are cooked. Drain, and purée them in a blender or push through a fine sieve. Cut the cucumber into matchstick-sized slivers; simmer in the remaining butter until tender.

Beat the egg yolks; add the cream and purée of peas. Heat the remaining chicken consommé. Stir in the purée mixture and cook over a gentle heat, stirring continuously, until the green-tinted soup is smooth and thick. Do not let the soup come to the boil or it will curdle. Just before serving, stir in the *julienne* of cucumber and add salt and black pepper to taste. Serves 4.

ROBERT CARRIER 1968

SORREL AND SPINACH SOUP

Put 2 handfuls of fresh sorrel, 6 handfuls of fresh spinach and 1 finely chopped onion in a large saucepan and cook in 2 ounces of butter until soft. Add salt and black pepper to taste. Stir in 1 heaped tablespoon of flour and add 2 pints of chicken stock (preferably homemade). If the soup is too thick add more spinach. Bring it to the boil, then put in a blender and blend roughly. Put the soup back in the saucepan, add 2 tablespoons of grated horseradish (not horseradish sauce) and Worcestershire sauce to taste. Reheat and serve with cream.

GAYLE HUNNICUTT 1974

Erté 1926

FRENCH ONION SOUP

A much-published soup in *Vogue* – five different versions are given here, including two from Doris Lytton-Toye.

LEONE B. MOATS 1921

2 pts strong beef or chicken stock
½ lb onions
2 tbsp butter
1 tbsp olive oil
salt and pepper
4 slices of buttered, dried bread
4 heaped tbsp Parmesan cheese

Heat the stock in a double boiler. While it is heating, sauté the onions, which have been sliced into half moons, in butter and oil. When they are a citron colour and almost transparent, put them in the double boiler with the stock. Cook the onions in the stock until very, very tender. Add seasoning, and then ladle the onions into the waiting casseroles, pouring in as much of the stock as each casserole will hold. On top of each, place a slice of buttered bread, with a tablespoon of Parmesan cheese on top. Place in the oven until the cheese is brown and serve piping hot in the same casseroles. Serves 4.

BOULESTIN 1923

Get some large white onions and slice them thinly; melt some butter in a pan, and cook them till they are a nice brown colour. Then add a pinch of flour, a teaspoonful of beef stock, salt and pepper and sufficient water. Stir well, bring to the boil, and let it simmer till reduced by a quarter – that is to say, about twenty minutes.

Meanwhile, cut some thin slices of French bread, the long roll kind being the best, and dry them till very crisp in the oven. Now pour your onion soup into

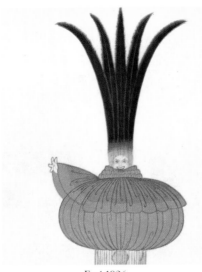

Erté 1926

little earthenware soup tureens, one for each person; put two or three pieces of dried bread on the top of each, sprinkle freely with grated cheese (Gruyère preferably), and put them in the oven till melted and golden.

CONSTANCE SPRY 1943

2 oz margarine
2 large onions, sliced
a short oz of flour
3 pts water
½ pt milk
salt and pepper
1 small round of toast for each person
3 tbsp grated cheese

Heat the margarine, add the sliced onion, and cook till it is soft and yellow. Sprinkle in the flour and stir till pale gold. Add the liquid gradually, bring it to the boil and simmer for 10 minutes. Season to taste. Pour into a casserole and lay slices of toast on top. Sprinkle with cheese and a dot of margarine and brown under the grill. Alternatively, toast and cheese can be put in the tureen first, and the soup poured over.

DORIS LYTTON-TOYE 1946

Slice the onions very finely; melt a good piece of fat or margarine in the pan. Put in the onions and cook over a fast flame till they take colour. Add a good pinch of flour, salt, pepper and cover with water. Bring to the boil and boil for several minutes. Dry some thinly cut bread in the oven. Put the bread in the soup tureen and pour the soup over it. Serve with plenty of grated cheese.

DORIS LYTTON-TOYE 1948

A pressure cooker recipe

Slice thinly 5-6 medium onions. Heat the pressure cooker and put in 1 ounce of margarine; when it melts, fry the onions gently until they are translucent and golden, but not burnt. Burnt onion gives the soup a bitter flavour. Season with a good dash of salt, pepper from the mill and a *soupçon* of sugar. Pour on 2 pints of beef, veal or chicken bone stock (not mutton) at boiling point. Cover the pan and allow it to reach pressure point; reduce the heat and cook at pressure for 5 minutes. Blend 2 eggs with 2½ fluid ounces of thin cream and pour into a tureen. Cool the soup by immersing the pan in cold water, but ensure that the pressure has subsided before removing the lid. Bring the soup to boiling point again in the open pan. Pour it on to the eggs and cream in the soup tureen, give a rapid stir and correct the seasoning. Strew grated cheese as liberally as you can allow over the surface. Serve at once. Alternatively, to serve it in the cooker itself, pour a little boiling soup on the liaison of cream and egg, then return the creamy mixture to the cooker. On no account should it boil again.

SOUPE AU POISSON

Most people usually associate the fish soup either with Marseilles or with America: indeed both the 'bouillabaisse' and the 'chowder' are well known and remarkably good when well prepared. But I came across some quite good fish soup at Boulogne last autumn during the famous 'fish week', and I tasted a very pleasant one only the other day in a small village near Dinard. Needless to say, these dishes never appear on the menu of even the smallest hotel, probably because the patron thinks, rightly or wrongly, that they are not civilized enough for visitors. As a matter of fact, the food the patron and his wife have on a corner of the kitchen table is often better than the more elaborate dishes which are sent to the *table d'hôte*.

The fish soup, which is very popular with Breton fishermen, is simple to make and very pleasant. It is very different from the Provençal dish of the same type as no oil is used for the cooking and it does not contain crab, saffron, tomato or any of the ingredients which give the 'bouillabaisse' its special flavour. You simply chop very fine and brown well in a good piece of the best butter what the Bretons call *les herbes*, that is, spring onions and sorrel (about a handful), one carrot, one potato, a little parsley, chives and (unexpectedly) mint. Add salt and pepper and boiling water; bring to the boil, put in some fish (it does not matter very much which as long as it is not a flat fish) and cook about twenty minutes. They eat this with bread and boiled potatoes, and as the man said all too modestly, *'Ca aide à faire passer le pain'*.

For a more civilized table, it would of course be better to pass it through a sieve, and remove the skin and bones of the fish before serving, but *les herbes* should be served with the pieces of fish.

BOULESTIN 1924

Erté 1926

NEW ENGLAND FISH CHOWDER

Ask the fishmonger to clean a nice fresh cod or haddock weighing about 4 pounds. Get him to skin it and remove the fillets and cut them in 2-inch slices. Be sure that he gives you the head and tail, bones and skin: put these in an enamel pan and pour over them 3 cups of cold water. Bring slowly to simmering point and simmer gently for 30 minutes.

In the meantime, peel and finely dice 3 white potatoes. Now put ½ pound of salt pork, cut in tiny little squares, in the bottom of a large enamel pan and cook it very slowly to draw out the fat. When it begins to colour, add 3 onions, very thinly sliced, and cook them without browning until tender. When the fish stock is ready, sprinkle the onions with 2 scant tablespoons of flour and stir well. Gradually add the hot fish stock, strained. Then add the fish and potatoes in alternate layers, season lightly and simmer very slowly for 30 minutes.

When cooked and ready to serve, add 2 pints of very rich hot milk in which you have melted a big lump of butter. Do not let the soup boil once the milk has been added. Serve at once in a big soup tureen, accompanied by toasted crackers. Serves 6.

1938

SHRIMP SOUP

2 cups cooked and shelled shrimps
1 small onion, grated
3 tbsp butter
½ tbsp flour
salt and pepper
2 pts milk
½ cup cream
¼ cup sherry
grated nutmeg

Put the shrimps through the meat grinder. Simmer the onion in ½ tablespoon butter for 5 minutes. Melt the remaining butter in a pan and add the flour, stirring until smooth. Add the shrimps, salt and pepper. Pour on the milk and cream gradually. Stir until the mixture begins to thicken. Cook over hot water for 30 minutes, stirring occasionally. Add the sherry and nutmeg just before serving; do not allow the soup to cool.

1938

GREEK FISH SOUP

Fish soup, as they make it in Greece, is excellent and unusual. Take the trimmings of any fish – heads, tails, fins, skins – and place in a saucepan with enough cold water to cover. Boil gently with 1 onion, a little parsley, celery, and a bay leaf.

Simmer till the flesh leaves the bones, then strain and measure. Return the stock to the saucepan, and to every pint allow 2 tablespoons of uncooked rice. Season with salt and pepper, and boil till the rice is tender. Beat 2 eggs, and add to them the juice of 1 large or 2 small lemons. Just before serving, lift the fish stock off the fire, and slowly add to it the eggs and lemon, stirring continuously. Cook very gently until the soup is the consistency of thin cream, and serve immediately. This soup will not keep hot, as the eggs will curdle, and it must not boil after they are added to the stock.

1939

> **'Classic bouquet garni: a stalk of parsley, a bay leaf and a sprig of thyme tied in a muslin bag to flavour sauces, soups and stews.'**

CREAM PRAWN SOUP

60 prawns
1 pt milk (more if necessary)
1 tbsp butter
2 pts meat stock
1 tbsp flour
salt and pepper
¼ pt sour cream
2 egg yolks
1 tbsp chopped chives
BOUILLON
3 pts water
1 pt vinegar
salt and pepper
1 onion, shredded
1 carrot, shredded
1 tbsp chopped thyme
1 tbsp pearl barley
1 sprig parsley

Place the washed but unshelled prawns in a bowl with enough milk to cover them and soak for 2 hours. Drain them and discard the milk. Mix together the ingredients for the bouillon in a saucepan and bring to the boil; throw in the prawns, and simmer until they are pink. Drain. Remove and discard the legs. Pick the meat from the shells and set aside. Pound the shells in a mortar (yes, really), and mix them with the butter. Rub the butter through a sieve.

Mix the bouillon with the meat stock. Stir in the flour, salt and pepper, and add the prawn butter made from the shells. Stir in the prawn meat. Simmer without boiling. Add the sour cream, egg yolks and chives just before serving.

1939

NORWEGIAN FISH SOUP

Cut 2 pounds of cod, hake or fresh haddock into pieces. Place in a pan with 3½ pints of water, a little salt, a few peppercorns and a bay leaf. Bring to the boil, then simmer for 1-1½ hours. Strain.

Melt 1½ ounces of margarine in a pan. Add 1½ ounces of flour and cook for a few minutes. Add the fish liquor gradually. When it is boiling, season and flavour to taste with a little sherry or Marsala. Some of the fish, sieved, can be put in to thicken the soup to a cream. Alternatively, flaked fish may be added.

DORIS LYTTON-TOYE 1947

LA BOUILLABAISSE

1 large onion
olive oil
3 large tomatoes
2 cloves garlic
salt and pepper
½ lb red mullet
12 oz lobster meat
½ lb sole
12 oz halibut
½ lb conger eel
2-3 tbsp freshly chopped parsley
2-3 threads saffron
2 bay leaves
1 sprig fennel
12 slices French bread

Mince the onion and fry it until light golden in olive oil. Add the peeled and chopped tomatoes and 1 clove of garlic, crushed with salt. When the tomatoes are well cooked, add all the fish (cut into large pieces), the chopped parsley, saffron, bay leaves, fennel and 2 dessertspoons of olive oil. Cover with water, add salt and pepper to taste and cook rapidly for 15 minutes. Fry the slices of bread in olive oil and rub them with the remaining clove of garlic, cut in half. Arrange the bread in a large terrine and pour over the soup.

PETER PIRBRIGHT AND GRETEL BEER 1950

MARYLAND CRAB SOUP

1 tbsp flour
2 tbsp melted butter
4 cups milk
1 stick celery, chopped
1 small onion, minced
1 tbsp chopped parsley
salt and pepper
2 cups crab meat
½ cup thick cream
paprika or chopped parsley to garnish

Stir the flour into the melted butter in a saucepan until smooth. Blend in the milk and add the celery. onion. parsley and salt and pepper to taste. Stir until it thickens. then cook for a further 15 minutes. Strain the sauce through a piece of muslin. return it to the pan and add the crab meat. Heat and add the thick cream. Stir well. but do not let it boil. Garnish with paprika or parsley.

MARIUS DUTREY 1955

SOUPE AUX MOULES

4 quarts mussels
2 onions, chopped
2 bay leaves
4 sprigs parsley
5 oz butter
1 pt white wine
salt and pepper
2 egg yolks
½ pt cream
a handful of chopped fresh chervil to garnish

Scrub and wash the mussels. Put them in a large pan with the onions. bay leaves. parsley. butter. wine. salt and pepper. Cover the pan and cook until the mussels open. Take them out of their shells and strain the stock.

Whisk the egg yolks into the cream and. off the stove. add this liaison to the mussel stock. Just before serving. put the mussels into the soup and heat it up slowly. but do not let it boil. Scatter the chervil over it.

MAPIE DE TOULOUSE-LAUTREC 1961

Tessa Traeger 1987

PRAWN BISQUE

½ lb cooked prawns
¼ pt tinned clam juice (more if necessary)
¾ pt double cream
¼ tsp paprika
salt and freshly ground black pepper
4-6 tbsp dry sherry
1 tbsp finely chopped parsley
1 tbsp finely chopped chives

Place the cooked prawns (saving one or two for garnish) and clam juice in an electric blender. and blend for 1 minute. Remove to the top of a double saucepan. add the cream and paprika. and season to taste with salt and pepper. Cook over hot water. stirring from time to time. until the soup comes to the boil. Thin to taste with additional clam juice. Add the sherry. and serve immediately in individual cups. garnished with chopped prawns and finely chopped parsley and chives. Serves 4 to 6.

ROBERT CARRIER 1966

POTAGE RUBIS

Chop finely 1 small onion; cook it gently in a covered pan with ½ ounce of margarine. When the onion is translucent, add 3 small cooked beetroot, grated, and sauté these together for 1 minute. Put in a piece of bay leaf, a sprig of thyme, salt and pepper, 1½ pints of boiling water, 2 or 3 bacon rinds and a pea of Marmite. Bring to the boil and simmer for 15 minutes. Slake 1 level tablespoon of arrowroot in a little water, pour it into the soup and cook till it is clear. Strain the soup into a bowl, and stir in just enough vinegar or lemon juice to sharpen it delicately. Add a pinch of sugar. Cool the soup completely and remove any fat. Freshen up the colour by the addition of some extra beetroot juice. Chill well before serving and garnish each bowl with a little freshly chopped parsley or a thin slice of lemon. *Note:* Iced cream soups, such as green pea or tomato, are made by adding the

Hamerschlag 1937

cooked purée to a béchamel sauce. This type of soup should just veil the back of the spoon at boiling point; they thicken up as they cool.

DORIS LYTTON-TOYE 1947

GAZPACHO

¾ pt water
¾ pt tomato juice
¾ oz aspic jelly
½ tsp Tabasco
paprika
¼ cucumber
12 oz tomatoes
4 oz green peppers
4 oz onions
¼ pt vinegar
¼ pt olive oil

Heat, but do not boil, the water and tomato juice, and add the dissolved aspic jelly, Tabasco and paprika pepper. Set aside to cool, then leave to chill in the refrigerator.

Peel and remove the pips from the cucumber, tomatoes and green peppers and dice them. Finely chop the onions. Marinate the vegetables in vinegar and oil overnight, and before serving add the chilled stock. Serve cold. Serves 6.

ELIZABETH KENDALL 1966

VICHYSSOISE

Doris Lytton-Toye said 'This is best as a very cold summer soup but it is also excellent hot. June Platt, over a decade earlier, considered it a hot soup 'equally good served cold . Hers is very rich.

JUNE PLATT 1935

12 hearts of leeks (white part only)
4 white onions
1 lb unsalted butter
8 pts chicken consommé
2 lb white potatoes
salt and pepper
2 pts cream

Split the leeks down the centre and wash them thoroughly. Peel the onions. Chop the leeks and onions very finely. Melt half the butter in an enamel pan and cook the leeks and onions very, very slowly, adding a few spoons of water, if necessary, to keep them from browning. Then add the chicken consommé and potatoes, which have been peeled and cut up very finely. Add salt and pepper and cook until the potatoes are thoroughly done. Put the soup through a very fine sieve. Add the remaining butter and stir until melted. When ready to serve, add the cream and heat in a double boiler. Never let it boil, once the cream has been added. If the soup is to be served cold, use a few less potatoes.

DORIS LYTTON-TOYE 1949

Cut away and discard the green part of 3 large leeks. Trim and wash the leeks upside down under the cold tap. (Splitting them lengthwise, but not quite through, helps to extract any lurking grit.) Slice them finely. Slice also 1 medium onion and 1 stalk of celery. Melt 1 ounce of margarine in a large pan and put in the leeks, onion and celery. Cover the pan and permit them to become tender over a low flame. Shake the pan occasionally, and add 3 large peeled potatoes, finely sliced, 1 pint of boiling water and a pinch of salt. Simmer, covered, until the vegetables are perfectly soft. Sieve or pass the soup through a fine strainer. Return it to the pan and thin it out with ¾ pint of light stock, preferably chicken, then simmer awhile and skim well. Season to your liking, and finish the soup with a breakfast cup of evaporated milk and some chopped chives or watercress.

SUMMER TOMATO SOUP WITH BASIL

2 lb tomatoes (about 16)
3 oz butter
1 bay leaf
salt and pepper
fresh basil leaves
½ pt single cream
½ cucumber

Skin the tomatoes and cut them up. Cook them in butter with the bay leaf very slowly for about 10 minutes until they are soft and mushy. Add salt and pepper. Put through a sieve into a bowl. Chop up the fresh basil and add it to the tomatoes. Mix in the cream and grate in the cucumber, skin and all. Serve very cold with poppadums.

KIRSTY MORLEY 1973

SPITALFIELD SOUP

½ lb leeks
2 oz butter
½ lb potatoes
½ lb cauliflower
1½ pts light chicken stock, heated
4 oz small carrots
2 bunches spring onions, bulbs only
4 oz shelled peas, fresh or frozen
⅓ pt single cream
sea salt and black pepper
3 tbsp chopped chervil or dill, or 1½ tbsp each
chopped parsley and chives

Slice the leeks and cook them gently in the butter for 5 minutes. Add the peeled and sliced potatoes and the cauliflower, coarsely chopped. Stir around for 1-2 minutes, then pour on 1 pint of the heated stock. Bring to the boil, cover and simmer for 30 minutes. While this is cooking, put the remaining ½ pint of stock in a small pan with the thinly sliced carrots; bring to the boil and cook for 5 minutes. Add the spring onions and the peas, and cook for another 5 minutes. Set aside.

When the first part of the soup has finished cooking, cool for 5 minutes, then purée in a food processor, adding the cream. Return to the clean saucepan and add the contents of the smaller pan. Reheat, stirring, and add salt and pepper to taste. Finally, stir in the chopped herbs, then cool and chill for several hours. Serve in small cups. Serves 6.
Note: This soup is also very good served hot, if preferred.

ARABELLA BOXER 1983

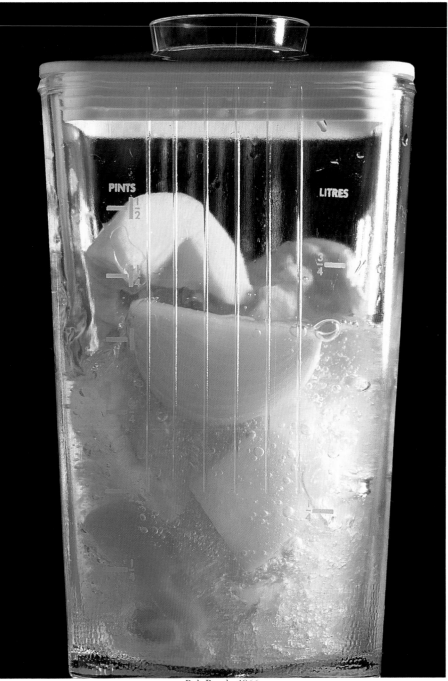
Bob Brooks 1966

PURÉE DE CIBOURE

This soup, which is of the 'rustic' kind, is much appreciated by the inhabitants of the Basque country; it is seldom made in the other parts of France.

Soak some haricot beans for twelve hours (if they are dry ones) and put them in salted water with an equal quantity of potatoes. Chop together finely two shallots, two heads of garlic, olives and two leeks. Bring everything to the boil together and cook for at least three hours on a moderate fire. Pass through a sieve, add a little beefstock, a good deal of freshly ground pepper, and just before serving, if you like, the yolk of one egg. This soup should be neither too thick nor too clear. It tastes pleasant.

BOULESTIN 1923

SOUPE DE CHASSE

This is a very good and useful soup, usually served in the east of France to men before starting on a shooting expedition. Put in a saucepan three or four onions, finely chopped, with a piece of butter the size of an egg. Melt the onions over a slow fire but do not let them get brown.

Add water (enough for five or six people, allowing a little more for reducing), bring to the boil, then put in one leek, a head of celery, parsley, thyme, bay leaf, a few cloves and a little garlic, salt and pepper, also a pinch of sugar; let it boil gently for at least two hours.

Cut thin slices of stale bread, fry them in butter, and dispose them two or three deep in a warm soup tureen. Take a tablespoonful of potato flour, add to it a small quantity of good stock, mix well and see that it is smooth. To this you add, stirring quickly, the yolks of three eggs; mix well again and pour this into the soup, stir once more and pour the finished mixture over the bread in the soup tureen. Serve at once.

BOULESTIN 1928

PETITE MARMITE

Take a clear consommé and add to it cooked peas, string beans, onions and some finely chopped pieces of breast of chicken. Pour into individual earthenware casseroles and place in each 2 of the thinnest slices of French bread (crust and all); sprinkle with Parmesan and place in the oven for 2 minutes.

LEONE B. MOATS 1934

BEEF BROTH WITH CABBAGE TOASTS AND CHEESE

½ small cabbage
salt and pepper
8 bread rolls
4 oz butter
1 cup grated Parmesan cheese
4 pts beef broth
finely chopped parsley

Shred the tender part of a green cabbage very finely. Boil some water and add the washed, shredded cabbage and salt to taste. Cook for 5 minutes, then drain thoroughly. The cabbage should be tender and green, not soft and mushy.

Slice the rolls thinly and toast them to a delicate brown. Butter them well, pile a little cabbage neatly on each and sprinkle liberally with cheese. Put a tiny piece of butter on top of each one and set under the grill until the cheese and butter have melted together to a light brown. In the meantime, heat the beef broth to boiling point. Season to taste with salt and pepper. Pour it into a hot tureen and sprinkle with a little parsley. Place the tureen in front of the hostess and bring the cabbage toasts piping hot on a separate dish. The hostess then places 2 or 3 of the cabbage toasts in each soup plate and pours over them a ladleful of the hot bouillon. Serves 8.

JUNE PLATT 1934

Opposite: Michel Certain 1966

POTATO SOUP

12 oz potatoes
1 tbsp fat
1 tbsp flour
pinch of marjoram
salt and pepper
2 pts stock (see method)
GARNISH
3 oz cooked diced potatoes
chopped parsley

Peel and quarter the potatoes and cook them to a pulp in salt water. Drain, reserving the water, and add the potatoes to a light roux made with the fat and flour. Flavour with a pinch of marjoram, and salt and pepper to taste. Add about 2 pints of liquid – use either stock or the water reserved after cooking the potatoes brought up to 2 pints with water. Simmer till well blended. Garnish with the diced potatoes and parsley.

PETER PIRBRIGHT AND GRETEL BEER 1950

POTAGE DE GARBANZOS

2 cups chick peas
2 *chorizos*
4-5 medium potatoes
1 lb spinach
2 cloves garlic
2 medium onions
2 tomatoes
salt and pepper

Soak the chick peas overnight in cold water. Change the water and put the peas to boil. Lower the heat and simmer until about three-quarters done. In the meantime, soak the *chorizos* in boiling water for 5 minutes. Slice them and add to the chick peas, together with the peeled and diced potatoes, well-washed spinach and crushed cloves of garlic. Cook until the vegetables are tender. Meanwhile, fry the chopped onions and skinned tomatoes gently in a little oil and add them to the rest. Add salt and pepper to taste.

PETER PIRBRIGHT AND GRETEL BEER 1952

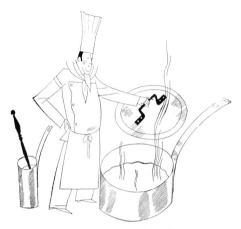

Roger de La\u{}vererie 1929

CHESTNUT SOUP

Slit the tops of 1 pound of chestnuts and boil them for 20-30 minutes – they should be well cooked but not squashy. Drain them, and as soon as they are cool enough to handle, skin them (the inside as well as the outside skin should be removed).

While they are cooking, chop 2 large onions coarsely and cook them gently in a little butter until they are soft but not brown. Add the chestnuts to the onions. Season with salt and pepper. Mash the chestnuts with a fork and moisten with a little stock (preferably chicken or veal) or milk. When the chestnuts are soft, put the whole mixture through a fine mill into a clean saucepan. Add more stock or milk so that there is a cupful of soup per person. Simmer it gently for 20 minutes. The soup is then ready for the next day. All it needs is to be brought nearly to the boil. You then add half a cup of cream. Remember to have your own glass of sherry in the kitchen.

ROBIN MCDOUALL 1955

CREAMY PEA SOUP

8-12 oz shelled peas
1 medium potato, sliced
1 medium onion, sliced
1 lettuce, cut into quarters
1 pt chicken stock
½ pt double cream
juice of ½ lemon
salt and freshly ground black pepper

Place the peas, potato, onion, lettuce and half the chicken stock in a saucepan and bring to the boil. Cover and simmer for 15 minutes. Cool slightly, then transfer to a blender and purée the vegetables; alternatively, press them through a fine sieve.

Return the soup to a clean saucepan; add the remaining stock and simmer for 5 minutes. Add the cream and lemon juice and season to taste. Serves 4.

ROBERT CARRIER 1966

CRÈME SÉNÉGALE

1 oz butter
1½ tsp light curry powder (Spice Islands, Sea Isle or Schwartz)
2 tbsp flour
1½ pts strong chicken stock, heated
juice of ½ lemon
sea salt and pepper
¼ pt single cream
4 oz cooked breast of chicken, chopped

Melt the butter in a saucepan. Stir in the curry powder, then the flour. Cook gently for 3 minutes, stirring often, then add the heated stock. Blend, stirring constantly, and simmer for another 3-4 minutes. Add the lemon juice, salt and pepper to taste, and the cream.

For a hot soup, stir in the chopped white meat at this stage, reheat gently, and serve. For a cold soup, cool quickly in a sink half-full of cold water, stirring now and then to prevent a skin forming. Chill for 2-3 hours and add the meat just before serving. Serves 4 to 6.

ARABELLA BOXER 1976

RIBOLLITA

4 oz cannellini beans
1 large onion
2 large carrots
3 sticks celery
1 head fennel
½ lb courgettes
½ lb tomatoes, skinned
4 tbsp olive oil
2 cloves garlic, crushed
2 pts stock
sea salt and black pepper
NEXT DAY
6-8 slices home-made bread
1 lb chard or green cabbage
a little extra olive oil

Start the day before. Put the dried beans in a pan, cover with cold water and bring to the boil. Cover the pan, turn off the heat, and leave for 1 hour. Chop the onion, carrots, celery, fennel, courgettes (unpeeled) and the skinned tomatoes. When the beans are ready, heat the oil in a large pan and stew the chopped vegetables gently for 8-10 minutes. Add the garlic towards the end. Heat the stock and add to the pan with the drained beans. Bring to the boil and simmer gently for 1 hour, or until the beans are tender. Add salt and pepper at this stage and leave until the next day.

Have some deep soup plates warmed, with a thick slice of bread – preferably home-made white bread, slightly stale – in each one. Cook the chard (which is the nearest equivalent I can find to the Italian *cavalo nero*) in boiling water; drain and chop coarsely. (A small green cabbage, cut in quarters and cut across in slices after cooking, also makes a good alternative.) Pile the green vegetables on top of the bread. Reheat the minestrone, boil for 2-3 minutes, then pour over the bread and greens. Have a small jug of olive oil, preferably the green virgin oil, on the table so that each person can pour a little on top of their soup. Serves 6 to 8.

ARABELLA BOXER 1978

LENTIL SOUP WITH DUCK SKIN

This fabulous soup is based on one made by a French chef from Gascony. The garnish of duck skin, or halved peeled broad beans, makes it unusual and elegant enough for a dinner party.

1 leek, sliced
1 tbsp olive oil
1 oz butter
1 carrot, sliced
1 stick celery, sliced
6 oz green lentils
sea salt and black pepper
STOCK
½ duck, or remains of a roast duck
1 lb chicken joints
vegetable trimmings
GARNISH
duck skin from ½ raw duck, or 4 oz broad beans, fresh or frozen
VARIATION
½ lb spinach
2 cartons (16 oz) Greek sheep's yoghurt
juice of 1½ lemons

First prepare the stock. If using half a raw duck, remove the skin before using the rest of the bird to make the stock. Place the duck in a saucepan, add the chicken joints and vegetable trimmings and cover with water. Bring to the boil, cover the pan and simmer gently for 3-4 hours. You will need about 1¾ pints, made in advance, with fat removed.

Soften the sliced leek in the oil and butter for 3-4 minutes, then add the carrot and celery. Cook gently for another 3 minutes, then add the lentils. Cook gently for 4 minutes, stirring often, while you heat the stock. Pour on the hot stock and bring to the boil slowly. Add sea salt and black pepper, half cover the pan, and cook until the lentils are soft, about 35 minutes. Leave to cool for a little, then purée in a food processor. Tip into a clean pan or bowl, and leave for a few hours for the flavour to develop.

Shortly before serving, reheat the soup and prepare the garnish. Cut the

Tessa Traeger 1976

duck skin in thin strips, paring away most of the fat. Fry gently in a non-stick pan, until it has rendered all its fat and become crisp and golden brown. Drain on soft paper. Serve this delicious soup in bowls, with the duck skins scattered over the top.

If you don't have any duck skin, cook fresh or frozen broad beans, then slip them out of their skins, split them in half, and lay them in a circle on the surface of each bowl. Serves 4.

Variation: For a delicious cold soup, make it in advance and leave to cool. Cook the leaf spinach briefly, then cool under the tap. Put in a food processor with the lentil soup, yoghurt and lemon juice. Process until smoothly blended, then chill well. This makes a delicious tart soup that is quite substantial. It can also be served hot; do not overheat or the yoghurt will separate. Garnish with broad beans. Serves 6.

ARABELLA BOXER 1987

EGGS AND CHEESE

The Irish poet Thomas Moore once wrote: 'Who can help loving the land that has taught us Six hundred and eighty-five ways to dress eggs?' He was referring to France, of course. Elsewhere, eggs have too often been relegated to the breakfast table where they usually arrive boiled, poached, fried or scrambled. The French have always excelled in turning them into feathery soft omelettes for luncheon or delectable soufflés with crisp golden tops and creamy centres for dinner. Following in the French tradition, this chapter includes Doris Lytton-Toye's golden rules for omelette-making and Elizabeth David's unbeatable instructions for successful soufflés.

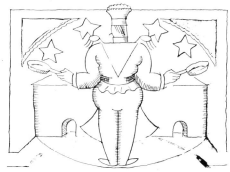

Above: Edward McKnight-Kauffer 1924
Opposite: Daniel Jouanneau 1984

It is said that France has a different kind of cheese for every day of the year (which was why, Winston Churchill informed General de Gaulle, it was so difficult to unite the country). In England, since medieval times, Cheddar has been the popular choice, so much so that at one time there was even a futures market in the commodity. The cheeses were huge: 120-pound monsters taking 5 years to mature.

Today there is an almost endless variety of textures and tastes in cheeses made throughout the world. It is one of the most fascinating foods with its subtle gradations of flavour and kindly disposition to blend so readily with other ingredients. Another important attribute is its readiness to partner fine wines. Frances Kornblum wrote: 'A very helpful guide I have found to follow in the service of cheese and wines is that the stronger the cheese, the stronger the wine should be. That, however, may not work out so comfortably for some of you who will be inclined to some such cheese classification as "inoffensive, offensive and brutal", while among many of us the grouping is "mild, moderate and strong".

'With Burgundy I find it excellent to serve Port Salut. Claret with Gruyère or any of the "running" types of cheese such as French Brie. With the stronger cheeses, such as the Cheddars and Cheshires, a light tawny Port forms a fine companionship, while old vintage Port and Stilton is nothing less than a heavenly match.

'And at any time that you are caught unawares with an empty cellar, don't hesitate to serve good, strong black coffee, which can be honestly used as a very good stop gap with practically all good cheese. The distinctive flavour of both these foods blends very harmoniously on the palate.'

> **'A tip for scrambled eggs (made with butter of course, not milk): when they are done, take them off the fire and stir in one more raw egg.'**
> ROBIN MCDOUALL

OEUFS BERCY

Take a few small French sausages and fry them till brown; then cut them in two and break some eggs over them (having left in the pan only a little of the fat); cook for a few minutes till the white is nearly set, add salt and pepper and put them, a minute only, under the grill.

BOULESTIN 1923

PIPÉRADE

This is a delicious dish, very popular in Béarn and in the Basque country. It can be partly prepared in advance as follows: take sweet peppers, cut them in slices and remove the seeds, and cook them in pork fat. If you are not certain of the quality of your pork fat (so few people nowadays fatten and kill their own pigs!), use a mixture of butter and olive oil, or butter and a little bacon fat. Cook in the same way the same quantity of tomatoes (peeled), adding them later, as they do not take so long to cook. Mix well, add seasoning, and let it simmer till it is all soft, melted and juicy.

When you want to finish the *pipérade*, you simply break in, one by one and without beating them, four or five eggs (this would do for ½ pound of each vegetable and for about six people), stir them in quickly over the spirit lamp or the electric stove 'full on'. After a few minutes you will get an exquisite mixture in which the eggs have entirely disappeared and to which, for a main dish, you can add some slices of Bayonne ham lightly tossed in butter and fried bread.

BOULESTIN 1928

OEUFS À LA DIABLE

In one saucepan make a rather thin béchamel sauce, properly seasoned with salt, pepper and nutmeg; in another one cook in butter two shallots, finely chopped. When the shallots are lightly browned, add a drop of wine vinegar, a tablespoon of French mustard, a pinch of paprika and a pinch of curry powder; stir all this well and add it to the béchamel sauce, into which you have incorporated the yolk of one egg and a small glass of fresh cream. Cook slowly *au bain marie*, whipping all the time and adding, one by one, little pieces of butter. See that it is highly seasoned, and if necessary rectify the seasoning. Keep the sauce as hot as possible, the saucepan still standing in hot water.

Meanwhile, fry your eggs either in butter, or in bacon fat according to taste, turning them once. They should be well fried outside and soft inside. Dispose them on toast previously fried. Just before serving, pour the *sauce diable* all round and all over the eggs.

BOULESTIN 1929

SCRAMBLED EGGS WITH ANCHOVIES

3 cleaned anchovies
2 small cups fresh butter
2 small cups white breadcrumbs
8 eggs, lightly scrambled
1 tbsp Parmesan cheese
extra butter for baking

Pass the anchovies and the butter through a sieve. Mix the breadcrumbs with the butter and anchovies. Line an ovenproof dish with this mixture; then add the lightly scrambled eggs. Spread the cheese thickly over the mixture and dot the top with butter. Bake the mixture in a very hot oven until it is lightly browned on the surface, but be careful that the eggs are not too firm.

COUNTESS BENIGNI 1934

OMELETTE ARNOLD BENNETT

For this omelette you chop finely a fillet of smoked haddock. Beat up with it as many eggs as required, adding a little salt and pepper. (Not too much salt as the haddock is already salty.) Melt a little butter in a pan and cook the omelette lightly. Do not roll the omelette when cooked, but turn it flat on to a plate. Spread over the top a little *sauce mornay*, sprinkle with grated cheese, and pass under the grill to brown.

THE CHEF OF THE SAVOY GRILL 1934

EGGS IN ASPIC

Hard boil 12 eggs. Cut lengthwise and remove the yolks. Press the yolks through a fine sieve. Also press through a fine sieve the contents of a medium-sized jar of *pâté de foie gras*. Mix the yolks and *foie gras* together, add salt and pepper to taste and a few drops of cream. Fill the centres of the eggs with this, and put the halves together again, being careful to wipe off any excess stuffing, so the whites are immaculate.

In the meantime, make the following aspic: heat 2 tins of Madrilène, and add to it ⅛ cup of cognac and ⅔ cup of dry white wine. Soak 3 teaspoons of gelatine in ½ cup of cold water for 15 minutes. Stir into the boiling Madrilène until dissolved. Strain and cool.

Decorate the bottoms of 12 individual moulds with a few leaves of tarragon dipped in the cold jelly, then pour in enough gelatine to make a ½-inch coating. When the gelatine has set, lay an egg in each one and pour the rest of the gelatine over them to fill the moulds.

Place on ice to set and thoroughly chill. Turn out on a platter and decorate with shredded lettuce before serving.

JUNE PLATT 1935

David Gittens 1965

POACHED EGGS À LA BOURGUIGNONNE

First prepare 6 round fried *croûtons*, about 3 inches in diameter, and keep them warm. Now make the sauce: chop finely 2 shallots and a little parsley. Put them in an enamel saucepan with a tiny pinch of thyme, a small piece of bay leaf, a pinch of salt, a dash of pepper, and cover with 2 cups of red burgundy. A few mushroom stems and peelings will improve the sauce but are not absolutely necessary. Reduce to one half by boiling rapidly, then pass the sauce through a hair sieve into another enamel pan.

In the meantime, cream 1 tablespoon of butter with 1 tablespoon of flour until smooth. Bring the wine liquid to the boil and add, little by little, the flour and butter, stirring well. Remove from the fire, add another 1½ tablespoons of butter, bit by bit, and stir until it is all incorporated. Keep warm while you poach 6 eggs in the usual manner. Put the hot *croûtons* on a hot dish, place a poached egg on each one and ladle the sauce carefully over the eggs. Garnish with fried parsley and serve at once. Serves 6.

JUNE PLATT 1936

OEUFS À L'INDIENNE

Cut in half as many hard-boiled eggs as are required and arrange them on the bottom of an ovenproof dish. Then chop up 2 Spanish onions very finely, put them in a fireproof dish with 3 dessert-spoons of olive oil. Season with salt, pepper, a little turmeric, a very little ginger, a bay leaf, and the juice of 1 lemon. Let this simmer for 30 minutes on a slow fire, stirring constantly. Then add 6 peeled and chopped tomatoes. Reduce till it is of a fairly thick consistency to cover the eggs. Pour over the eggs in the dish and reheat in a moderate oven. Add fried breadcrumbs and a little cheese, and return to the oven for a few minutes.

MRS ROBIN WILSON 1952

LES OEUFS ELIZABETH

This is one of the recipes created by well-known restaurants to celebrate the Coronation of Queen Elizabeth II.

1 large walnut of butter
4 oz Gruyère cheese
2 eggs
salt

Cut the butter into small pieces so that the whole of the bottom of a fireproof dish is covered. Slice half the Gruyère into fine wafers and make a layer over the butter. Place over gentle heat until the cheese begins to melt.

Separate the yolks of the eggs from the whites and put the yolks into the dish without breaking them. Leave on gentle heat until nearly set.

While the yolks are setting, beat the whites until stiff, having added a pinch of salt. Spoon a layer of stiffly beaten white over the egg yolks, then cover the egg white with a layer of finely sliced Gruyère and place in the oven until it turns golden.

PÈRE AUGUSTE 1953

Anthony Denney 1957

OMELETTES TO ORDER

DORIS LYTTON-TOYE 1952

High tide, full moon at Mont St. Michel, followed by an omelette *chez la Veuve Poulard*: an exquisite experience that still vibrates in my memory. Deservedly, the Widow Poulard held an unchallenged reputation in Brittany. In her lofty kitchen, women in traditional Breton costume wielded fantastically long-handled heavy pans over a raging furnace, the butter spurting almost to a flame before the eggs went in. Gossips whispered that the secret of the velvety texture of her omelettes was due to a spoon of cream in the whisked eggs: no one knew for certain. However, the golden rules for omelette-making were obvious in that kitchen for anyone who wished to learn. Here they are:

1. A really heavy pan, preferably of iron: never washed, simply wiped out with a clean cloth.

2. The pan made sizzling hot first, then the butter (or clarified fat, not margarine) added and swirled round until the sides are well greased.

3. The seasoned eggs, beaten lightly, are tipped all at once into the pan, then, while the pan is shaken by the left hand, the eggs are stirred with the back of a fork until they begin to set loosely.

4. Next (this can be done away from the fire since the heat in the metal is enough to continue the cooking), tilt the pan slightly and, with the fork, fold the omelette delicately over to the far side of the pan, pressing any untidy edges together.

5. Holding the pan still tilted away from you, give two or three sharp bangs on the handle with the right fist: the omelette will slip into position for turning out.

Alan Cracknell 1967

6. Grasp the pan in the right hand, knuckles underneath, hold a plate or dish in the left and quickly reverse the pan over the plate.

The classic omelette is oval in shape, has a creamy inside and a very thin uncoloured overcoat. Supposing our omelette lacks shapeliness, a tip given to me by a chef will put matters right. Lay over it a clean cloth and between the palms coax it to the desired oval. Wipe any trace of egg from the dish, add a touch of finely chopped parsley and serve. Another tip: avoid too hot a dish. It will toughen the omelette, cooking the eggs over again. Any omelette will taste better when seasoned with pepper ground from a mill and with ground rock salt. The usual white pepper and table salt is flat by comparison.

When omelettes stick the pan needs 'proving'. Set it on the flame with a layer of coarse salt: leave until the salt begins to brown. Throw away the salt; wipe the pan. I keep scraps of tissue paper for this purpose. Put some clear fat in the pan and heat thoroughly: once more wipe out the pan. A new pan should be 'proved' in the same manner.

OMELETTE AU FROMAGE

Add some grated cheese and a *pointe* of cayenne to the egg mixture. Sprinkle the finished omelette with some extra cheese and add a parsley spray.

OMELETTE AU JAMBON

To 3 eggs allow 1 dessertspoon of diced ham: whisk this into the eggs and seasoning. When the omelette is made, garnish with a diamond of lean ham.

OMELETTE FINES HERBES

This is an ordinary omelette with finely chopped parsley, chervil and tarragon included in the mixture.

OMELETTE AUX CROÛTONS

Fry some tiny dice of bread and add them to the beaten eggs. Make the omelette in the usual way; decorate with chopped parsley or chives.

OMELETTE AUX CHAMPIGNONS

To 4 eggs allow 3-4 small mushrooms. Wash the mushrooms in several waters; peel them if the outdoor kind. Mince the stalks and cook them gently in a little margarine for a few minutes. Add them to the beaten eggs. Slice the mushroom caps across thinly, keeping their original shape; lay them on a greased plate, season with salt and pepper, dot with little bits of margarine and grill slowly. Make the omelette, turn on to its dish, then dispose the mushroom slices along its length. Put 2 tufts of parsley on either side and serve immediately.

OMELETTE À LA REINE

Make an ordinary omelette. Slit it down the centre and fill the cavity with a mixture of diced chicken and mushrooms held together with a tablespoon of creamy sauce.

SOUFFLÉS

ELIZABETH DAVID 1959

The most tricky part of soufflé cooking is getting the whites of the eggs to the right consistency. They must be stiff, but creamy rather than grainy. The utensil which all professionals used to keep especially for beating egg whites was a hemispherical, untinned copper bowl. There seems to be little doubt that, in this bowl, egg whites can be whipped quicker and to a better, more airy – and at the same time creamier – consistency than in a china bowl. I do not know exactly why this should be so, I only observe that it is. But these copper bowls are expensive and most people can do well enough with an ordinary kitchen mixing bowl, so long as it is roomy enough for the number of eggs with which you are dealing. See that it is scrupulously clean. Specks of grease may spoil the chances of the eggs rising.

Personally, I can come to terms with neither rotary nor electric whisks for egg whites; I can't control them, and they produce too solid a mass. I use an old sixpenny spiral whisk for small quantities, and a long looped wire whisk for anything over 4 or 5 whites.

As to the oven, it must be really hot before you put in your soufflé. Have a baking sheet ready on the shelf on which the soufflé is to stand. The heat from this metal sheet helps to cook the egg mixture at the bottom of the dish.

Don't worry too much about the correct soufflé dishes. The ones we use nowadays are quite different from those at one time considered suitable for soufflés, and which were usually oval and made of metal. So you can use a pie dish or an old-fashioned metal entrée dish for soufflés, but the timing depends to a certain extent upon the depth of the dish and whether the mixture is spread out or piled up – a soufflé in a wide, shallow dish naturally cooks a good deal quicker than in a deep one.

I don't myself go in for tying paper collars around the dish; this system, except for cold soufflés, is a complication and a nuisance. If you fill your dish almost to the top with the mixture, and time it properly, all will be well. A terrific, towering soufflé is sometimes overcooked and empty inside. High and dry, as you might say, which is worse than one which is too liquid. The ideal, of course, is a well-risen soufflé which is creamy in the centre as you dip into it. If it is cooked too dry to start with, it will be quite withered by the time it reaches the third or fourth person. But practice is more useful than theory.

VANILLA SOUFFLÉ

This is typical of the kind of soufflé based on a thickened white sauce.

Ingredients are: 1½ ounces of butter, 2 level tablespoons of flour, ½ pint of milk, 3 ounces of white sugar, a vanilla pod, 4 whole eggs and 1 extra white.

Put the milk, sugar and vanilla pod into a saucepan and let it simmer gently for about 10 minutes. Melt the butter in a thick saucepan, stir in the flour, and when this is smooth gradually add the hot milk mixture. Cook over gentle heat, with a mat under the saucepan, for another 10-15 minutes until the sauce is quite smooth and thickish. Remove the vanilla pod and, off the fire, stir in the very well beaten yolks of the eggs. All this can be done in advance.

To cook the soufflé, preheat the oven to Gas Mark 4, 350°F, and have ready a 2-pint soufflé dish. Whip the whites, fold them into the main mixture, and turn into the dish. Make two deep cuts across the top, so that the soufflé is divided into four, strew with a little caster sugar and cook for 25-30 minutes.

This soufflé mixture can be used as a basis for other flavourings. Grated lemon or orange peel or a sherry glass of liqueur can be substituted for an equal proportion of the milk, and added to the basic mixture just before the yolks of the eggs are stirred in.

CHEESE SOUFFLÉ

There are dozens of different recipes for cheese soufflés. I give this particular one to show the system of cooking a soufflé slowly, so that it can be got ready in plenty of time.

Start off with the same basic mixture as for the vanilla soufflé, i.e., 1½ ounces of butter, 2 level tablespoons of flour, ½ pint of milk. The other ingredients are 2 ounces of grated cheese, the ideal being a half-and-half mixture of Parmesan and Gruyère; salt, plenty of freshly milled pepper, nutmeg, cayenne, 4 eggs, separated, and 1 extra white.

Having prepared the basic sauce of butter, flour and hot milk, and simmered it for 10 minutes, stir in your cheese and seasonings and, off the fire, the well-beaten yolks. When cool, fold in the 5 whipped whites. Turn into a 1½–2-pint soufflé dish. Have the oven heated to very moderate (Gas Mark 3, 325°F), and, having made the cuts across the top of the soufflé (as explained for the vanilla soufflé), cook it with the dish standing on a baking sheet in the centre of the oven for 30-35 minutes. A cheese soufflé nearly always smells cooked some while before it in fact is, so don't be taken in. And it is wiser not to sprinkle grated cheese on the top, for during the long cooking it gets too browned.

von Alvensleben 1982

OMELETTE AUX COQUILLES SAINT-JACQUES

16 scallops
4 oz butter
2 liqueur glasses brandy
2 tbsp flour
½ pt cream
16 eggs
COURT BOUILLON
½ pt water
¼ pt dry white wine
1 carrot, sliced
1 onion, sliced
1 clove garlic
1 sprig thyme
1 bay leaf
juice of 1 lemon
salt and pepper

Place all the ingredients for the *court bouillon* in a pan, simmer for 1 hour and then set aside to get cold.

If possible, buy unopened scallops and set them, round side down, in a baking tin over heat. When they have opened, remove them from the shell, cut off and throw away the black parts and wash the rest thoroughly.

Put them in the *court bouillon*, bring to the boil, then simmer for 5 minutes. Drain them and reserve the stock. Heat up half the butter, sauté the scallops in it for a minute or two, then pour in the brandy and light it. When the flames have died, set the scallops aside while making the sauce.

Make a velouté sauce with the remaining butter, the flour and the hot strained stock, then add the cream and, if the sauce is too thin, reduce it by boiling, stirring all the time. Remove from the heat, add salt and pepper if necessary, then put the scallops into the sauce.

Beat the eggs thoroughly and make an ordinary omelette, slide it on to a hot dish and pour the sauce and scallops over it.

MAPIE DE TOULOUSE-LAUTREC 1961

OEUFS AU CAVIAR

1-2 eggs per person
a little double cream
1 dessertspoon caviar per egg
pepper

Carefully cut the tops off the raw eggs and keep aside. Separate the whites from the yolks, leaving the yolks inside the shell. Put the eggs in ovenproof egg cups in a medium oven (Gas Mark 4, 350°F) for 5 minutes (the yolks must be warm but still liquid). Take out of the oven, and add a little cream and the caviar to each shell. Replace the tops on the eggs and serve with buttered toast.

NATHALIE HAMBRO 1974

EGG CROQUETTES

6 eggs
1 small onion
butter for frying
4 tbsp flour
½ pt milk, heated with ½ bay leaf and a pinch of mace or nutmeg
2 oz ham or 2 tbsp chopped parsley
salt and pepper
1 egg yolk, beaten
dry breadcrumbs for coating

Hard boil the eggs, cool them under cold water and remove the shells. Chop the onion and brown it slowly in butter. When soft and lightly coloured, stir in 2 tablespoons of flour and the strained, flavoured milk. Blend well.

Chop the eggs finely, and the ham or parsley. Stir both into the sauce, season and pour into a lightly greased dish. Cool, then chill for several hours or overnight. The next day, shape the mixture into oval egg shapes, and roll them first in the remaining flour, then in the beaten egg and dry breadcrumbs. Fry the croquettes in butter and drain them on absorbent paper. Serve with fresh tomato sauce, pepper sauce or fried parsley. Serves 3 to 4.

ARABELLA BOXER 1976

OEUFS À L'ESTRAGON

¼ pt double cream
3-4 sprigs tarragon
4 eggs

Heat the cream in a small pan and when it is nearly boiling put in the sprigs of tarragon, saving 4 nice leaves. Cover the pan and leave by the side of the fire until the cream is well flavoured, about 15 minutes.

Break the eggs into buttered cocotte dishes and bake in a moderate oven (Gas Mark 3, 325°F). When almost set (after about 8 minutes), strain the cream and pour a little over each egg. Lay a tarragon leaf on top of each, and return to the oven for 2 minutes. Serves 4.

ARABELLA BOXER 1976

CURRIED EGGS

1 medium onion
2 oz butter
1 tbsp light curry powder (Schwartz, Spice Islands, or Sea Isle)
1 tbsp flour
¾ pt hot chicken stock
¼ pt thin cream
1½ tbsp lemon juice
1½ tbsp orange juice
2 oz chopped (nibbed) almonds
8 hard-boiled eggs

Chop the onion and fry in the butter until golden. Add the curry powder and the flour and cook gently for 2-3 minutes, then add the heated stock. Stir until blended, then simmer for 12 minutes. Add the cream, then the fruit juices. Add the nuts and stir until all is well mixed. Cut the eggs in quarters and stir gently into the sauce. Reheat gently. Serves 4 to 6 as a first course, or 4 as a main course with rice and a green salad.

ARABELLA BOXER 1979

CROQUE MONSIEUR

Melt a piece of butter the size of a walnut in a saucepan, and add, before it gets brown, little by little, and stirring well, two tablespoons of flour, then a teacup of boiling milk. Cook this mixture for a quarter of an hour, and let it rest ten minutes. Then add two eggs, pepper and salt, and a quarter of a pound of grated cheese, preferably Gruyère and Parmesan, mixed in equal quantities.

Cut small pieces of stale bread, about two inches square and half an inch thick: put on each a thin piece of lean ham and over it about a teaspoon of the mixture previously described. Fry in very hot fat till golden brown (without turning them): drain well, sprinkle with a little red pepper and serve at once. The best fat to use is that part of the beef fat which is around the kidney.

BOULESTIN 1923

CHIPPENHAM CHEESE SAVOURY

A favourite of King Edward

For this you will require 2 eggs, 1 wine glass of cream, 2 tablespoons of milk and 6 ounces of grated Parmesan.

Beat the eggs, less one white, with the cream and milk in a saucepan. Add the cheese and keep stirring on a slow fire until the mixture is thick and creamy. Serve, if possible, in the vessel in which it has been cooked, handing hot toast to each guest and allowing him to pour over it a spoonful of cheese.

MRS ASPINALL-OGLANDER 1934

BRILLAT-SAVARIN'S FONDUE

Take as many eggs as are required for the number of your guests and weigh them: a piece of good Gruyère weighing a third and a piece of butter weighing a sixth. Break and beat up the eggs in a casserole, add the butter and the cheese, grated. Set the casserole over a brisk fire and stir with a wooden spoon until the mixture is suitably thick and soft. Salt, or none, according to whether the cheese is more or less old, and a strong dose of pepper. Send for your best wine, and let the same be quaffed – when you will see marvels.

JEANNE OWEN 1939

Ray Williams 1963

TANTE MARIE'S FONDUE

Melt 2 tablespoons of butter in the chafing dish. Add 2 scant tablespoons of flour and blend well. Slowly add 1 cup of milk and stir continuously as it thickens. The mixture must be the consistency of thick cream. If it is too thick, add a little more milk.

Add paprika and a pinch of cayenne, then stir in 2 cups of freshly grated cheese, first one of Parmesan and then one of Gruyère. Do not let it boil after the cheese has been added but keep it just hot enough to melt the cheese. Add the yolks of 3 eggs mixed with 3 tablespoons of cream. Keep stirring till quite hot and, as a final touch, put in a pinch of freshly ground nutmeg.

Serve in heated ramekins with small cubes of toasted bread, which are dipped into the fondue to be coated with the cheese by the individual guests.

This recipe serves 6 and must be well timed and made with care.

JEANNE OWEN 1939

FROMAGE À LA TRUFFE

Take three 6-ounce cakes of slightly salted cream cheese and mash with a silver fork. Add ½ cup of thick cream very slowly, beating it in with the fork.

Peel and slice 3 large truffles and cut in strips. Fold the pieces of truffle into the cream cheese, being careful not to break the truffle into bits. Pile high in your most beautiful glass dish and leave in the refrigerator till needed. Prepare this at least 3 or 4 hours in advance to allow it to become firm and for the perfume of the truffle to permeate the cheese. Serve with very thin wafer biscuits. A dry chilled sherry or a chilled Moselle as an apéritif goes beautifully with this cream cheese and adds to a very unusual dish.

JEANNE OWEN 1939

Evans 1984

GAUFRETTES FROMAGÉES

This is a savoury that is always appreciated – the only trouble is there's never enough! Cream some margarine. Work into it the same amount of grated cheese. Spread the creamed cheese liberally on unsweetened ice wafers. Place them in a hot oven till just browned and crisp. A little anchovy essence in the mixture varies the flavour. Allow at least 3 for each person. To serve with cocktails, cut the wafers in half.

DORIS LYTTON-TOYE 1949

AIGRETTES

These puff balls are delicious: beat 2 egg whites to a stiff froth (you could perhaps use egg whites left over from making mayonnaise) and fold in 2 ounces of grated cheese, adding salt and cayenne as desired. Shape into balls the size of marbles. Fry in smoking hot fat till golden brown; they swell as they cook. Drain well and sprinkle with grated cheese to serve.

DORIS LYTTON-TOYE 1949

MOZZARELLA ALLO SPIEDO

This is a homely Italian supper dish akin to Welsh rarebit, eaten with a cold anchovy sauce. The traditional way to cook it is to spear on a skewer alternate slices of bread and Mozzarella (or some similar buffalo or cows' milk cheese), and grill them over the red embers of a wood fire on a cold winter evening. The sauce is made by pounding a few fillets of anchovy in a mortar and diluting them with olive oil (I usually add a little milk as well). You then dip your sizzling hot slice of toasted bread and cheese into the cold anchovy sauce before each mouthful – a simple dish that is nevertheless worthy of the land which gave birth to Lucullus.

It can easily be adapted to canapés for cocktail parties by spearing small cubes of bread and cheese alternately on toothpicks and browning them under a hot grill. Serve them piping hot in a shallow earthenware dish with a pot of cold anchovy sauce alongside, into which guests can dip their toothpicks.

GEORGINA MASSON 1954

34

CHEESE D'ARTOIS

Roll out ½ pound of flaky or puff pastry thinly into an oblong shape and divide in half. Beat up 2 eggs and mix them with ½ cup of grated Gruyère cheese. 1 tablespoon of melted (not hot) margarine, salt, pepper and cayenne. Spread this mixture on one half of the pastry, leaving a ½-inch margin all round. Dampen this and then lay the second half on top. Press well, brush over with beaten egg and mark across in long thin fingers. Bake in a hot oven (Gas Regulo 7, 425°F) until crisp and golden. Cut into fingers and serve hot or cold.

IRIS SYRETT 1954

FRENCH MACARONI CHEESE

This makes a useful supper dish. Cook the macaroni in the usual way and toss in butter. Add 1 pound of skinned and diced tomatoes, 1 crushed clove of garlic and 6 chopped anchovies. Mix well together with 3 ounces of grated English Cheddar cheese and put in a buttered ovenproof dish. Dot with butter, add a sprinkling of cheese and heat through.

ELIZABETH KENDALL 1968

FRESHLY HERBED CREAM CHEESE

Pour fresh double cream (not pasteurized or homogenized) into a clean damp cloth (a bowl will hold the cloth while it is filled). Tie the edges to make a bag and hang in a cool place where the cheese can drip for a week.

Re-wrap the cheese in a fresh cloth. Put it in a mould with a weight on top for 2-3 days; turn the cheese twice a day. Season with salt and black pepper, and sprinkle with chopped fresh herbs – dill, parsley, tarragon or basil. Wrap in a cheesecloth and tie with raffia.

MAXINE MCKENDRY 1970

WELSH RAREBIT

Anything as traditional as Welsh Rarebit is bound to have many variations. Here are four, the third by Mary Bromfield, wife of the author Louis Bromfield.

JEANNE OWEN 1939

Melt 1 pound of freshly grated cheese – mild or strong according to taste – with 2 tablespoons of butter in the top of a double boiler. When it begins to melt, add slowly ½ glass of good ale, stirring continuously. Blend it carefully, then add paprika and a generous pinch of dry mustard. When the mixture is creamy, add 2 egg yolks that have been broken and mixed with a little ale. When very hot, serve on toast. For 6 people.

DORIS LYTTON-TOYE 1948

Slice thinly 4 ounces of dryish Cheddar and put it in a pan with ½ ounce of butter, ½ teaspoon of made mustard, a little pepper and salt, 1 dessertspoon of milk and a drop or two of vinegar. Place the pan in another pan of hot water. Allow to melt very, very slowly, but without stirring overmuch – stirring a rarebit makes the cheese ropy. Toast the bread on one side only; butter the untoasted side, pour over the rarebit and grill immediately. Send to the table sizzling.

MARY BROMFIELD 1953

Place in a frying pan a good-sized lump of butter and heat it until melted and turning brown. Then stir in, slowly, grated or finely cut cheese, stirring continuously with a fork. When the cheese has melted, stir in heated cream until the mixture is about right to spread on toast.

Denton Welch 1947

(The cream should be heated before adding to prevent the cheese from separating.) Then add pepper, Worcestershire sauce, and any other flavouring ingredients, and serve on very dry toast.

The whole trick of the dish is the speed and dexterity with which it is made. It should be ready within 2 or 3 minutes after the cheese has been added. If a Golden Buck is preferred, stir in a well-beaten egg. Rarebit for 4 persons is nearly the limit. In the case of a larger quantity, speed and dexterity lose out and the cheese may separate.

ROBIN MCDOUALL 1955

Take 1 pound of best English Cheddar, very fresh, and cut it in paper-thin slices. Put them in the chafing-dish with some made mustard, a generous dash of Worcestershire sauce, a dessertspoon of sherry and 2 tablespoons of beer. Stir it until it reaches the consistency of well-chewed chewing gum. An obliging guest should, in the meanwhile, have made some toast. Put a piece of toast on each plate and spoon on to it some of the Welsh Rarebit.

Edward McKnight-Kauffer 1925

MACARONI CHEESE

This is one of those comforting dishes we remember with pleasure from childhood. Far removed from Italian food despite its ingredients, it could not be more English in character.

½ lb macaroni
4 oz streaky bacon
2½ oz butter
3 tbsp flour
⅔ pt milk, warmed
4 tbsp cream
4 oz Cheddar cheese, grated
sea salt and pepper
½ lb tomatoes

Cook the macaroni as usual; drain well. Chop the bacon and fry until crisp; drain on absorbent paper. Melt 2 ounces of butter, stir in the flour and cook for 1 minute. Add the heated milk and stir until blended. Stir in the cream and the grated cheese, reserving 2 tablespoons to scatter over the top. Add plenty of sea salt and black pepper and simmer for 4 minutes. Stir in the macaroni and the chopped bacon and pour half the mixture into a buttered ovenproof dish. Skin and slice the tomatoes and cook briefly, just until softened, in the remaining butter. Lay them over the macaroni in the dish, pouring the juices over them, and cover with the rest of the macaroni. Scatter the reserved cheese over the top and bake in a moderately hot oven (Gas Mark 6, 400°F) for 20 minutes. Serve with a green salad. Alternatively, prepare in advance and reheat for 35-40 minutes at Gas Mark 4, 350°F. Serves 4.

ARABELLA BOXER 1979

CHEESE DREAMS

These are especially good when made with toasted muffin bread.

4 slices wholemeal bread or muffin bread
1 oz butter
4 slices Cheddar cheese
8 rashers streaky bacon, rinds removed
3 small tomatoes, sliced
sea salt and black pepper

Toast the bread and spread each slice with butter. Cover with a piece of cheese, and lay 2 rashers of bacon over each one, crossing diagonally. Intersperse with tomato slices. Sprinkle with sea salt and black pepper and grill until the bacon becomes crisp and the cheese melts. Serve immediately. Serves 4.

ARABELLA BOXER 1982

CHEESE, POTATO AND ONION PIE

1lb potatoes, peeled and sliced
1 small onion, peeled and chopped
4 oz Cheddar cheese, grated
1 wine glass stock or cider
salt and pepper
about 12 oz pastry

Put the potatoes, onion and cheese in layers in a pie dish. Moisten with the liquid and season to taste. Cover with the pastry and bake in a preheated hot oven (Gas Mark 7, 425°F) for about 45 minutes or until brown. Good hot or cold. Serves 4 to 6.

MARWOOD YEATMAN 1985

CHEESE CUSTARD

1 pt milk
4 oz fresh white breadcrumbs
8 oz Cheddar cheese, grated
2 eggs, beaten
salt and pepper
pinch of nutmeg (optional)

Put the milk and breadcrumbs in a pan, bring up to the boil and remove from the heat. Stir in the cheese and beaten eggs, season to taste and mix well.

Grease a pie dish, pour in the mixture and bake in a preheated hot oven (Gas Mark 7, 425°F) for 25 minutes or until turning brown and firm. Good with mustard. Serves 4 to 6.
Note: This recipe comes from Kent, where it was a popular supper dish. Originally, it contained the local hard cheese, which is no longer made. The custard will rise but not as much as a soufflé.

MARWOOD YEATMAN 1985

CHEESE STRAWS

3 oz flour, sifted
1½ oz butter
3 oz Cheddar cheese, grated
2 egg yolks
salt and pepper

Put the flour in a bowl with the butter and work the two lightly together with the fingertips to the consistency of breadcrumbs. Add the Cheddar and egg yolks and season to taste. Mix well, adding a little water to bind the dough, if necessary. Roll out on a floured board or slab to a ¼-inch thickness and cut into straws, about 3 inches in length. (Cut out a few rings if you want to bind them.) Bake in a preheated moderate oven (Gas Mark 4, 350°F) for about 45 minutes.

MARWOOD YEATMAN 1985

Tessa Traeger 1983

PÂTÉS AND PIES

Today, the word pâté is often used to describe any mixture of finely ground meats, liver, game, fish — or even vegetables — seasoned and baked. Terrines, potted meats and meat loaves are all similar in that they are minced, chopped or pounded and cooked. Strictly speaking, a mixture cooked in a terrine (shallow earthenware dish) is called exactly that; something cooked in a pastry crust (*en croûte*) is a pâté; and a mixture of minced fowl or game bird meat is a galantine. In years gone by, the French aristocrats ate pâtés made of various kinds of meat while the peasants made do with the giblets, heavily seasoned. Today, pâtés and terrines of all descriptions are an essential part of French cuisine.

Pâté de foie gras is reputedly the invention of an eighteenth-century pastry cook from Normandy, Jean-Joseph Close, who was taken by his master to Alsace where he created this rich dish of goose livers, veal and truffles wrapped in pastry. Later he was able to market his creation and make his fortune.

While the French were enjoying their pâtés, the British were concentrating on potting, one of the oldest methods of preserving. Originally, the ingredients were cooked in a pot, cooled, then made airtight with a layer of suet. As time went by, butter replaced the suet and only the best meat was used, pounded to a fine texture and tightly packed in the pot to exclude all air.

The original French word for pastry is *pâte* and this is still used for Pâte de Paques — a traditional Easter pie made in the Poitou region.

Some people are born pastry cooks. They have a flair for making pastry of such lightness it literally melts in the mouth. Not for natural cooks, scales and measures and temperature charts: they know by instinct that deftness and lightness of touch are everything; that over-anxiousness and coaxing only make for leaden, sulky dough.

Arabella Boxer recommends setting aside a whole afternoon for this occupation: 'With two or three pounds of pastry one can make a series of pies, tarts and linings for quiches. One can be eaten the same day, the others stored in the refrigerator or frozen. It is a lovely feeling to have more food than one actually needs at any given time, and a perfect incentive to ask round some friends. Viewed in this way, cooking becomes enjoyable again; the pleasure of doing things for fun rather than necessity is regained.'

Above: John Minton 1946
Opposite: Tessa Traeger 1985

GAME TERRINE

Take whatever game you have, either partridge, pheasant or hare, and carve nice fillets out of it; also cut some lean veal and pork in thin slices, the proportions to be two of game to one of butcher's meat. Prepare some minced meat as follows: small pieces of game, streaky bacon, a few truffles, parsley, a little stale bread, onions and shallots, finely chopped. Rub through a fine sieve, add salt and a good deal of pepper and, if you like, the yolk of one egg.

Take a terrine, grease it with pork fat, and dispose in it a layer of game and meat, then a layer of minced meat, and so on till full.

Put in a small saucepan full of water the bones from the partridge or pheasant, one small onion, one sliced carrot, parsley, thyme, bacon rind, salt and pepper, and a calf's foot. Bring to the boil and let it simmer till well reduced, then pass the stock through a strainer and keep it warm.

Put your terrine into a *bain marie* and bake in a moderate oven for about two hours. When cooked, remove it and pour over it the gravy obtained by the boiling described above, which will eventually become a delicious jelly. Put a weight over the pâté and keep it in a cool place for twelve hours. It will keep for weeks if you pour melted pork fat over it, then cover it with a piece of greased paper and the terrine lid.

BOULESTIN 1923

PÂTÉ VENDÉEN

This pie or galantine is a near relation of the *pâté de jambon* they make so well in Burgundy. It is more or less the same preparation, except that the *pâté Vendéen* contains rabbit.

Take a rabbit, cut fillets out of the saddle and the legs; take the rest of the meat, the liver, a little piece of garlic, parsley, and chop all this together. Sea-

Gordon Davey 1940

son well and add spices, then marinate for an hour in a pint of white wine and a little brandy. Parboil a piece of ham in a stock prepared in the following manner: water, a tumbler of white wine, one calf's foot, and a good bouquet garni (there should be, in addition to the usual herbs, tarragon and chervil). Remove the ham when it is a little less than half cooked, then chop it and mix it well with the chopped rabbit.

Then fill a terrine with alternate layers of chopped meat and fillets of rabbit, sprinkling with seasoning after each layer of meat is placed: finish with a layer of minced meat and cook *au bain marie* in the oven.

While it is cooking, let the stock (with the calf's foot in) reduce thoroughly; this you will pour over your pâté to form, when cold, a delicious jelly.

BOULESTIN 1926

CHICKEN LIVER PÂTÉ

½ lb chicken livers
2 oz butter
1 clove garlic
1½ tbsp sherry
1½ tbsp brandy
salt and black pepper
pinch of mixed spice

This quick and easy pâté can be kept in the refrigerator for several days.

Clean and rinse the livers well. Melt 1 ounce of butter and sauté the livers until firm but still pink inside. Drain and transfer to a basin rubbed with the garlic. Add the sherry and brandy to the juices remaining in the pan, bring just to the boil and remove from the heat. Mash the livers to a paste, add generous seasoning, the remaining ounce of softened butter and the liquid. Mix thoroughly, then pack into small pots and chill. Serve with hot, thin toast or crisp bread.

ELIZABETH KENDALL 1960

PÂTÉ MAISON

12 oz calves' liver
4 oz fat bacon
4 rashers streaky bacon
salt and pepper
SAUCE
1 shallot
piece of carrot
1 bay leaf
1 sprig parsley
blade of mace
½ pt milk
1 oz butter
1 oz flour

To make the sauce, put the vegetables, herbs and mace in a saucepan with the milk, bring gently to the boil, then leave to stand off the heat for 10 minutes. Melt the butter in a pan, cook the flour for several minutes then stir in the strained milk. Simmer until thick and smooth and leave to cool.

Put the liver in a pan with water to cover and simmer for 5 minutes. Strain, then mince twice with the fat bacon. Add the liver and seasoning to the sauce and beat well. Line a 1 pound bread tin with the streaky bacon, fill with the mixture and cover with greaseproof paper. Put the tin in a *bain marie* and cook in the oven at Gas Mark 4, 350°F, for 2 hours. Let the pâté cool but do not chill. Serve with thin toast and unsalted butter.

ELIZABETH KENDALL 1966

BLENDER LIVER TERRINE

12 oz liver sausage
2-4 tbsp mayonnaise
2-4 tbsp cream
1 tbsp finely chopped onion
1 tbsp finely chopped parsley
salt and freshly ground black pepper
lemon juice or brandy
toast, crackers, or thin slices of rye or
pumpernickel bread
sieved hard-boiled egg yolks or chopped
parsley to garnish

Combine the liver sausage, mayonnaise, cream, onion and parsley in a blender and flavour to taste with salt, freshly ground black pepper, and lemon juice or brandy; whirl until smooth.

Serve on toast, crackers or thin slices of rye or pumpernickel bread; alternatively pack into small individual crocks or a terrine. Garnish with sieved hard-boiled egg yolks or chopped parsley.

ROBERT CARRIER 1966

TERRINE OF VEGETABLES

1½ lb chicken breasts
4 egg whites
4 oz very small French beans
1 lb very small carrots
1 lb broccoli
1 lb small courgettes, sliced lengthwise
1½ pts double cream
salt and pepper

Process the chicken in a blender for 1 minute. Add the egg whites and beat for 2 minutes. Sieve through a tamis and put into a deep-freeze until half frozen. Put the blender bowl in the refrigerator. Prepare the vegetables and cook them separately until *al dente*. Refresh in iced water and dry carefully on absorbent kitchen paper.

Remove the chicken from the deep-freeze and put into the chilled blender bowl. Add half the cream and process for 20 seconds. Scrape down the sides of the bowl and add the remaining cream.

Ray Williams 1962

Beat until mousse-like. Season to taste.

Line a terrine tin with tinfoil. Starting with a layer of chicken mousse, add a layer of French beans and continue with alternate layers of mousse and vegetables, finishing with mousse.

Place the terrine in a *bain marie* and cook in a moderate oven, Gas Mark 4, 350°F, for 1½ hours. Remove the terrine from the *bain marie*. When cool, place in the refrigerator and leave to chill for 12 hours. Serve the terrine with a fresh tomato sauce. Serves 12.

ALISON PRICE 1984

VOL-AU-VENTS FINANCIÈRE

Cut two or three truffles in small pieces and chop the peelings. Put them in a saucepan with a glass of Madeira, and let it reduce by half. Put in another saucepan a piece of butter the size of an egg, a tablespoonful of flour, and cook till brown; add a tablespoonful of good stock, stirring all the time, then your truffles and Madeira, mushrooms, *quenelles, fonds d'artichauts* (all things which you can buy already prepared in jars), a few pieces of sweetbread previously cooked in butter, and cook the whole thing a little while without bringing it to the boil.

Spoon the mixture into *vol-au-vents* (the pastry should be very light) which you have kept hot in the oven.

BOULESTIN 1923

SQUAB PIE

The story goes that there was once an old man and his wife who lived quietly in their little cottage. They had a tiny garden in which he grew onions, leeks, potatoes, wallflowers and hollyhock, and she cooked some of these (not the flowers) for their modest meals. She never complained and he never grumbled; they only quarrelled at dinner time because the one liked sweet pie, the other savoury pie; and, as they were old people without money or children, their daily food was their only interest in life. So the squabble about the pie became every day more noisy and passionate. In fact, they were on the verge of what the daily press would call a 'domestic tragedy' when, one day, while cooking the famous pie, the wife had an inspiration – why not mix the ingredients and make a combined pie, partly sweet, partly savoury? The ingredients were good, thought she, the result ought to be good. Indeed it was, and so was born the 'squab pie', and they lived happily for ever after, the old man, his wife and the

Georges Lepape 1931

squab pie – of which here is the genuine recipe:

Put in a pie dish leeks and potatoes cut in slices and a few pieces of either beef or mutton, salt, pepper and a little water, and cook on a moderate fire till it is partly cooked; then add apples cut in quarters, and sugar (it should be noticeably sweet). Finish cooking, cover with pastry of a flaky kind, and bake the pie in a quick oven. The apples should be put in so that they are cooked precisely at the same moment as the meat and vegetables.

BOULESTIN 1924

CARROT FLAN

Line a flan ring with cheese pastry – ordinary short pastry flavoured with grated cheese and a little cayenne pepper. Rather less fat than usual can be rubbed in – 2 ounces to 6 ounces of flour and 1½ ounces of cheese. Bake it blind, lined with paper and filled with dry beans or peas to keep its shape.

Cook ½-¾ pound of carrots, cut in fine slices, with salt, pepper, a pinch of sugar, and water just to cover. Make a sauce with ½ ounce of margarine, 1 level tablespoon of flour, and ¼ pint of carrot juice. Add a little more liquid if neces-

sary, season well, and finish the sauce with 1 dessertspoon of grated cheese. Arrange the carrots in the baked case, pour the sauce over them and bake in a hot oven for 10-15 minutes.

DORIS LYTTON-TOYE 1948

AMERICAN CHICKEN PIE

Place a 4-pound chicken in a pan (a good boiling fowl will do, but not the athletic kind), also its giblets, reserving the liver for a savoury some other time. Cover the bird with cold water and bring to boiling point; skim thoroughly. Add to the pot a carrot cut in half, an onion stuck with cloves, a bouquet garni, a little salt and 5 crushed peppercorns. Simmer till the fowl is tender, then let it cool in its liquor. When it is cold, carve the chicken meat in nice strips. Have also 4 ounces of York ham in strips (failing ham, use grilled bacon) and 4 ounces of tiny white mushroom caps. Dispose the chicken, ham and mushrooms in a pie dish, seasoning as you go. Fill the dish three-quarters of the way up with strained chicken stock. Cover with rough puff pastry and gild it with beaten egg. Bake the pie in a hot oven (Gas Mark 8, 450°F) till the pastry is a good golden brown. Half an hour before serving, put a small funnel through the centre of the crust and pour in a teacup of cream and reheat in a cool oven. *Note:* Return all the chicken bones to the liquor in the pan; cook gently for 3-4 hours and you have a lovely stock for another day. Store in the refrigerator.

DORIS LYTTON-TOYE 1950

Tessa Traeger 1980

STEAK, KIDNEY AND MUSHROOM PUDDINGS

12 oz shin of beef
4 oz kidney
2 oz mushrooms
lard or margarine for frying
1 small onion, chopped
1 clove garlic, crushed
finely chopped herbs
salt and pepper
½ lb flour
1 tbsp tomato purée
stock
½ lb chopped suet

Cut the beef, kidney and mushrooms into dice ⅓ inch in thickness and fry them gently in lard or margarine for 20 minutes. Add the chopped onion, herbs and salt and pepper to taste. Add a little flour and the tomato purée. Mix well with sufficient stock to cover, and cook slowly for 2 hours.

Mix the suet, remaining flour and seasoning with just enough chilled water to make the crusts and line 8 individual moulds. Fill them with the meat mixture and cover the tops with the suet pastry. Steam for about 1 hour. Serves 8.

ROYAL ANCHOR HOTEL, LIPHOOK 1952

CHICKEN PIE MASSACHUSETTS

4 broiling chickens, 2 lb each
salt and pepper
4 tbsp butter
4 shallots, chopped
3 tbsp flour
2 cups dry white wine
2 cups chicken stock
16 small onions, peeled
16 small white mushrooms, wiped
1 cup diced, boiled salt pork
4 medium potatoes, diced and parboiled
1 cup cream
puff pastry
2 eggs, slightly beaten
4 tbsp milk

Tod Draz

Cut the chickens into 4 pieces each, season them with salt and pepper and put them in a saucepan with the butter. Cook the chicken pieces gently for a few minutes but do not allow them to brown. Add the shallots and flour, stir till smooth, then add the wine and stock and bring to the boil. Add the onions and mushrooms and cook for 20-25 minutes or until the meat is tender. Remove the mushrooms after 12 minutes. When the chicken is done, remove the skin and bones from the meat and put the meat into a deep porcelain pie dish with the diced pork, onions, mushrooms and potatoes.

Cook the sauce till reduced to the consistency of thick cream. Now add the cream, correct the seasoning and strain through cheesecloth. Pour the sauce over the chicken and cover with puff pastry. Brush the top with the egg and milk mixed together to give a rich colour when done. Bake in a hot oven until the pastry is brown. Serves 8.

MARIUS DUTREY 1955

QUICHE LORRAINE

The classic Quiche Lorraine is an open-faced tart filled with a rich savoury custard and baked until puffed and golden brown. These variations from *Vogue* have the added flavour of onion, ham, bacon and cheese.

DORIS LYTTON-TOYE 1949

Line an 8-inch flan ring thinly with shortcrust pastry. Brush the pastry with melted margarine. Lay upon this some ham, finely chopped, or a rasher of bacon cut in thin strips and fried. Whisk 3 eggs with a touch of French mustard; beat in ½ pint of creamy milk, a cup of grated cheese, salt, pepper, a pinch of sugar. Pour into the pastry case and cook in a moderate oven for about 25 minutes. Reduce the heat once the pastry has set. The surface should be a rich golden brown, the inside soft and savoury.

Robin Jacques

Note: A piece of chopped onion may be fried and added with the bacon. Half evaporated milk and half ordinary gives a richer custard.

DORIS LYTTON-TOYE 1951

Line a flan case with thin flaky or half-puff pastry. Fill it with beans placed on aluminium foil. Bake in a hot oven (Gas Regulo 6, 400°F) to a light golden brown. Remove the beans and foil half-way through so that the bottom crust is cooked. Mix together 2 ounces of grated Parmesan, the same amount of Gruyère cheese, a beaten egg, a rasher of grilled bacon chopped in small pieces, 7½ fluid ounces of cream and milled pepper. Pour this mixture into the pastry case; replace in the oven at Gas Regulo 4, 350°F, for about 12-15 minutes; that is, until the top of the tart is golden and the custard firm but still creamy.

IRIS SYRETT 1954

Line a 6- or 7-inch flan ring with your favourite flaky pastry. Cover the bottom with diced bacon or ham, then a layer of thinly sliced onions, softened (but not browned) in butter or margarine. Beat 2 eggs, pour on 7½ fluid ounces of milk and cook in a double saucepan, stirring constantly until the custard thickens enough to coat the back of a wooden spoon. Remove at once, stir in 3-4 table-spoons of grated Gruyère, season with black pepper, salt and a *pinch* of nutmeg. Allow to cool slightly, pour into the flan and sprinkle with a dusting of cheese. Cook in a moderately hot oven (Gas Regulo 5 or 375°F) until set and brown. Serve just warm.

CHICKEN AND HAM PIE

A good, solid main course is chicken and ham pie. While you're about it, you may as well make one that will do for more than one meal. Cut the legs off a 4-5 pound roasting chicken, and cut the meat from them in as large pieces as possible. Cut off the breasts and slice them into thin fillets. Beat all these pieces out as flat as possible. Make a pint of chicken stock with the bones and giblets (well seasoned). Strain it, dissolve in it 1 ounce of gelatine, and let it cool.

Sprinkle some chopped onion and parsley in a pie dish and cover the bottom with thick slices of fat bacon (collar is best), from which you have removed the rind. Moisten with stock, sprinkle with more onion and parsley, then cover with a layer of chicken. Season, moisten, and cover with a layer of halved hard-boiled egg. Continue with these layers of chicken and bacon — seasoning and adding stock as you go — until the pie dish is full, with a layer of bacon on top.

Make a pie crust with 8 ounces of flour, 4 ounces of butter or dripping, a pinch of salt and as much water as you need to make a paste. Roll it out and cover the pie with this crust. Make a hole in the middle and make a pastry rose which will fill the hole while the pie is cooking. Brush the crust with egg yolk. Cook for 30 minutes in a moderate oven and then for another 2½ hours in a slow oven. When cooked, remove the rose and fill up with stock. Let it get cold and put it in the refrigerator for 2-3 hours.

ROBIN MCDOUALL 1955

'Lord Houghton, a noted Victorian gourmet, sighed on his deathbed, "My exit is the result of too many entrées".'

CHEESE AND APPLE TART

6 oz wholemeal biscuits
3 oz butter, melted
FILLING
small tin evaporated milk
grated rind and juice of 1 lemon
½ lb cream cheese
small stick celery, chopped
2 tbsp sultanas
2 tbsp chopped walnuts
1 apple, chopped
pinch of nutmeg

This pretty plateful needs no toiling over a hot stove. Even the shell is uncooked. First crush the biscuits and mix with melted butter. Line an 8-inch plate and leave until firm.

Meanwhile, put the evaporated milk into a basin, add the grated rind and juice of the lemon and whisk until thick. Whisk the cream cheese and add the finely chopped celery, the sultanas, nuts and apple. Add nutmeg to taste. Pile the mixture into the case and, if wished, add a sprinkling of paprika.

ELIZA MITCHELL 1961

QUICHE AUX POIREAUX

1 lb whites of leek
2 oz butter
salt
2 large eggs
½ pt cream
pepper
pinch of nutmeg
an 8-inch partially cooked shortcrust pastry flan
1 tbsp grated Gruyère or Emmenthal cheese
a little extra butter

Slice the leeks thinly, using only the white part; blanch for 5 minutes in boiling water. Pour off the water, leaving only a spoonful, then simmer gently in the butter and a little salt with the lid on the saucepan. In about 30 minutes the leeks will be very tender and the liquid

Tessa Traeger 1975

Denton Welch 1945

all absorbed. Beat the eggs, cream, pepper, salt and nutmeg together. Cool the leek purée and add to the cream gradually; correct the seasoning and pour into the partially cooked pastry case. Sprinkle with grated cheese and dot all over with small flakes of butter. Bake for about 25 minutes on the top shelf of a hot oven, Gas Mark 5, 375°F, until puffed up and golden brown.

VERONICA MACLEAN 1969

SMALL GAME PIES

1 brace pheasants, or 2 grouse and 1 pigeon,
or 1 pheasant and 1 grouse
2 oz butter
2 tbsp brandy
1 stick celery
2 stalks parsley
salt and pepper
1 bay leaf
1 oz dripping or butter
3 oz salt pork or fat green bacon
12 pickling onions
12 tiny carrots
4 small leeks
1½ tbsp flour
½ pt game stock (made from carcasses)
sea salt and black pepper
12 oz short pastry
1 egg yolk

I cook the birds in the pressure cooker as follows: put ½ ounce of butter inside each bird and melt the remaining butter in the pressure cooker. Brown the birds (which should be covered with bacon by the butcher) and *flambé* with the brandy. Add the celery, parsley, salt and pepper, and the bay leaf and cover the pan. Cook for 15 minutes (for a 2-pound bird). (Alternatively, the birds can be roasted for 35 minutes in a moderate oven.) Lift out and cool slightly, discard the flavouring vegetables, and allow the stock to settle prior to removing the fat. Later, cut the meat off the bones and cut in neat square pieces. Make a strong stock (again in the pressure cooker) with the carcasses. Strain and reduce till well flavoured.

Melt the dripping and brown the salt pork or bacon, cut in strips, in a casserole. Add the whole peeled onions, carrots cut in chunks, and leeks thickly sliced. Add the flour, then blend with ½ pint of the strained stock mixed with the liquid left after cooking the birds. Simmer until smooth, then add the cubed meat. Leave to cool while you make the pastry. Line 6-8 small tins like muffin tins, and fill with the meat and vegetables, moistened with the sauce. Cover with more pastry, decorate with trimmings, and brush with egg yolk. Bake the little pies for 25 minutes at Gas Mark 5, 375°F. Serves 6 to 8.

Note: A simpler version can be made by filling a pie dish with the filling and covering with a lid of pastry.

ARABELLA BOXER 1978

1926

yolk and bake for 15 minutes at Gas Mark 6, 400°F, and then a further 45 minutes at Gas Mark ½, 250°F. These can be served hot, cold or reheated. Serves 4.

ARABELLA BOXER 1980

GAME PUDDING

1 partridge
½ lb rump steak
sea salt and black pepper
6 oz mushrooms, sliced
3-4 tbsp chopped parsley
⅓ pt stock and red wine, mixed
SUET PASTRY
1 lb self-raising flour
pinch of salt
½ lb shredded suet
½ pt very cold water

Make the pastry as usual, and roll out two thirds of it to line a 1½-pint pudding basin. Cut the partridge in 4 pieces and cut the steak in strips. Make a layer of rump steak in the bottom of the basin, and sprinkle with sea salt and black pepper. Cover with half the sliced mushrooms, half the chopped parsley and more salt and pepper. Lay the quartered partridge on top, then cover with the rest of the steak, salt and pepper, sliced mushrooms and chopped parsley. Pour over the stock and wine so that the bowl is about three-quarters full, then cover with the remaining pastry, rolled out into a circle. Make a generous overlap and press the edges together to seal.

Tie in a cloth and stand in a pan with boiling water coming half-way up the bowl. Cover and steam for 3 hours, adding more boiling water as needed. Serve with boiled cabbage or carrots.
Note: This makes a delicious small pudding, enough for 3-4 people: for 5-6, use 2 partridges, ¾ lb rump steak, and ½ lb mushrooms in a 2-pint bowl.

ARABELLA BOXER 1980

CORNISH PASTIES

These can be made with either a suet mixture pastry or a plain short pastry. If to be eaten hot, I prefer to use one made with suet, but if for eating cold, the short pastry is lighter. In any case it should be fairly solid, firm and not too thin.

SUET MIXTURE PASTRY
½ lb flour
2 oz suet
2 oz butter
pinch of salt
iced water
SHORT PASTRY
½ lb flour
3½ oz butter, or 2 oz butter and 1½ oz lard
pinch of salt
iced water
1 egg yolk, beaten, to glaze
FILLING
6 oz rump steak
3 oz potato
1 oz onion
sea salt and black pepper

Make whichever pastry you prefer and chill for 20 minutes, wrapped in cling-film. Roll out until about ⅛ inch thick, then cut 4 circles 6 inches across, using a large saucer as a guide. Chop the steak into little cubes, and the potato likewise. Chop the onion finely and mix all together, adding lots of salt and pepper and 1 teaspoon of water. (If liked, 1 ounce of chopped carrot or turnip may be added.)

The old way of filling Cornish pasties was to pile the filling in the centre of the pastry and gather up the edges to meet (best done by holding the pastry in the palm of the hand). The inner edges were moistened with water and pinched together, then the pastry was laid down sideways and the edges crimped to make a rough edge. By filling them in this way the pasty would stand upright when baking, thus avoiding the possibility of the gravy leaking out.

You may find it easier to fill them by placing the meat mixture on one side of the circle, and folding the second half over it; it makes little difference. The crimping is done by first sealing the two edges, then making regular folds, like turning back the corner of a page of paper. Brush the pasties with beaten egg

FEUILLETÉ OF CRAYFISH

1 lb puff pastry
1 egg yolk
1 tbsp milk
48 crayfish, shelled

Preheat the oven to Gas Mark 7, 425°F.

Roll out the pastry into a rectangle 12 inches by 8 inches. Cut into 4 smaller rectangles. Place on a floured baking sheet and put in the refrigerator for 30 minutes.

Beat the egg yolk and milk together and glaze each rectangle carefully, making sure none of the egg yolk mixture runs down the sides of the pastry. Place in the oven for 12-15 minutes. Remove from the oven and keep warm.

Split the rectangles and remove any soft pastry from inside. Arrange the shelled crayfish on the pastry bases and on the plate around them. Top with the glazed covers. Serve with a sauce such as hollandaise or *beurre blanc*. Serves 4.

ALISON PRICE 1984

INDIVIDUAL PORK PIE

3 oz pork trimmings or belly (more lean than fat, minus skin, rind, bone, gristle)
salt (or anchovy essence) and pepper
pinch of mace and/or freshly chopped herbs (optional)
4 oz hot water crust pastry
jellied stock or aspic

Put the pork through the medium blade of the mincer. Season and add the mace and/or freshly chopped herbs, if used. Mix well.

Take 3 ounces of pastry (keep 1 ounce for the lid) and either fashion into a well shape, like a potter, or press into a greased tart tin of about 3 inches diameter. Pack the case with the pork (the filling will hold it in position). Cover with the remaining pastry and pinch the edges together. The hole in the top is important. Bind the sides with greaseproof paper secured with string. Bake in a preheated oven, Gas Mark 4, 350°F, for 1 hour. Check after 40 minutes to make sure it is not burning. Serve hot, or allow the pie to cool a little and fill to the brim with melted jelly. Be careful, it may leak.

MARWOOD YEATMAN 1985

Norman Eales 1965

'If green fingers make for successful gardening, certainly light cool fingers achieve good pastry.'

FISH

The new cry in England is "Eat More Fish" ' – this is not a current TV commercial but Marcel Boulestin writing in *Vogue* in 1923. The *Semaine du Poisson* was already an attraction in Boulogne where cheap weekend tickets, a calm sea, and the promise of delightful dishes were tempting visitors across the Channel. At home the Ministry of Agriculture and Fisheries issued a report stating, 'If the home market is to expand it is essential to educate the consumers to the dietetic value of good fresh fish, and at the same time ensure that supplies of such fish, at prices which will enable it to compete with all classes of meat, are continuously available.'

Oysters were frequently in *Vogue* in the early part of the century – 'throughout the lenten weeks there is perhaps no food in higher esteem than oysters,' according to an anonymous writer.

The kipper is at the other end of the fishy scale but another writer, explaining to his readers the kind of breakfast foods that appealed most to masculine tastes, wrote in 1938: 'Only a grilled kipper will make a man's mouth water. Cook the back first and don't get annoyed when it tries to turn up and burn its tail. This breakfast dish makes a very

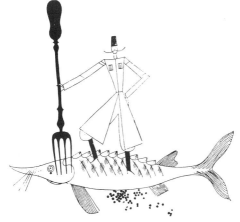

Above: Roger de Lavererie 1929
Opposite: Von Alvensleben 1986

good hot supper snack but recently I was caught late at night by some hungry men who had dined early. But I had some bread, butter and a good thick smoked haddock, so I cut the haddock in very thin slices, washed them with vinegar and made what everyone declared to be the best smoked salmon sandwiches they had ever tasted!'

Arabella Boxer, writing in the seventies, described her favourite ways of preparing fish: 'I much prefer fish cooked absolutely plainly, either grilled, fried or poached, and served with a separate sauce . . . There are many simple and delicious sauces that can be quickly made at home; I like a creamy horseradish sauce with fried fillet of plaice or sole, while a semi-frozen sauce of tomatoes and sour cream is quite delicious with *goujons* of sole.'

However, she also lamented, 'England is no longer the fish-eating nation it once was; more and more fish shops are disappearing, and most people seem content to restrict their fish-buying to the frozen compartments of the nearest supermarket. I don't know why we are so lazy about cooking fish, for the actual cooking time is short – even the largest fish can be cooked in half an hour – and the results are so delicious.'

Edward McKnight-Kauffer 1926

POISSON FARCI AU VIN BLANC

Take a good-sized carp, or a pike, and remove the head; wash the fish and clean it and wipe the inside. Sprinkle it with salt and pepper, both inside and outside, and leave it in a cloth till the following day.

Prepare stuffing in the following way: streaky bacon and ham, a little cold roast veal, a small slice of stale bread, parsley, two shallots, salt and pepper, all passed through a sieve or a mincing machine. Add a drop of white wine and stuff the fish with this mixture.

Put the fish in a fireproof dish, cover it with white wine and cook it in the oven. When it is about half cooked, sprinkle over it some of the stuffing and a few breadcrumbs and finish cooking, being careful to regulate the heat so the wine sauce does not evaporate altogether.

BOULESTIN 1923

'We have to eat to live so we might as well also learn to enjoy it.'

FISH IN ASPIC

The best kind of fish to use is freshwater fish such as trout, carp, pike or bream. Failing these, the nearest substitute would be conger eel. Sprinkle a teaspoon of gelatine over ½ cup of cold water and set aside. Halve an onion and put in a saucepan with 2 cups of water, 3 or 4 sliced carrots, a few peppercorns, a bay leaf, a teaspoon of sugar and a pinch of salt. Bring to the boil, then simmer gently for 15 minutes. Add the fish and continue simmering for another 10-15 minutes until the fish is soft but not overcooked, adding a little more water if necessary.

Lift out the fish carefully so as not to break it. Place in a shallow dish and surround with the carrots. Strain the liquid and stir in the gelatine, until it is dissolved. Pour the gelatine liquid over the fish and leave in a cool place to set. When completely set, turn out and serve decorated with parsley.

In Moravia, where this dish originates, a handful of chopped nuts is added to the liquid before it is poured over the fish. You may or may not be tempted to try it – personally we love it, because it brings out the full flavour.

PETER PIRBRIGHT AND GRETEL BEER 1949

STUFFED CARP

1 medium carp
margarine for baking
STUFFING
2 rolls
milk for soaking
2 anchovy fillets, finely chopped
salt and pepper
1 egg yolk
1 small onion, chopped
2 oz mushrooms, chopped
chopped parsley
1 tbsp margarine

Prepare the fish by removing the scales and slitting it open lengthwise. Take out the inside, and keep the roe for stuffing.

Soak the rolls in milk, then press out all moisture. Add the finely chopped anchovies and roe, salt and pepper and egg yolk. Fry the chopped onion, mushrooms and parsley in the margarine, add to the stuffing and mix well. Stuff the fish with this mixture and secure with thread. Heat margarine in a baking dish, add salt and pepper to taste and bake the fish at Gas Regulo 6, 400°F, until well done (about 1 hour), basting frequently.

PETER PIRBRIGHT AND GRETEL BEER 1950

GALANTINE DE SAUMON

Take some fillet of salmon (three pounds would do for about six to seven people), cut the best part of it in slices about one inch thick and put these in a dish for two hours with salt, pepper and enough sherry to cover them. Mince very finely together (or pass through a wire sieve) the flesh of any white fish (say about one pound to three pounds of salmon), the rest of the salmon and a slice of stale bread dipped in milk. Add salt and pepper, the yolks of two eggs, a small piece of butter, a few chopped truffles and a certain amount of the sherry in which the fillets of salmon have been soaking. Place in a buttered terrine the fillets of salmon and stuffing in alternate layers, adding here and there a slice of truffle. Cook with the lid on for about an hour and a quarter in a moderate oven.

This dish, which is delicious, is, of course, all the better for being a large one, as somehow the subtle flavour of the ingredients seems to increase with the size; also, the small ones would be apt to be too dry.

BOULESTIN 1924

BRANDADE DE SAUMON

1½ lb fresh salmon
1 clove garlic, crushed
6 tbsp double cream
¼ pt olive oil
juice of ½ lemon
salt and freshly ground black pepper
toast triangles fried in olive oil or butter
(optional)

Poach the salmon until tender. Remove from the water; drain and flake, removing the bones and skin.

Place the salmon flakes in an electric blender or food processor with the crushed garlic, 2 tablespoons of the cream and 4 tablespoons of the olive oil. Blend this mixture, adding the remaining cream and olive oil, alternately, from time to time, until the oil and cream are completely absorbed and the *brandade* is creamy smooth. When ready to serve, simmer the mixture in the top of a double saucepan. Stir in the lemon juice and season to taste with salt and pepper.

Brandade de saumon may be served either hot or cold. If to be served hot, place in a mound on a warm serving dish and surround with toast triangles fried in olive oil or butter. Serves 4.

ROBERT CARRIER 1966

Picasso plate 1950

TRUITES AU CHABLIS

Have some small trout, dispose them in a small fireproof dish, with, all round, tomatoes cut in quarters, one banana cut in thin slices, tarragon and shallots finely chopped. Pour over all this a glass of Chablis (or Pouilly), season well, and cook very slowly; turn them carefully when they are about half done. When they are ready, remove the skins and keep the fish hot; let the sauce reduce a little more, then pass it through a fine sieve. Dispose the trout in the fireproof dish; add some *sauce hollandaise* to the sauce, little by little, over a very slow fire and whipping all the time. When it has the right consistency pour over the trout and serve at once.

BOULESTIN 1928

Martin 1925

TROUT IN RED WINE

This is practically unforgettable, it's so good. Make a *court bouillon* in an enamel pan by simmering together for 30 minutes, 2 cups of red wine, 2 cups of water, 1 small bouquet of parsley, a tiny pinch of thyme, a small piece of bay leaf, 1 scant teaspoon of coarse salt, a few black peppercorns, and 4 little white onions finely chopped with 1 shallot.

Strain the *court bouillon* through cheesecloth into a shallow enamel baking pan just large enough to hold 6 trout side by side. Poach the trout in the *court bouillon* for 10 minutes, then pour off most of the liquid, putting the fish on the back of the stove to keep warm. Reduce the liquid by two thirds by simmering fast. In the meantime, cream 4 tablespoons of butter with 1½ tablespoons of flour. Add it, bit by bit, to the reduced liquid, stirring well until all is incorporated. Pour the sauce over the trout and place for a second under a very hot grill to brown lightly. Garnish with parsley and serve immediately. Serves 6.

JUNE PLATT 1936

FINGER TROUT MEUNIÈRE

Wash, dry, then lightly flour the fish. Fry them in a mixture of olive oil and margarine until browned and cooked through, turning them once. Lift the fish out on to hot plates. Pour off the fat in the pan, put in 1½ ounces of butter or margarine, 1½ tablespoons of lemon juice and a good grating of nutmeg. Let this sauce just colour, and pour over the fish while still sizzling. Scatter with some chopped parsley. Any fillets of fish can be treated *à la meunière*. Garnish as you wish, with lemon or orange sections, stewed olives or cucumber, capers or mushrooms.

A quick and pleasant way with fillets of fish is to dip the dried and seasoned fillets in egg, then in a mixture of crumbs and grated cheese. Bake them in a buttered dish in the oven and serve a tomato sauce, *maître d'hôtel* butter, or chive butter which is less usual.

DORIS LYTTON-TOYE 1951

TROUT FILLETS IN OATMEAL

4 trout
sea salt and black pepper
a little milk
coarse oatmeal for coating
about 2 oz butter
1-2 lemons to serve

Cut off the heads and tails of the fish and lift each side carefully from the central bones, leaving on the skin. Sprinkle each fillet with salt and pepper, dip in milk, then in coarse oatmeal. They can then be fried in butter or grilled, in which case they should be dotted with the butter cut in small pieces. In either case, turn the fish carefully, and try to avoid knocking off the oatmeal. Serve nicely browned, with cut lemons and grilled tomatoes. A mustard sauce goes well with this dish.

ARABELLA BOXER 1979

Robert Freson 1964

FILETS DE CABILLAUD MARINÉS

Take a small cod, fillet it carefully, seeing that there are no bones left, then marinate the fillets for a day in the following mixture: a tumblerful of dry white wine and Madeira mixed, a liqueur glassful of brandy, salt, pepper, chopped shallots and two or three small bouquets of thyme, bay leaf and parsley.

Take an ovenproof dish, butter it well, dispose your fillets of fish and garnish them with slices of fresh mushroom. Pour over the mixture in which they have been soaked (less the bouquets) and cook about twenty minutes in the oven, basting often. See that it is well seasoned, add two tablespoons of fresh cream, a few small pieces of butter, shake well so that the sauce is evenly bound and serve. Any fish of a moderate size with a rather dry flesh can be treated in the same way, including such fresh-water fish as carp and pike.

BOULESTIN 1926

BROWN NUT FISH

This recipe will turn the plebeian cutlet of cod or hake into a succulent morsel. Obtain even-sized cutlets, wipe them and remove the skin and centre bone. Place them in a well-buttered dish and sprinkle with a little curry powder, some chopped capers (if possible) and chopped blanched almonds. Season them and put small pieces of butter and tiny shreds of bacon on top. Pour a few tablespoons of stock into the dish and bake in a moderate oven (Gas Mark 4, 350°F) for about 20 minutes, basting occasionally. Now sprinkle with breadcrumbs and return to the oven for 5 minutes to crisp the crumbs. Serve the cutlets with slices of lemon.

DORIS LYTTON-TOYE 1942

COD CHOWDER

3 lb cod
12 oz salt pork, diced
3 onions, sliced
6 large potatoes, diced
1½ cups chopped celery
2 bay leaves
3 pts milk
3 tbsp butter
1½ tsp salt
¾ tsp freshly ground black pepper

Heat 2 cups of water, and poach the cod in it for 15 minutes. Drain the cod and flake the flesh. Retain the stock. Sauté the pork until it is crisp, then remove it from the pan and set aside. Fry the onion gently in the pork fat until just turning colour. Add the cod, potatoes, celery, bay leaves, 1 cup of stock and 2 cups of boiling water. Now simmer together for 30 minutes.

Add the milk, butter, salt, pepper and pork and reheat, but do not boil. Crumble dry crackers on top, if you like, before serving. Serves 8.

MARIUS DUTREY 1955

BROCHETTES OF COD AND SOLE WITH MUSTARD SAUCE

2 thick cod steaks
2 small sole, filleted
salt
flour
oil for deep frying
MUSTARD SAUCE
1 tbsp butter
1 tbsp olive oil
1 onion, coarsely chopped
1 bunch parsley stalks
salt and freshly ground black pepper
1 tbsp flour
½ pt tinned clam juice
¼ pt dry white wine
1 tbsp mustard

To make the mustard sauce: heat the butter and oil in a saucepan and add the chopped onion, parsley stalks and salt and freshly ground black pepper to taste. Sauté, stirring continuously, until the onion is transparent. Sprinkle with flour and stir until well blended; add the clam juice and wine, and simmer gently for 20 minutes.

Place the mustard in the top of a double saucepan and strain the stock over it, pressing the onion and parsley stalks well against the sieve with a wooden spoon. Mix well, over simmering water, and continue to cook until the sauce is thick and smooth.

When ready to serve, cut the fish into 1-inch squares and arrange them on small skewers. Salt and flour them and deep fry in very hot oil until golden. Serve immediately, accompanied by the sauce. Serves 4.

ROBERT CARRIER 1965

BAKED COD

2½-3 lb cod on the bone
juice of 2 lemons
4 oz butter
sea salt and black pepper
3-4 tbsp dry breadcrumbs

Put the piece of cod in a fireproof dish and pour over the juice of the lemons. Cut the butter in pieces and scatter over and around. Cover with a buttered piece of aluminium foil and bake for about 1 hour at Gas Mark 4, 350°F. Half-way through, remove the paper and skin the top side of the fish. Baste with the butter and lemon and cover with a thick layer of breadcrumbs. Return to the oven and baste two or three times during the rest of the cooking. Serves 4 to 6.

ARABELLA BOXER 1977

FISH PIE

1½ lb haddock fillet
¾ pt milk
sea salt and black pepper
1½ oz butter
2 tbsp flour
2 tbsp cream
2 hard-boiled eggs
2 tbsp chopped parsley
POTATO PURÉE
1½ lb potatoes
2 oz butter
⅓ pt milk
sea salt and black pepper

Put the fish in a broad pan and add the ¾ pint of milk. Add enough water to almost cover the fish, and some salt. Bring to the boil and simmer until the fish flakes easily, about 10 minutes. Lift out the fish and strain the cooking liquor. Measure ½ pint and reserve it; keep the rest for a soup.

When cool enough to handle, flake the fish, discarding all skin and bones. Melt the butter, stir in the flour and cook for 1 minute. Add the reserved ½ pint of fish stock and stir until blended. Simmer for 3-4 minutes, adding salt and black pepper to taste, and the cream. Stir in the flaked fish and the chopped hard-boiled eggs and reheat gently. Add the chopped parsley and pour into a buttered soufflé dish. Have a potato purée made before-hand and kept hot. Spoon over the fish and serve with broccoli. Serves 4.

Note: If made in advance, reheat very gently or the sauce will boil up and merge with the purée.

ARABELLA BOXER 1979

Robert Freson 1964

HALIBUT SOUFFLÉ

I cup flaked halibut
I cup thick white sauce
I tsp lemon juice
I tsp Worcestershire sauce
salt and pepper
I egg white, beaten stiff
I cup breadcrumbs
I oz butter, melted
2 tbsp grated Parmesan cheese

Mix together the flaked fish, white sauce, lemon juice, Worcestershire sauce, salt and pepper, then fold in the beaten egg white. Three-quarters fill a buttered glass baking dish with this mixture. Mix the breadcrumbs with the melted butter and Parmesan cheese, and strew them on top. Bake the soufflé in a hot oven for 10-15 minutes.

LEONE B. MOATS 1933

HALIBUT STRACHUR

3½-4½ lb halibut
6 oz butter
juice of 2 lemons
½ pt cream
I tbsp Worcestershire sauce (optional)
salt and black pepper

Get your fishmonger to give you a well-shaped piece of halibut weighing over 3 pounds. Half a small fish looks better than a slice from a large one. Remember it will be a lot smaller when cooked.

Clean and trim the halibut but do not skin or bone it. Cook it in the butter in a large frying pan, with the juice of one of the lemons sprinkled over it while it is cooking. Cook until it is golden brown on both sides and the flesh comes away easily from the backbone. Turn the fish very carefully so as to keep it whole. It will need about 15 minutes' gentle cooking on both sides. When ready, remove the fish from the pan. Skin and collect as many bones from the edges of the fish as you can: transfer it to a shallow entrée dish and keep hot. Add the cream to the juices in the pan, then the Worcestershire sauce (if liked) and lemon juice, salt and pepper to taste. Pour the sauce over the fish. Serve with deep-fried straw potatoes arranged in little bundles around the edge of the fish.

VERONICA MACLEAN 1970

> '**Cookery is as old as the world, but it must also remain, always, as modern as fashion.**'
>
> PHILEAS GILBERT

Anthony Denney 1960

SPECIALLY SOUSED HERRING

Remove the heads, backbones and fins from the herrings and wash thoroughly. Season their insides: lay in each a wafer of onion: roll up from head to tail. Pack together closely in an ovenproof dish, tails erect. Pour over a mixture of wine vinegar and water, laced with white wine or port. Strew more onion rings, also carrot slices, a few peppercorns, 2 cloves and a bay leaf, cut in two, on top. Cover with a baking tin and cook in a moderate oven for about 45 minutes. Cool before serving.

DORIS LYTTON-TOYE 1948

HERRINGS BAKED WITH APPLES AND POTATOES

4 herrings
4 oz smoked streaky bacon, thinly sliced
4 cloves
2 bay leaves
1 sprig fresh rosemary (or 1 tsp dried)
mustard
1 oz unsalted butter
1 small onion, finely chopped
1 clove garlic, crushed
2 tbsp chopped parsley
salt and pepper
4 sweet apples
juice of ½ lemon
2 tbsp medium fine oatmeal
3 tbsp olive oil

Clean the herrings and remove the heads. Slice down the sides of the backbones of the fish, cutting them in two. Remove the spine by pulling it back from the tail end and easing it away from the flesh. Trim each piece carefully, cutting off the very bony bits of flesh at one side.

Line a shallow casserole dish with bacon. Add the cloves, bay leaves and rosemary. Spread the herrings generously with mustard and lay on top of the bacon – flesh side up. Dot with butter.

1924

Sprinkle with the finely chopped onion, garlic, parsley, salt and pepper. Peel, core and slice apples and lay them over the herrings to cover them completely. Pour over the lemon juice, sprinkle with oatmeal and finally dribble olive oil over the top. Bake in preheated moderately hot oven (Gas Mark 5-6, 375-400°F) for 35-40 minutes. Serves 4.

JANE LONGMAN 1985

ROUGETS PROVENÇALE

Take 6 small fresh red mullet, each weighing about 4 ounces. Alternatively, use river trout, small Dover sole (their black skin removed), or fillets of sole. Do not empty the fish, but remove the gills and clean the outside. Dry and season them well.

Chop a shallot finely and crush a clove of garlic in coarse salt. Peel the skin and remove the seeds from 8 tomatoes: cut the flesh into dice. Melt a knob of butter in a saucepan, put in the shallot, then cover the pan and cook over a low flame until it is transparent, but don't let it burn or it will have a bitter taste. Add the tomatoes and garlic, continue cooking for a few minutes and then add 2 tablespoons of fine salad oil, a small glass of white wine, a coffee-spoon of saffron, a pinch of basil, a dash of sugar, and salt and freshly ground pepper. Boil together until the sauce is reduced by half. As the reduction proceeds, sauté the mullets in hot oil for a couple of minutes on either side.

Place a little of the sauce in a shallow ovenproof dish. Dispose the fish elegantly thereon, season again, pour the cooking oil over them, then mask completely with the remainder of the tomato sauce. Cover the dish with greaseproof paper and bake in a fast oven for about 15 minutes. Lay a slice of lemon, previously freed from rind and pith, and a strip of anchovy on each fish before serving. This dish can be prepared beforehand and baked just before dinner. It is delectable either hot or cold.

DORIS LYTTON-TOYE 1949

ROUGETS GRILLÉS

Except for the gills, the sea woodcock (red mullet) is usually left whole and not emptied. Preferably, choose fish weighing 4-6 ounces.

Wipe the fish carefully, then make shallow incisions, on either side, into the flesh. Place the fish in a flat dish, season with salt and pepper and sprinkle over a little oil and lemon juice, a few parsley stalks and half a bay leaf. Allow the fish to marinate for 1 hour, turning them occasionally. Grill them under a fast grill for about 20 minutes, basting them often with the marinade. Lay a pat of *maître d'hôtel* butter on each fish and serve at once.

DORIS LYTTON-TOYE 1951

Douglas 1933

SOLE BRETONNE

Skin the sole, remove the fins and slice it the whole length in the middle. Lift the fillets and insert little pieces of salt butter worked with a little parsley and lemon juice. Cook it in butter in a frying pan, turning it once. Before serving, add more salt, pepper and a little more lemon. This way of cooking a sole is very simple and delicious, being a little more than a fried one and a little less than a sole *meunière*.

BOULESTIN 1924

Opposite: Tessa Traeger 1983

PAUPIETTES DE SOLE ELISABETH

Take some fillets of sole, roll them and fill them with the stuffing described below; tie them and cook them slowly in Chablis or any other dry white wine mixed with fish stock. Drain them well and keep them hot.

Cook the stock a little longer till it has reduced by half, then add a glass of *sauce béchamel* and a glass of fresh cream, a little grated Parmesan and a few pieces of butter. Season well, cook for a few minutes and squeeze through a muslin. Keep hot in a *bain marie*.

Have as many *fonds d'artichauts* as there are fillets, previously sautéd in butter. Put on each a few chopped truffles, lay over this one *paupiette* of sole, pour some sauce over, sprinkle with a little grated cheese, brown quickly and serve at once.

Should you want to have this dish served absolutely correctly, the *paupiettes* should be disposed in a circle in the serving dish and the centre afterwards filled with a *ragoût* of truffles.

The stuffing should be prepared in the following manner: take some stale breadcrumbs and soak them in milk; reduce this mixture to a pulp and 'bind' it with the yolk of an egg. Add double the quantity of raw fish (pike or whiting), salt it and pound well together for a few minutes. Add one or two more yolks of eggs, according to the quantity of stuffing wanted, some fresh butter worked to a cream, and seasoning; and before using see that the stuffing is smooth.

For the fish stock necessary for this dish (also very useful for cooking other kinds of fillets of sole), put in a small saucepan the head and bones of the fish, slices of mushroom and carrot, thyme, bay leaf, parsley, cloves, salt and pepper, a glass of water, a glass of white wine, bring to the boil and reduce on a slow fire.

BOULESTIN 1925

FILETS DE SOLE DOROTHÉE

The sole having been filleted, put in a small saucepan the head and bones, one onion in slices, one carrot, a sprig of thyme, a bay leaf, a clove, salt and pepper, a glass of water and a glass of dry white wine. Bring this to the boil and reduce it on a slow fire for about twenty minutes. Pass it through a muslin and keep it warm.

Sprinkle the sole fillets with salt and paprika and cook them in butter; then *flambé* with a little good brandy. Mix together this butter and brandy and the sauce previously prepared; add small mushrooms, a glass of fresh cream and a little lemon juice, and pour it very hot over the fillets. It is advisable for this dish, as for all dishes which are *flambés*, to use really good brandy, and not the kind generally sold as cooking brandy, which has no strength and no flavour.

BOULESTIN 1925

SOLE MONICA

Properly prepared, this is the most perfect of the dishes in which sole is used as a base. Six or eight fillets of sole are poached in a pint or less of milk. A quarter of a pound of white grapes of the firm-fleshed variety are peeled and seeded, and an equal quantity of mushrooms are sliced, cooked in butter and seasoned with salt, black pepper and cayenne. Then a tablespoon of flour and a tablespoon of butter are creamed together and added slowly to the milk from which the fillets have been removed. This should be stirred constantly until the mixture thickens, and 2 tablespoons of grated mild cheese and ½ pint of cream should be added gradually. The fillets are arranged in a casserole, in layers with the grapes and mushrooms, covered with sauce, and baked for 12 minutes in a hot oven.

1934

FILLETS OF SOLE OR FLOUNDER IN RED WINE

Finely chop 6 white onions and cook them gently in butter until soft but not brown. Spread the onions in the bottom of an enamel baking dish, just large enough to hold 8 fillets of either sole or flounder. Lay the fillets on this bed, salt and pepper lightly, pour over them 1½ cups of good red wine and dot with 3 tablespoons of butter. Place the pan on the fire and bring the fish to the boil, then place the pan in a moderately hot oven to bake (Gas Mark 5, 375°F), basting very frequently. When the juice has reduced to about ½ cup and the fish is no longer transparent, it is ready to serve. Sprinkle very lightly with very finely chopped parsley and serve at once.

JUNE PLATT 1936

SOLE MEUNIÈRE À L'ORANGE

Cut off the heads, obliquely, from two small sole. Remove the black skin, scrape the white skin; snip away the side bones. Wash and dry the fish, season with salt and pepper, and roll in flour. Melt some margarine or clarified fat in a flat pan and, when the fat is hot, lay in the fish. Cook the fish slowly for about 6 minutes, then turn them and cook the other sides. Meanwhile, peel an orange, remove all the pith and cut into segments. Warm the segments in a pan.

Dress the sole in a hot dish, sprinkle each with a good pinch of chopped parsley and some lemon juice. Dispose the segments of orange down the centre of the sole. Melt a piece of butter in the fish saucepan and, when it begins to froth and turn golden brown, pour it over the fish and serve immediately.

DORIS LYTTON-TOYE 1949

Pierre Brissaud 1934

FILETS DE SOLE À L'INDIENNE

2 Dover sole or lemon sole, skinned and filleted, with their bones
vegetable trimmings (ends of leek and celery, ½ small onion and sliced carrot)
½ bay leaf
1 stalk parsley
salt and black pepper
⅛ pt white wine
3 tbsp desiccated coconut
½ oz butter
1 small onion, chopped
1 small eating apple (Granny Smith or Cox), peeled, cored and chopped
1 medium tomato, skinned and chopped
1 small clove garlic, finely chopped
1½ tsp light curry powder (Schwartz, Spice Islands, or McCormick)
¼ pt double cream
1 tsp flour
1 tsp sweet fruit syrup (optional)
2 tsp lemon juice

Put the fish bones and skins in a saucepan with the vegetable trimmings, bay leaf, parsley, salt and black pepper. Pour over the white wine and enough cold water to just cover. Bring to the boil and simmer for 25 minutes, then strain. You will need just under 1 pint. Measure ½ pint of the strained stock and pour it over the desiccated coconut in a bowl. Leave to stand for 30 minutes, then drain, squeezing the coconut which you then discard.

Melt the butter and cook the chopped onion until it softens and starts to colour. Add the chopped apple, then the tomato and garlic. Stir in the curry powder and cook for 1 minute, stirring. Add the strained coconut milk and simmer gently for 10 minutes. Towards the end of the time, heat the remaining fish stock in a pan. Cut the fish fillets into diagonal strips about 1 inch across. Poach them in the fish stock, for 2 minutes only, then remove from the heat. When the sauce has finished cooking, put 1 tablespoon of the cream into a teacup and stir in the flour, to make a smooth paste. Add this by degrees to the sauce, stirring constantly, and simmer gently for 3 minutes. Then add the rest of the cream, the fruit syrup (if you have it) and the lemon juice. (I use syrup from pickled fruit but you could use tinned fruit syrup or omit it altogether. In this case, use only 1 teaspoon of lemon juice.) Drop the little strips of fish into the sauce and reheat. Simmer all together for 1 minute, then serve with boiled rice.

This makes a delicious light main dish for a luncheon or late supper served with a green salad. Serves 4.

ARABELLA BOXER 1983

TURBOT KEBABS

Wash and dry a piece of turbot, about a pound, and cut it in chunks or gobbets of 1½ inches square. Put them in a basin with a little oil, seasoning and a bay leaf, and leave to marinate for 30 minutes. Then spear the pieces on skewers, with small bay leaves between each, and grill under a hot grill. Cook until lightly browned, turning them and seasoning once or twice. When cooked through, serve at once on a hot dish, with herb butter. Boiled rice, tossed in margarine, makes a good basis for these kebabs. *Note:* Melted margarine will do instead of oil.

DORIS LYTTON-TOYE 1945

TURBOT AUX CHAMPIGNONS

4 turbot or halibut steaks
½ cup milk
½ lb mushrooms
1⅓ tbsp margarine
handful of parsley sprigs, chopped
2 tsp flour
2 egg yolks
juice of 1 lemon
salt and pepper

Poach the fish in salted water to which the milk has been added. Drain well and keep hot.

Clean and slice the mushrooms. Melt the margarine in a large frying pan, add the sliced mushrooms and chopped parsley. Cover with a lid and simmer gently until the mushrooms are tender. Sprinkle with flour and stir well. Gradually add 2 cups of cold water (a little more if necessary) and simmer until well blended. Beat together the egg yolks and lemon juice, and gradually add to the mushrooms. Keep on a very low flame; on no account should the sauce boil. Add salt and pepper to taste. Add the fish to the sauce and cover to keep hot.

PETER PIRBRIGHT AND GRETEL BEER 1949

FISH SMOORE

For this fish curry, from Galle in Southern Ceylon, rub 2 pounds of turbot (the best substitute for seer fish) with pepper, salt and turmeric. Fry it in butter until light brown, then add 2 chopped cloves of garlic, 1 sliced onion and a large knob of preserved ginger cut into tiny dice. When the onion softens, add 1 dessertspoon of curry powder, 1 teaspoon of cinnamon, 2 or 3 pounded dried red chillies, and a bay leaf. Cook for 5 minutes, then add 3 ounces of desiccated coconut, which has been soaked for 2 hours in 2 tablespoons of vinegar and ½ pint of water. Simmer very slowly till the fish is tender. Break up the fish and serve with plain rice.

BERYL GOULD-MARKS 1954

GRILLED LOBSTER

Parboil 3 big lobsters for 5 minutes in plenty of actively boiling, salted water. Remove from the water and, with a sharp knife, split them in two, lengthwise down the back. Remove and throw away the stomach and intestines. Remove and keep, separately, the green part and the red coral, if there is any. Butter the meat and shells with soft butter and place, shell side up, on a buttered pan. Place under a hot grill for 12 minutes; then turn, reduce the heat slightly and cook, meat side up, for about 7 minutes.

In the meantime, clarify ¾ cup of butter by melting it slowly, pouring off the clear part into a saucepan and throwing away the milky part. Add to the butter the juice of 1 lemon, a dash each of Tabasco and Worcestershire sauce, the chopped coral and salt and pepper. Put the green part you have saved back into the lobster. Place the lobsters on a hot platter, garnish with lemon and serve at once with the butter sauce which you have heated slightly. Serves 6.

1937

Pierre Brissaud 1934

KEDGEREE

As Mrs Plunket-Greene pointed out in 1960, no two people make kedgeree the same way, and some like it hot while others prefer it cold. Some people have it for breakfast, others serve it for supper.

DORIS LYTTON-TOYE'S COLD SALMON KEDGEREE 1948

Wrap a 1 pound cut of salmon in muslin. Lower it into a pan of boiling salted water and simmer gently until the fish is tender. Let it cool in the liquid.

Cook a small teacup of well-washed rice in salted boiling water, with a clove of garlic and a bay leaf, till the grain is soft but unbroken. Drain the rice and rinse under the cold tap, removing the garlic and bay leaf.

Prepare a white sauce from ¾ ounce of butter, ¾ ounce of flour and ½ pint of liquid (half milk, half fish liquor). Season the sauce with salt and pepper, a few drops of anchovy essence and a pinch of curry powder. Stir the sauce as it cools.

Drain the salmon and flake the flesh. Blend the rice and fish gently with a fork; fold in the cooled sauce and a tablespoon or so of top of the milk. Be certain the seasoning is enough; cold foods require higher seasoning. Chill in the ice box. Pile the creamy kedgeree on a dish garnished with knots of watercress or quartered lettuce hearts.

ROBIN MCDOUALL'S HADDOCK KEDGEREE 1956

Cook 2 haddock in milk until the flesh begins to fall off the bones. Remove the skin and bones and flake the flesh. Heat the flaked flesh in butter and add about the same quantity of cold boiled rice. Add 2 hard-boiled eggs, cut in quarters, and season with a little salt, some black pepper and a good deal of cayenne. Add a raw egg and a cup of cream – not so much, however, as to make it runny. Stir lightly with a fork.

MRS PLUNKET-GREENE'S HADDOCK KEDGEREE 1960

For 6 people take 12 ounces of long-grain rice, 12 ounces of smoked haddock and peeled shrimps, 1 tablespoon of chopped fresh parsley, 2 tablespoons of chopped chives, mayonnaise, pepper, 4 hard-boiled eggs and 12 anchovy fillets. Poach and flake the haddock, then cook the rice: rinse and drain thoroughly and stir together with a fork. When cold, add the shrimps, parsley and chives and stir in enough mayonnaise (real is a must) to make a not-too-moist mixture. Add pepper to taste and serve it garnished with chopped eggs and anchovies.

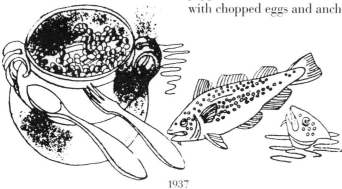

1937

HOMARD AU CHAMPAGNE

This is one of Prunier's recipes: cut up just over 1 pound of lobster meat in small pieces. Toss it in butter, and season with salt and pepper. Moisten the lobster with Madeira and a little fish stock and, if possible, add a truffle. Let it cook for 20 minutes with the cover on, then remove the lobster and slice the truffle. Put them both in a covered serving dish and keep warm.

Strain and reduce the stock in which the lobster was cooked. Add ½ pint of double cream and heat without bringing it to the boil. Throw in 2 sherry glasses of still champagne, and bind with the yolks of 2 eggs. Pour over the lobster, and serve immediately. This dish must not be kept waiting.

JUNE PLATT 1937

LOBSTER THERMIDOR

Split 2 freshly boiled lobsters down the back. Remove the meat from the claws and body and cut it into dice. Melt 1 ounce of butter in a saucepan, stir in ¾ ounce of flour and cook for a few seconds. Moisten with ½ pint of stock and ¼ pint of cream or rich top of the milk. Whisk the sauce until it boils, then put in the lobster meat, together with any creamy part and coral from the carapace. Simmer the mixture for a good 10 minutes, stirring frequently. Season with salt, paprika, and a few grains of cayenne. At the end of the cooking time, add a little sherry.

Wash the lobster shells, fill them with the mixture and cover with a thickish layer of buttered crumbs. Set in a moderately hot oven (Gas Regulo 6, 400°F) for about 5 minutes. If the crumbs are not browned, place under a blazing grill for a second or so. Serve on a dish garnished with crisp sprigs of watercress and wedges of lemon.

DORIS LYTTON-TOYE 1951

HOMARD FRAPPÉ

With a fork, shred the flesh of a well-cooked lobster finely. Make some very thin, well-seasoned mayonnaise, faintly coloured with some of the coral from the lobster. Add it to the lobster meat. Mix together so that it is quite loose. Pile it up in a bowl, roughly, and sprinkle a little more of the coral over it. Place on a large dish with cracked ice around the bowl. Serve sandwiches of mustard and cress with this.

LOELIA DUCHESS OF WESTMINSTER 1952

FITZ'S LOBSTER RISOTTO

2 medium freshly boiled lobsters (about 1½ lb each)
about 2 tumblers rice
about 4 oz butter
a little olive oil
salt and pepper
a little paprika
¼ pt sour cream
4 hard-boiled eggs
1 tbsp freshly chopped tarragon
1 tbsp freshly grated Parmesan cheese
1 wine glass medium dry sherry

When the lobsters are cold, crack the claws, cut the tails in two and remove all the meat. Skim the water in which the lobsters were boiled; bring the water once more to the boil and throw in the rice. Boil briskly for about 12 minutes (start testing after 11; it should be *al dente*, or firm but not hard) and, when ready, turn immediately into a large sieve or colander and run cold water over the rice until the starch is washed away and the water runs clear. Leave to drain and dry in a very cool oven, with the door open, or on top of the cooker: it will take from 1-2 hours. Meanwhile, cut the lobster meat into convenient pieces.

Fifteen minutes before serving, melt the butter and a little olive oil in a large sauté pan. Stir in the rice, the cut up lobster and lobster coral, and any bits you can scrape from the shell. Add salt, pepper and paprika to taste, the cream, hard-boiled eggs, tarragon, Parmesan and sherry. Mix all the ingredients together carefully, adding more butter and oil, if necessary, to prevent sticking. Correct the seasoning and turn on to a very hot serving dish.

VERONICA MACLEAN 1969

Alan Cracknell 1966

65

MOULES MARINIÈRES

I pt mussels
I small onion, finely chopped
salt and pepper
I tbsp finely chopped parsley
a few drops of lemon juice

Scrape the mussels and scrub in several changes of water, discarding any that are not firmly closed. Put them in a pan with about 2 tablespoons of water, the finely chopped onion and a sprinkle of pepper. Cover with a lid and cook over a brisk flame, shaking the pan from time to time until the shells have opened. Discard the top shells, arrange the mussels in a serving dish, and sprinkle with finely chopped parsley. Add a few drops of lemon juice to the liquid in the pan, adjust the seasoning (adding a little salt, if necessary) and pour hot over the mussels.
Note: This is not the classic recipe where the sauce should contain some white wine and also be thickened, but a 'slimming' version.

GRETEL BEER 1953

SHEFFIELD ISLAND BISQUE

Here is an American recipe with which to ring the changes on *moules marinières*. Begin by washing 3 dozen mussels (in our measures this would be about 4 pints) and discard any that are not tightly closed. In a large kettle (pan to us), heat ¼ cup of olive oil and add 1 sliced clove of garlic, a pinch of cayenne, 6 sprigs of parsley and 1 teaspoon of marjoram. Add the mussels, mixing them thoroughly with the seasoned oil. Pour in 1 cup of dry white wine and add ½ teaspoon of freshly ground black pepper. Cover the kettle and steam the mussels until the shells open. Remove the mussels from the shells, chop them and reserve them.

Cook the liquid until it is reduced to about 1 cup, add to it ½ cup of white wine and set aside. Sauté 1 tablespoon of chopped shallots in 3 tablespoons of butter and blend in 2 tablespoons of flour. Gradually, add to the roux 3 tablespoons of the strained mussel liquor. When the sauce thickens, add the mussels and 1 cup each of cream and milk, and cook for 2 minutes longer or until the sauce is heated through. Before serving garnish the bisque with freshly chopped parsley.

ELIZABETH KENDALL 1958

Anthony Denney 1957

MUSSELS AU GRATIN

6 pts mussels
¼ pt white wine
1 small onion or shallot, finely chopped
½ pt water
1 teacup stale breadcrumbs
1 teacup grated Parmesan cheese
1 tbsp freshly chopped parsley

Wash and scrub and beard the mussels. Discard any that are not tightly closed. If you're worried, leave them in a pail of fresh water overnight, with a spoonful of oatmeal sprinkled into the water. This, the old wives tell us, is *guaranteed* to purify them.

Cook the mussels in a large pan with the wine, the onion or shallot and the water. Cover the pan, bring to the boil, and boil for 1 minute. Drain away the liquid into a shallower pan. Put this pan on the fire and boil briskly to reduce. Meanwhile, pull away the upper half of each mussel shell. All the mussels should have partly opened in the boiling, so throw away any that have not. Place the mussels in their remaining shells, side by side, on a sheet of foil in a shallow oven-proof dish. You can make 2 layers as long as you sprinkle each layer first with the breadcrumbs, then the grated Parmesan and parsley. Add the liquid in which you boiled the mussels, which should have reduced to about ¼ pint. Enclose this with the mussels in the foil like a huge parcel. Bake in a hot oven (Gas Mark 8, 450°F) for 15 minutes, and split the parcel at the table.

VERONICA MACLEAN 1970

HUITRES AU GRATIN

Put in a small saucepan two shallots, two or three mushrooms and parsley, all very finely chopped, and cook them in butter till brown. Add some breadcrumbs, salt and pepper, a little dry white wine and a small piece of fresh butter, and boil this for a few minutes. It should be rather thick.

Open some large oysters, leave them in the hollow shell and cover each of them with the stuffing. Sprinkle them with breadcrumbs, add a little melted butter, and brown in a moderate oven.

BOULESTIN 1923

Denton Welch 1946

BROILED SHRIMPS

Wash 1 pound of shrimps in cold water. Then, with little scissors, snip the shells open along the centre of their backs and remove every bit of black intestines with a little knife. This is definitely a bore but absolutely necessary. When finished, rinse them once more in cold water and dry them well. Now pour 4 ounces of melted fresh butter, mixed with ½ cup of olive oil, over the bottom of a flat fire-proof meat platter. Sprinkle the dish with 1 heaped tablespoon of chopped shallots and 3 cloves of garlic, also finely chopped. Now place the shrimps on the platter in a single layer, and roll them over in the butter and oil so that they are well coated. Squeeze the juice of ½ lemon over them.

Place the platter under a hot grill for 5 minutes, then sprinkle the shrimps lightly with salt and heavily with coarsely ground black pepper. Turn them over and grill them so that they actually brown lightly. Sprinkle again lightly with salt and heavily with pepper, and pour over them 1 cup of reduced, hot, dry white wine. Place under the grill again for just a few seconds. Sprinkle with finely chopped parsley and serve at once with plenty of French bread. They are eaten with the fingers (the shells have to be removed) and are definitely messy, but oh so good.

JUNE PLATT 1939

SIAMESE CUCUMBER AND PRAWNS

Cut a medium-sized cucumber into quarters, lengthwise, then slantingly into 1-inch pieces. Shell ½ pound of prawns and split them in two. Cut 4 ounces of mushrooms into wafer-thin slices.

Fry a crushed and chopped clove of garlic in 2 tablespoons of peanut oil until brown. Add the prawns, turn a few times, then add the mushrooms, a pinch of salt and ½ teaspoon of sugar. Push the ingredients to the side of the pan out of the direct heat. Put in the cucumbers and fry them for 5 minutes, then blend in with the other ingredients.

Mix together 1 tablespoon of sherry, 1 tablespoon of soya bean sauce (1 teaspoon of yeast extract diluted with 3 teaspoons of water and a dash of Worcestershire sauce will do instead), and 1 tablespoon of water; pour over the mixture. Stir thoroughly, cover closely and simmer for 10 minutes. Serve with rice.

BERYL GOULD-MARKS 1954

RICE WITH PRAWNS AND CREAM SAUCE

Suppose the dish is for just 2 people as a main course, to be followed by a salad and a sweet: measure out a full teacup (about 6 ounces) of Patna rice, and pour it into a saucepan containing 10 cups of boiling water to which you have added 1 tablespoon of salt and, after the water comes back to the boil, a tablespoon of olive oil, which helps to disperse the scum and prevent the water from boiling over. Boil for 13-15 minutes, then rinse and strain as usual in a colander. Turn into a lightly oiled or buttered tin or small soufflé dish, cover with a folded cloth and leave in the lowest oven while you attend to the prawn mixture.

For this you need about 6 ounces of peeled prawns (you can buy 4-ounce and 2-ounce packets of frozen prawns which usually have a better flavour than the ubiquitous scampi). Preferably they should be thawed out by the time you start to cook them, and sprinkled with lemon juice, pepper and nutmeg. Probably no salt will be needed.

Heat 1½ ounces of butter in a small, thick frying pan. In this cook the prawns, very gently, for a minute or so. Pour a small glass of brandy (4-6 tablespoons) into a soup ladle or little saucepan. Warm it over a low flame, catch light to it and pour it flaming over the prawns. Shake and rotate the pan so that the flames spread, and when they go out, turn the heat low and let the mixture simmer for a couple of minutes so that the brandy loses its crude taste. Increase the heat again, pour in a scant ¼ pint of thick cream and let it bubble until it starts to thicken, again shaking the pan and spooning the cream up and round. Stir in a little chopped parsley. Turn your prepared rice out on to a hot dish and pour the prawn mixture over and round it.

ELIZABETH DAVID 1959

John Minton 1947

GRILLED DUBLIN PRAWNS

5 large langoustines or scampi prawns per person
lemon quarters to serve
HERB BUTTER SAUCE
¼ pt double cream
3 oz unsalted butter
juice of 1 lime
pinch of paprika
finely chopped tarragon
chives (or soft green herbs)
salt and pepper

To prepare the sauce, bring the cream to the boil. Take to the side of the stove and whisk in the butter, piece by piece, then the lime juice. Add a pinch of paprika, the fresh herbs and salt and pepper to taste. Grill the prawns for 3-4 minutes under a very hot grill (no need to turn them). Serve the grilled prawns on a bed of seaweed with quarters of lemon and hand the sauce separately. It may be useful to have finger bowls.

MICHAEL QUINN 1983

CRAB JAMBALAYA

Chop two onions very finely and brown them in a pan; add a pudding-spoon of flour (and stir well), also, chopped together, thyme, bay leaf, parsley and one clove of garlic. Fry these for a few minutes, then add chilli pepper and 3 large tomatoes cut in very small pieces. Let the mixture simmer for about 10 minutes, after which you add the necessary quantity of boiling stock, that is, about half a pint; also a glass of dry white wine. (The recipe I have by me says 'three quarts' of stock, which seems to me a rather large quantity, especially seeing that the finished article, which I have tasted, is a kind of dry pilaff. These 3 quarts of stock are, I take it, meant to disappear during the process of cooking the rice, which is a rather extravagant method; and I think the same excellent result can be obtained in cooking the rice separately in water and giving the finishing touch in a much smaller quantity of stock.)

Bring it to the boil, throw in your already cooked rice, about half a pound, the flesh of 2 crabs (previously boiled), see that it is highly flavoured and seasoned and cook for about 20 minutes, stirring occasionally. Serve very hot.

BOULESTIN 1926

CRAB MOUSSE

1 lb crab meat
¼ pt mayonnaise
¼ pt creamed cheese
freshly ground pepper
¼ pt gelatine
2 tsp lemon juice

Ask the fishmonger to boil your crab and let you have the meat as soon as possible. Combine the white and brown meat together, carefully removing any sinews or shell. Combine the mayonnaise and creamed cheese, then mix in the crab meat and season well with pepper. Prepare the gelatine according to the packet instructions, add the lemon juice and stir into the mixture. Put in a soufflé dish to set. This fresh mousse is delicious. It can be made with frozen crab but the flavour is not quite the same. Serves 6.

VISCOUNT EDEN 1973

COQUILLES ST JACQUES

This recipe comes from the famous *Chapon Fin* at Bordeaux. It is a delicious dish and by far the best way of serving this excellent shellfish. Wash the scallops well, boil them in salted water and chop the red part and the white part together with a tomato, a little onion, parsley, a few mushrooms, salt and pepper. Cook this for a few minutes in butter and bind it with a little *sauce béchamel*. Fill the scallop shells with the mixture and brown in the oven.

BOULESTIN 1924

FRIED SCALLOPS WITH TARTAR SAUCE

Marinate 1 pint of scallops in 3 tablespoons of olive oil, the juice of 1 lemon, 1 teaspoon of salt and a little pepper for 30 minutes. Meanwhile, prepare some rolled and sifted cracker crumbs; beat 1 egg with a little milk. Roll each scallop in crumbs, then dip it into the egg and back into the crumbs.

Heat some lard in a deep iron pan fitted with a wire basket. When the fat is about 350°F, or just below the smoking point, put a few of the scallops in the basket so that they do not touch each other. Put the basket into the fat and cook the scallops until they are a light golden brown, about 2 minutes. Remove them and place on absorbent kitchen paper in a pan in the oven to drain and keep warm while you fry the rest. Serve the scallops with tartar sauce made in the following manner:

To 1 cup of mayonnaise (preferably home-made) add 1 teaspoon of finely minced shallots, 1 teaspoon of well chopped fresh parsley, ½ teaspoon of chopped onion, 2 teaspoons of chopped capers and 2 teaspoons of chopped pickle. Serves 6.

JUNE PLATT 1938

Tessa Traeger 1977

STEAMED SCALLOPS

This unusual dish has a lot to recommend it. It is elegant, healthy, quickly made, and very appetizing.

2 tsp sesame oil
2 cloves garlic
1 sq inch piece root ginger
4 spring onions
12 scallops, with 4 curved shells, cleaned
sea salt
2 tsp soy sauce

Lay 4 pieces of foil on a flat surface and rub with a few drops of sesame oil. Slice the garlic and ginger finely, and lay half the slices on the pieces of foil. Cut the spring onions into 1-inch lengths, then cut each piece into very thin slivers. Lay half of these on the foil. Cut the scallops into quarters and lay on top of the onions. Sprinkle with sea salt, the remaining sesame oil, and the soy sauce. Cover with the remaining garlic, ginger and spring onions. Wrap up the foil packages and lay them in a steamer. Cook for 8 minutes over boiling water, covered. Serve the foil packages lying in the shells, as a first course, or light main dish. Serves 4.

Note: A perfect start to a dinner party, this goes well before a rich main dish.

ARABELLA BOXER 1984

ANSJOVISOGA

8 anchovy fillets
1 small onion
1 egg yolk

This delicious hors d'oeuvre is very simple to prepare: finely chop the anchovy fillets and onion. Place the raw egg yolk in the centre of a round serving dish, surround first with a circle of chopped onion, then with a circle of chopped anchovies. Serve with crispbread. The first person to be served stirs the ingredients until well blended.

PETER PIRBRIGHT AND GRETEL BEER 1950

JANSSONS FRESTELSE

This means 'Jansson's Temptation' and well it might be....

1 onion
1½ tbsp butter
2 potatoes
10 anchovy fillets
¾ cup cream or top of the milk

Slice the onion and brown lightly in ½ tablespoon of butter. Peel and cut the potatoes into strips. In a buttered baking dish arrange first a layer of potatoes, then a layer of onions and anchovies, and finish with a layer of potatoes. Add a few drops of the oil from the tin of anchovies and dot with the remaining butter.

Place in a preheated oven (Gas Regulo 6, 400°F) and after 10 minutes add half the cream. Pour in the remaining cream after another 10 minutes. Continue baking for 20 minutes, then reduce the heat to Gas Regulo ¼, 225°F. Bake for another 20-30 minutes, when the potatoes will be soft and the dish ready to serve.

PETER PIRBRIGHT AND GRETEL BEER 1950

CREAMED FINNAN HADDIES

Use the small smoked haddocks that have very few bones, and cut them in halves. Blanch them by pouring boiling water over and letting them stand awhile. Put the blanched fish in a buttered dish, pour over some fresh boiling water and add a little pepper. Cook them till tender in the oven, then pour away the water. Spread over the fish a little butter, cream and sherry, and replace in the oven. When this is absorbed, repeat the butter, cream and sherry, and again place in the oven for a few minutes. Shake the sauce rather than stir it. Add a dash of red pepper just before serving.

DORIS LYTTON-TOYE 1937

KIPPER MOUSSE

4 oz butter
½ lb kipper fillets, skinned
½ small onion, finely chopped
¼ pt milk
blade of mace
3 peppercorns
curl of lemon rind
bay leaf
1 oz flour
1 dessertspoon lemon juice
1 dessertspoon dry white wine
salt and cayenne pepper
5 oz double cream
GARNISH
cucumber slices
¼ pt aspic jelly

Melt 1 ounce of butter in a frying pan and fry the kippers and onion gently. Strain, keeping the juices, and mince the fish and onion together. Infuse the milk with the mace, peppercorns, lemon rind and bay leaf. Make a roux using 1 ounce of butter and 1 ounce of flour, then add the strained milk. Leave until cold.

Pound the cold minced kipper and onion with the remaining 2 ounces of butter; add the lemon juice, wine, kipper juices and the cold sauce. Season with salt and cayenne pepper to taste. Whip the cream fairly stiffly and fold into the mixture. Turn into individual soufflé dishes and chill. Garnish each one with cucumber slices and aspic jelly. For 6 people.

ELIZABETH KENDALL 1969

von Alvensleben 1985

MEAT

The cost of meat has worried people for more than 500 years: 'Befe and motton is so dere. that a penny worth of meet wyll scant suffyse a boy at a meale.' complained one cook in 1524. In those days appetites were enormous: piles of different kinds of meat and birds were all served up together. England was a vast grill room with shepherds and soldiers roasting oxen and sheep by the fires of the forest.

By the end of the sixteenth century appetites had become a little more sophisticated and the fashion evolved for mixing spices and scents with everything: marjoram and rosewater, musk and ambergris were sprinkled over stews and grilled meats. The Crusaders brought back from the Near East the secrets of oriental cooking and the idea of mixing sweet and savoury. So today we have the very 'English' mint sauce and redcurrant jelly with lamb, and sweet pickles with honey-roasted ham.

'Tell me what you eat and I will tell you who you are.' goes an old Italian saying. There is often sound logical reason behind national cuisine: the ubiquitous veal in Italy is due to Italian methods of cattle-rearing which make it more economical to

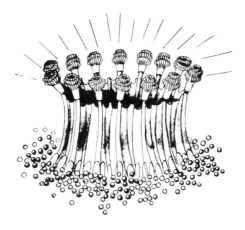

Above: 1938
Opposite: Daniel Jouanneau 1984

kill the calves young. The Hungarian *gulyas*, anglicized to goulash. dates back to migratory days of civilization when it was the principal form of nourishment for the male population as they grazed their cattle over the great plains.

Through the decades cookery writers in *Vogue* promoted the virtues of cheaper cuts of meat: in 1931. *Vogue* readers were told that. 'the alternative to that small fine piece of meat is the good hearty bourgeois dish. A country hostess can obtain an enviable reputation for keeping a gourmet's table by collecting a dish from each county.' In 1940 *Vogue* informed its readers: 'stew has the sturdy peasant virtues which win wars'. Just as well — during the Second World War meat was the first food to be rationed (1940) and the last to be removed from rationing (1954).

Today there tends to be less meat in our diet and many of the old wartime recipes using a minimum of meat are coming into their own. Also included here are rarer and richer dishes using marinades. stuffings and wine but. as Paul Gallico said, 'The only difference between cooking with wine and not cooking with wine is that you pour some wine in.'

PEPPER-POT

This dish is given here *à titre de curiosité*. Very likely it will not be of any use to Londoners, but it used to be a typical West Indian dish. One does not come across it very often now even in Jamaica, probably because people are not equal to the effort. There is no harm in trying.

Take a small quantity each of kale, callalu, okroes, beef and salt pork; a few tomatoes, one white coco, one 'country pepper', thyme, skellion, onion to taste and fresh meat bones. Put all on with two quarts of water, having tied the callalu and kale together. When they are boiled tender, rub them through a colander and return to the pot. Strain before serving. Shrimps or black crabs may be boiled with this. (Callalu is really spinach, and there are several kinds native to the country; 'country pepper' is the real article with the 'pep' in it. It is so called to distinguish it from black pepper. Kale is another type of edible leaf.)

BOULESTIN 1923

RAGOÛT DE BOEUF

The preliminary frying of the vegetables for this dish, and for many others, makes all the difference and gives a flavour quite apart from that of ordinary stews.

Clean and peel the following vegetables, and cut them into slices: three medium-sized carrots, three onions and a few tomatoes. Place them in an earthenware stewpan and fry them in olive oil – or in butter if you prefer it – until almost cooked. Meanwhile, you should have browned your beef in butter. Add the meat to the vegetables, and then one tumbler of cold water, salt and pepper (a little drop of claret would not do any harm). Cover and let the *ragoût* simmer for at least one hour and a half.

BOULESTIN 1924

BOEUF EN DAUBE FROID

This would do very well for a *pièce de résistance*. Take 4 or 5 pounds of the best fillet steak. Cut it in thin slices and beat and season them well. Prepare some *hachis* in the following way: 1 pound of pork, half fat, half lean, two onions, parsley, shallots and chervil, all finely chopped together and highly seasoned. On one slice of beef put a layer of mincemeat, then a few slices of bacon, then another slice of beef, and so on till you have used the whole lot, ending with a slice of beef. Having tied the piece all round with fine string, put it in a fireproof dish on a bed of butter, bones, onion, and carrots (in slices). Add the classical bouquet, a glass of water, salt and pepper, a little nutmeg, also a tablespoon of tomato purée and a glass of dry white wine. Cook this slowly for about four hours with the lid on. When it is thoroughly cooked, place the piece of beef in a deep dish, remove the string and pour over it, through a sieve, all the gravy, which, when cold, will be a succulent jelly. It is advisable to make this dish a day before so that the meat is well flavoured.

BOULESTIN 1924

RED FLANNEL HASH

Cut 6 boiled beets into tiny squares. Do the same with 6 boiled potatoes. Mix together and add 1 cup of ground hamburger. Season with salt and pepper. Put 2 tablespoons of bacon fat or butter in a frying pan. When it has melted add the mixture and pour over all a little hot water. Cook slowly in a covered pan for 15 minutes. Then remove the cover, pour over all 3 tablespoons of melted butter to which you have added 1 tablespoon of cream. Brown quickly, turn out on to a hot platter, and serve at once. Serves 6.

JUNE PLATT 1938

BEEF STEW

Brown slowly, in a little margarine, ½ pound of scalded salt pork cut in little squares. Transfer the pork to a stewpot and, in the remaining fat, brown lightly 2 pounds of skirt of beef cut in little squares. Add this to the stewpot. Add to the first pan 12 small onions sliced finely. Cook them slowly for a minute or two, then add 1¼ cups of hot consommé. Stir well and pour over the beef. Season to taste and add 1 tablespoon paprika. Cover tightly and simmer for about 1 hour (Gas Regulo 1, 275°F), then add 2 pounds of potatoes cut in squares. Cover and simmer for 1 hour longer.

JUNE PLATT 1940

GULYAS

Gulyas (generally mis-spelt goulash) is the staple Hungarian dish. It can be prepared with beef, with veal, or pork, or with all three combined; and with chicken, known as Chicken Paprika.

To make it, cut 1 pound of lean beef and 1 pound of veal into fair-sized cubes. Melt some pork fat in a saucepan. Add 1 ounce of finely cut bacon. Chop finely 1 large onion and sauté it in the fat. When the onion is golden, the meat – with 1 level teaspoon of paprika and 1 teaspoon of vinegar – goes in. Cook for a minute or two, stirring. Add 1 cup of strained tomatoes, a pinch of salt and enough water to cover, just. Bring to the boil, then simmer with the lid on for 1 hour. When the juice is clear, blend 1 dessertspoon of flour with a little sour cream or milk, and pour it in while shaking the pan. Continue to simmer for another 15 minutes. After the first 30 minutes of cooking, put in 8-12 small parboiled potatoes. Transfer to a casserole and finish in the oven. Correct the seasoning, adding paprika for colour.

DORIS LYTTON-TOYE 1946

CURRIED BEEF

3 onions
2 cloves of garlic
2 tbsp olive oil
2 tbsp curry powder
pinch of cinnamon
pinch of nutmeg
1 lb rump steak
½ apple, sliced
2 tomatoes, chopped
1 pt stock
1 tbsp desiccated coconut
1 tbsp mango chutney
salt and pepper
sugar
lemon juice
handful of raisins (optional)

Chop the onions coarsely and the garlic finely and cook them until they are soft, but not brown, in the olive oil. Add the curry powder (less than 2 tablespoons, if you do not like a very hot curry). Cook very gently, stirring well, adding more oil (or butter), if necessary. Add the cinnamon and nutmeg, then the meat (from which you have cut off the fat), cut into cubes a little larger than lumps of sugar. Add the apple and tomatoes. Moisten with some of the stock. Add the coconut and chutney and the rest of the stock. Cook slowly over a gentle flame, adding more stock – or water – if the curry gets dry. Add salt and pepper, sugar and lemon juice if, after tasting, you think them desirable, and raisins if you like them. Serve with boiled rice, Bombay duck and poppadums, dried in the oven, and mango chutney.

ROBIN MCDOUALL 1956

ROAST WING RIB OF BEEF

Having bought, say, a 5 to 5½ pound piece of wing rib on the bone (much less than this does not make a successful roast), place it on a grid standing in a roomy baking tin. The grid is important, for it keeps the meat from stewing in its own fat. It is also important to remove the joint from the refrigerator, if you have been obliged to keep it there overnight, several hours before the cooking time. Preheat the oven to a moderate heat (Gas Mark 4, 350°F). Brush the top surface of the meat with olive oil. No other fat is necessary. Above all, no mixed-up fat saved from the past seventeen years of roasting. Place the meat in the centre of the oven and leave it completely alone for 1 whole hour. Then turn it over. Cook another 1¼ hours if you like the beef *very* underdone all through, 1½ hours if you like it well done on the outside and red in the centre and 1¾ if you want it well done, and red only in a small patch right in the middle of each slice. Remove the beef to the hot serving dish and let it stand before carving.

Potatoes boiled in their skins and all but cooked, then peeled and halved lengthways, can be nicely roasted in the fat underneath the meat during the last 1¼ hours of cooking. They will emerge pale golden, soft inside and just crisp on the outside.

I cannot see myself that any sauce, other than the lovely and plentiful juice which comes from the meat as you carve it, can be needed, but if you feel you must have one, probably the nicest is the traditional horseradish – a very mild and creamy one rather than the more usual ferociously hot concoction. The comparatively slow roasting, no basting method of this recipe is unorthodox by cookery school rules. That it is the method which ensures the retention of the maximum of natural juice in the meat you can see for yourself.

ELIZABETH DAVID 1959

André Marty 1924

BOEUF STROGANOFF

2 lb absolutely lean fillet of beef
3 oz butter
3 tbsp brandy
½ lb mushrooms, roughly chopped
I medium onion, finely chopped
I tsp tomato purée
I tbsp flour
I pt meat stock (you can use bouillon cubes)
salt and freshly ground pepper
5 fl oz sour cream

This is a wonderful show-off dish, yet it is quite easy to cook and so good to eat. Have ready on a side table your hot-plate, heavy sauté pan, a large plate, cooking spoon and fork, and all the ingredients in separate containers.

Cut the beef into fingers about 1½ inches long by ½ inch wide and ½ inch thick. Melt about 2 ounces of the butter in the pan and when it is really hot put in just as many slices of beef as the pan will hold comfortably, and brown them quickly on all sides. Remove each lot to the plate as they are done.

When you have taken out the last of the beef, pour the brandy into the pan, heat it, set it alight and shake the pan until the flame goes out. Now sauté the mushrooms in the pan for about 3 minutes. Remove them and add to the plate of meat.

Heat up the remaining butter and put in the onion and sauté gently until it is light brown. Stir in the tomato purée and flour. Put the pan back on the hot-plate and cook fairly quickly, stirring all the time, for a few minutes. Now, still stirring, add the stock little by little.

Put the meat and mushrooms into the pan, add salt and pepper and simmer very gently for 10 minutes. Stir in the cream and leave the pan over the lowest possible heat for another few minutes. Serves 6 to 8.

CHRIS HASKETT-SMITH 1961

von Alvensleben 1983

Roger de Lavererie 1937

SOUVLAKIA

2 lb fillet steak, or *noix de veau*, or lean meat from a leg of lamb
3 large green pimientos or I small tin of red pimientos
MARINADE
I wine glass white wine
I coffee-cup olive oil
I medium onion, grated
I tbsp oregano
2 bay leaves
grated rind of I lemon
juice of ½ lemon
I tsp sugar
freshly ground pepper and salt

Cut the meat in 1-inch chunks. Mix all the ingredients for the marinade in a bowl. Put the meat in the marinade, mix well and leave overnight. Remove the meat from the marinade. Cut the fresh green pimientos or red tinned ones in 1-inch squares. String the meat and pimientos alternately on skewers, allowing 6 to 8 chunks of meat for each individual skewer. Grill them till cooked as required, turning over the skewers a few times during the process.

Souvlakia are served in Greece with French fried potatoes and a salad. I prefer them with rice pilaf and tomatoes glacées. Serves 8.

LADY FLEMING 1961

GRILLED STEAK WITH ROQUEFORT BUTTER

I rump steak (about 1½ inches thick)
freshly ground black pepper
2-4 tbsp softened butter
salt
ROQUEFORT BUTTER
I oz Roquefort cheese
2 oz butter
juice of ½ lemon
2 tbsp finely chopped parsley, chervil or chives
salt and freshly ground black pepper

Remove the steak from the refrigerator at least 30 minutes before cooking. Slit the fat in several places around the side to prevent the meat from curling during cooking. Preheat the grill for 15-20 minutes. Sprinkle both sides of the steak with freshly ground black pepper and spread with softened butter.

Rub the hot grid with a piece of suet. Place the steak on the grid and grill for 8 minutes on each side for a rare steak: a few minutes more if you prefer steak to be medium rare. Sprinkle the meat with salt to taste.

To make Roquefort Butter, cream the cheese and butter with lemon juice and finely chopped parsley, chervil or chives. Season to taste with salt and freshly ground black pepper.

To serve, transfer the steak to a hot serving platter and top with the Roquefort Butter. Serves 4.

ROBERT CARRIER 1965

STEAK WITH CORIANDER

Put 1 tablespoon of coriander seeds in a mortar with 1 teaspoon each of black peppercorns and coarse sea salt. Crush roughly with the pestle and use to coat 2 steaks. Leave for 1 hour before cooking. Heat butter and oil in a heavy frying pan and cook the steaks briefly each side. Serves 2.

ARABELLA BOXER 1977

SHEPHERD'S PIE

1 medium onion
1 oz butter
1½ lb minced beef
2 tsp flour
½ lb carrots
POTATO PURÉE
1½ lb potatoes
2 oz butter
⅓ pt milk
sea salt and black pepper

Chop the onion and cook slowly in the butter in a sauté pan with a lid. When it starts to turn golden, add the minced beef and break it up with 2 wooden spoons. Cook slowly, stirring often, until browned all over. Stir in the flour and add ¾ pint of hot water. Simmer gently with the lid on, stirring now and then, for about 30 minutes, adding more water if needed. At the end of the cooking time, there should be a small amount of slightly thickened gravy. Slice the carrots and boil until tender; drain. (Some of the carrot water can be used for adding to the minced beef.)

To make the potato purée: peel the potatoes and cut in halves. Boil until tender, drain and dry well. Push them through a medium food mill and stir over low heat to make a dry purée.

Melt the butter in the milk, adding sea salt and black pepper. Pour by degrees into the potato purée, beating until all is smooth. When the meat is ready, spoon it into a serving dish and cover with the

Bob Brooks 1966

sliced carrots. Pile the potato purée over all, so that it covers the dish completely.

Serve immediately or reheat briefly in the oven, if necessary, or brown slightly under the grill. If made in advance allow 35-40 minutes at Gas Mark 4, 350°F. to reheat. If preferred, a drier purée can be made by halving the amount of milk, and the dish browned to a crisp crust under the grill or in a quick oven. Serves 4 to 5.

ARABELLA BOXER 1979

STEAK AND KIDNEY STEW

1½ lb best stewing steak
½ lb ox kidneys
1 large onion, halved and sliced
2 carrots, sliced
salt and black pepper
SUET DOUGH
½ lb flour
pinch of salt
4 oz shredded suet
a little cold water

Cut the beef and kidneys into small pieces and put them in a broad saucepan or a sauté pan with a lid. Add the sliced onion and carrot, salt and black pepper, and enough very hot water to come level with the meat. Bring to the boil, cover, and cook for 30 minutes.

Make the suet as usual and roll out thickly. Using the lid of the pan as a guide, cut out a circle slightly smaller than the pan, and lay on top of the meat. Cover and cook steadily for another 1½ hours. To serve, cut the suet in quarters and lift on to a plate. Spoon the steak and kidney stew into a round serving dish, and lay the pieces of suet on top. Serves 4.

ARABELLA BOXER 1983

POACHED SIRLOIN STEAK

4 thin slices sirloin steak, about ¼ inch thick, weighing about 3 oz each
¾ pt good beef or chicken stock
3 spring onions, cut in 1-inch lengths, to garnish
SAUCE
2 tbsp beef or chicken stock
2 tbsp medium dry vermouth or dry sherry
2 tbsp soy sauce
2 tsp grated horseradish
½ oz root ginger, peeled

Trim the steaks, cutting away the fat. Heat the ¾ pint of stock in a sauté pan or deep frying pan. Mix the sauce ingredients in a jug, pressing the ginger through a garlic press, and adding the juice to the sauce. Cut the spring onions into very thin slivers. When the stock boils, lower the heat and put in the pieces of meat, 2 at a time. Poach them for exactly 1 minute, then lift them out and lay them on a hot flat dish. When all are cooked, pour over a little of the sauce, and scatter the spring onions over all. Serve the rest of the sauce in a small jug. Serves 4, as a light main dish, with a carrot, fennel and celery salad. For larger appetites, allow 2 steaks each.

ARABELLA BOXER 1984

BRAISED BEEF WITH GLAZED VEGETABLES

The combination of the tender beef with the vegetables in their sticky glaze is quite irresistible.

3 lb rolled rump, or topside, larded whenever possible
1 large onion, sliced
2 large carrots, sliced
2 cloves garlic, peeled
2 bay leaves
2 sprigs thyme
1 bottle red wine
1½ oz butter
1 tbsp olive oil
4 oz mushrooms, coarsely chopped
1 calf's foot, split in 4
sea salt and black pepper
GARNISH
12 oz small onions, pickling onions, or shallots
½ lb thin carrots, cut in 3
1 oz butter
1 tbsp sugar
4-6 oz chanterelles (when available)

Start a day in advance. Put the beef in a deep dish with the sliced vegetables, garlic and herbs scattered over it. Pour over the wine and leave overnight in a cool place, basting once or twice. Next day, drain the beef and wipe dry with kitchen paper. Strain the wine and reserve both it and the vegetables and herbs. Melt the butter and oil in an oval casserole and brown the meat all over. Then remove it and put the sliced vegetables in the pan. Add the chopped mushrooms and cook gently, stirring for 4 minutes, then replace the beef with the calf's foot tucked in around it. Heat the strained marinade and pour it over, adding sea salt and black pepper. Bring to the boil, then cover the pan and cook for 2½ hours at Gas Mark 3, 325°F.

About 30 minutes before the time is up, put the whole peeled onions and carrots cut in chunks in a small pan. (If baby carrots are available, they can be left whole.) Take about ½ pint of stock from the casserole, using a bulb-type baster, and pour over them. There should be enough almost to cover them. Bring to the boil and cook quite fast, covered, until the vegetables are tender, 15-20 minutes; then drain, reserving any stock that remains. Put 1 ounce of butter and the sugar in the pan. Put back 2 tablespoons of the same stock and cook all together gently, shaking the pan from time to time, until the sauce has reduced to a sticky glaze and the vegetables have browned slightly.

If you have some chanterelles, put them in a small pan with a little of the stock from the vegetables, or from the main casserole. Cook gently, covered, until they have softened – about 6 minutes – then set aside.

When the meat is cooked, remove it and carve in fairly thick slices. Strain the stock and make a bed of the sliced vegetables on a shallow dish. Lay the slices of beef on this, and arrange the glazed onions and carrots along either side of the dish. Scatter the chanterelles over the meat, and moisten with a little of the stock from the vegetables. Remove as much of the fat as possible from the surface of the main body of stock, and reduce a little, if necessary, by boiling fast. Serve in a sauceboat.

This needs only potato purée or fresh noodles to accompany it, with a green salad to follow. Serves 5 to 6.

ARABELLA BOXER 1988

BEEF OLIVES

This is one of my favourite dishes of this sort, perfect for Saturday lunch in the country, after a walk in the woods. Your butcher will cut the beef for you if you ask him in good time.

6 thin slices topside or buttock steak, beaten
I oz soft white breadcrumbs
2 oz shredded suet
beef trimmings, finely chopped
2 rashers streaky bacon, chopped
I tbsp chopped parsley
½ tsp finely chopped orange rind
sea salt and black pepper
½ tsp chopped fresh thyme or ¼ tsp dried thyme
I egg, beaten
I oz butter
I tbsp sunflower oil
I medium onion, halved and thinly sliced
I medium carrot, thinly sliced
I medium leek, thinly sliced
I stick celery, thinly sliced
½ tbsp flour
½ pt chicken or beef stock
2 tbsp chopped parsley
potato purée, to serve

Beat out the slices of beef to the required thinness and trim them to a neat rectangular shape. Chop the trimmings and reserve for the stuffing. Put the breadcrumbs into a large bowl and mix with the shredded suet, chopped beef trimmings, chopped bacon, parsley and orange rind, sea salt and black pepper and thyme. Bind with a beaten egg and divide into 6 portions. Lay one on each piece of beef then roll up and tie with coarse thread, or fasten with a wooden toothpick.

Heat the butter and oil in a casserole and brown the sliced vegetables, stirring constantly. Then push them to one side, or remove altogether, and brown the beef olives all over. Remove them from the pan and sprinkle the flour into the pan. Stir till smooth, then pour on the heated stock, stirring till smooth, adding

John Barbour 1929

salt and pepper to taste. Put the sliced vegetables back in the pan and lay the beef olives over them. Cover with foil and the lid, then cook gently for 1½ hours, either on top of the stove, or in a moderate oven (Gas Mark 3, 325°F).

Towards the end of the cooking, make a creamy potato purée and spread it in a thick layer down the centre of a shallow (or flat) serving dish. When the olives are cooked, remove the thread or toothpicks, and lay them on the potato purée. Scatter the sliced vegetables over them with the chopped parsley over all. Skim the fat from the surface of the sauce, and serve separately, or spoon some over the top if you prefer. Serves 6.

ARABELLA BOXER 1988

> **'The Frenchman's pleasure is the appreciation of quality, not the consumption of quantity.'**
> BOULESTIN

SAUCISSES AUX CHOUX

Put a piece of bacon, about half a pound in weight, in a large saucepan with water, broken pepper, salt and the classical bay leaf, thyme and parsley tied together: cook it for about one hour and a half. Then remove the bacon if you are a careful person and want to use it at its best for something else (or cold in the Irish peasant fashion) – or recklessly leave it in if you do not mind. Anyhow, the water is sufficiently flavoured by now for our purpose. Bring it once more to the boil and then throw in your cabbage, cut in smallish pieces.

While the cabbage is cooking, grill the sausages (the long French ones made of pork are the only possible ones for this dish) and keep them warm. Drain the cabbage well, add more salt and pepper, a little grated nutmeg, a small piece of butter, and put half of it in a fireproof dish, then the sausages on this bed, then the rest of the cabbage. Pour a cupful of good beef stock over it. Cook in a moderate oven with the lid on for about half an hour or so. This dish, if properly prepared, is quite delicious.

BOULESTIN 1924

HAM LOAF

A good supper dish served with horseradish cream sauce.

Pass 2 pounds of lean fresh pork and 1 pound of lean smoked ham through the mincer. Roll some crackers into fairly fine crumbs, enough to give 1 cup to add to the meat mixture. Then add 2 well-beaten eggs and mix in with the fingers, adding gradually 1 cup of milk. Season to taste with salt and pepper if needed. Pack closely into a buttered brick-shaped tin, and bake for 1½ hours in a moderate oven. Pour off superfluous fat and turn on to a dish. Put the loaf back in the oven for a few minutes to dry off.

DORIS LYTTON-TOYE 1933

BOILED HAM BAKED WITH BROWN SUGAR AND CLOVES

Soak a Virginia ham for 24 hours in enough cold water to cover it. Take it out and scrub it well with a brush. Put it (skin down) in a big broiler and cover it completely with cold water. Add 1 table-spoon of whole mixed spices and several apples cut up. Cover it and put it on the fire to boil. When it is boiling. add another pint of cold water and when it boils up. skim it carefully. Cook about 15 minutes to the pound. When it is tender through. uncover it and let it cool in its liquor. Then pull off the skin care-fully. leaving about 3 inches of it on at the shank. Cut with a sharp knife in points or scallops. Put it in an enamel baking pan. mark it in a criss-cross pat-tern with a knife but don't cut down deep into the fat. Pour some cider over it if you have some. sprinkle lightly with red pepper. stick cloves into the squares and spread light brown sugar thickly all over it. Put in the oven at Gas Regulo 5. 375°F. and bake for about 1 hour. bast-ing frequently. until it is rich and brown all over.

JUNE PLATT 1938

POTTED HAM

Take the remains of a baked gammon. Mince all the lean meat with about a quarter as much fat. Stir in some made mustard (English). a little powdered mace and some nutmeg. Then add enough melted butter to bring it to the consistency of potted meat. Put it into a terrine. the terrine into a *bain marie*, and bake in a slow oven for 30 minutes. When cold. cover the top with more melted butter.

ROBIN MCDOUALL 1956

GRATIN OF HAM

8 good slices of cooked ham
½ lb Cheddar cheese, grated
1 wine glass white wine or cider
5 fl oz cream
pepper

Stack the ham in a close-fitting fireproof dish. and cover with the cheese. Moisten with the liquid and pour the cream over the top. Dust with pepper and bake in a preheated oven for 45 minutes at Gas Mark 4. 350°F. or until the cheese is melted and turning brown. Serves 4. *Variation:* If preferred. you can put the ham and cheese on a bed of freshly cooked spinach.

MARWOOD YEATMAN 1985

Tessa Traeger 1979

COLD CROWN ROAST OF PORK

Try serving a well-cooked crown roast of pork cold, accompanied by a big bowl of mayonnaise and a delicious French bean salad with French dressing.

Order ribs of a young pig, and get the butcher to make a crown with no stuffing in the centre. Make a note of how much it weighs. The tip of each bone should be covered with a square of salt pork. Ask the butcher to supply the frills separately.

Sprinkle the roast copiously with salt and pepper. Place it on a rack in a roasting pan in a hot oven (Gas Regulo 8, 450°F) for 20 minutes to brown; then reduce the heat to Regulo 5, 375°F, and continue roasting, basting frequently, for 25 minutes to the pound. Remove the meat from the oven. Let the roast get cold, then place it in the refrigerator. When you are ready to serve, put the frills on, and garnish with parsley and slices of lemon.

JUNE PLATT 1938

PORC À LA FLAMANDE

3 lb fillet of pork
butter or margarine for frying
2 onions
3 tbsp flour
2 pts milk
1 bouquet garni
salt and pepper
3 turnips
2 tbsp sugar

Cut the pork into pieces and sauté to a golden brown in a little butter or margarine. Add the onions, well chopped, and simmer very slowly for 10 minutes with the lid on the saucepan. Add the flour and stir until it begins to thicken. Add the milk (already heated), bouquet garni and salt and pepper to taste. Cook for a few minutes, stirring all the time, then transfer to a casserole. Cook with the lid on in the oven for 1½ hours.

Tessa Traeger 1977

Serve with this, the turnips prepared in the following manner: peel and dice them, and sauté in 3 ounces of butter. When the turnips are done to a golden colour, place a piece of brown paper on top, put the cover on the saucepan and cook very slowly. When cooked, add the sugar, and salt to taste. Shake the pan over the fire until the sugar becomes caramel. Stir with a fork, adding more butter if needed.

MARY BROMFIELD 1953

ROAST LOIN OF PORK WITH WINE AND HERBS

Pork. being a fat meat. is best moistened with stock or wine rather than any extra fat. and should preferably be slow roasted. It is not spoilt if left a little longer than the specified time.

For a small pork roast. the neck end of the loin. comprising 7 or 8 cutlets. is admirable. It is excellent cold if it is not all eaten at one meal. Get the butcher to pare off the rind. without removing any of the fat unless the joint happens to be a very fat one. and to chine the bones.

Rub the meat well with salt. pour a glass (4-6 fl oz) of red or white wine over it. strew it with a little thyme or marjoram and a few slivers of garlic. and leave to steep for a minimum of 2 hours.

Put the meat. fat side up and covered with oiled paper or foil. into a baking tin with the rind underneath and the marinade poured over. Cook it in a preheated moderate oven (Gas Mark 4. 350°F). simply checking from time to time that the liquid is not drying up. If it is. add a little warm stock or water. After 1 hour's cooking. remove the paper and have ready 2 tablespoons of chopped parsley mixed with 2 tablespoons of fine breadcrumbs. Spread this mixture over the fat side of the pork. pressing it gently down with a knife. Lower the oven to Gas Mark 2. 300°F. and cook for another 40 minutes. basting it now and again with its own liquid. The breadcrumbs and parsley will form a nice golden coating.

The best potato dish to serve with this is a very smooth purée. rather runny. which you put into a deepish dish. pouring all round the edges a ring of the delicious wine and herb-scented juices from the pork. In France. a dish of the potato purée and meat gravy is sometimes served as a separate course. the meat itself coming afterwards. either hot or cold. with a green salad. The pork is. I think. much better when cold.

ELIZABETH DAVID 1959

CÔTES DE PORC WITH ROSEMARY

about 3 lb boneless loin of pork
1 tsp salt
black pepper
2 tbsp bacon fat or cooking oil
1 oz butter
3 or more sprigs rosemary
1 lemon
¼ pt or ½ cup dry white vermouth
MARINADE
3 tbsp lemon juice
3 tbsp olive oil
6 sprigs rosemary
1 clove garlic, crushed (optional)

Get your butcher to trim the pork and cut it into 6-8 chops about 1 inch thick. Rub salt and pepper into the pork and pour over the marinade. Marinate it in a covered enamel or china bowl for at least 4 hours. if possible overnight. Turn over and baste the meat several times during marination. Discard the marinade. dry the meat thoroughly. then heat the fat or oil in a large sauté pan which has a lid until it is nearly smoking. Sear the chops quickly. in 2 lots. cooking them on each side for about 3 or 4 minutes or until brown. then take them out of the pan and keep them warm. Pour away any fat. then put a good ounce of butter and the second lot of rosemary. which you shred a little. into the sauté pan. Return the chops. which will slightly overlay each other. reheat until sizzling. then cover the pan and simmer gently for another 20-25 minutes. basting with the butter and juices every now and then. Remove the chops to a hot serving dish and squeeze the juice of the lemon over them. and scatter with as much rosemary as you can collect from the pan. Skim off some of the fat from the pan juices. Pour in the vermouth and boil it rapidly to reduce it. Pour over the chops. Serve with a smooth potato purée and a simple green salad.

VERONICA MACLEAN 1969

LOIN OF PORK WITH PRUNES

2 lb loin of pork with crackling
butter
2 tbsp orange juice
1 sprig rosemary
20-25 good prunes, soaked in red wine
1 glass white wine
5 fl oz jellied stock
salt and pepper

Rub the pork with butter. Roast it with the orange juice and rosemary in a hot oven (Gas Mark 6. 400°F) for 1-1½ hours. Cover at first with paper. and when the fat begins to run remove it. and baste frequently until brown and crisp.

Simmer the prunes until tender in the wine. Put the pork on to a warmed serving dish. Pour off the fat from the roasting tin and add the white wine and the jellied stock. Reduce a little. season. thicken with butter and reboil before straining into a gravy boat. Place the prunes around the pork and serve.

MRS RUPERT HAMBRO 1974

PORK CHOPS WITH CHEESE

4 pork chops without the skin
6 oz Cheddar cheese, grated
2 egg yolks
salt and pepper
½ wine glass white wine or cider
2 heaped tsp mustard powder

Grill the chops on both sides in a pan until just firm. Meanwhile. combine the cheese in a bowl with the egg yolks and seasoning. Stir the wine or cider into the mustard powder with a fork until smooth. Add to the cheese mixture and mash together. Spread one quarter of the cheese over each chop and return to the grill until melted and turning brown. Serves 4.

MARWOOD YEATMAN 1985

NAVARIN PRINTANIER

Fifty years separate Boulestin's recipe for Navarin Printanier and Prue Leith's Spring Lamb Stew but the recipes vary little. More elaborate versions are by Constance Spry and Mapie de Toulouse-Lautrec. Shoulder of lamb or middle neck can be substituted for mutton.

BOULESTIN 1925

Brown in butter some pieces of mutton (the same kind of pieces as used for Irish stew), sprinkle with flour, stir well, add a tumbler of good stock, a bouquet as usual, salt and pepper; bring to the boil and then cook on a slow fire. Meanwhile, fry lightly a few small onions, carrots and turnips cut in little pieces; add them to the *navarin* together with a few small potatoes, also a little more stock if necessary, and cook slowly till well reduced. Skim off the fat before serving. You can also add, just before serving, a few peas or French beans previously boiled.

CONSTANCE SPRY 1943

You need from 2 to 3 pounds of mutton, dripping for frying, 1 ounce of flour, 3 pints of water or vegetable stock, a bouquet of herbs with a bay leaf, 1 small clove of garlic, 5 fresh tomatoes, sliced, or 2 tablespoons of tomato purée, salt and pepper to taste and a teaspoon of sugar. In winter, use carrots and turnips, and in summer, peas and beans. You also need small onions and potatoes.

Cut the meat in pieces. Season it with salt, pepper and sugar (which gives a good colour). Heat the dripping in a pan, and put in the meat so that each piece touches the bottom; otherwise cook it in relays. When the meat is browned on each side, sprinkle it with flour, continuing to cook until the flour is slightly coloured. Add enough water or vegetable stock to cover the meat. Bring it to the boil, stirring well. Add the tomatoes, crushed garlic, seasoning and bouquet. Cover the pan, bring the liquid to the boil and simmer for 1 hour, in the oven if possible. Now prepare the vegetables: brown the onions and keep them hot. Peel and cut up the potatoes, and place them in cold water. Scrape the carrots; peel the turnips and wipe them; do not wash them. Brown the latter in fat after the onions have come out. Take out the bouquet and put the mutton in a fresh saucepan. Skim off any fat and strain the liquid over the meat. Bring to the boil and add the onions, carrots and turnips. Simmer for 20 minutes; add the potatoes and any other vegetables. Cover closely and continue to simmer for 45 minutes. Cool for a minute, then skim off excess fat. Transfer to a serving dish and serve at once.

MAPIE DE TOULOUSE-LAUTREC 1961

The ingredients are 4½ pounds (weight after boning) of boned shoulder of lamb cut into pieces of about 3 ounces, 4 ounces of lard, 1 heaped teaspoon of caster sugar, 4 tablespoons of flour, 3 large tomatoes, peeled and chopped,

Denton Welch 1946

1 clove of garlic, a bouquet of parsley, thyme and a bay leaf tied together, 1 pound of new peas, 20 each of small young turnips, carrots and potatoes, salt and freshly ground pepper. Have ready some hot water or, better still, if you have it, some well-flavoured stock.

Melt the lard in a heavy stewpan, put in the lamb and sugar and season with salt and pepper. Brown the meat well all over then take it out of the pan and pour away three-quarters of the fat. Roll the meat in the flour until it is well coated, then put it back in the pan. Sauté it for a minute or two while you stir, then add the tomatoes, garlic and the bouquet and enough water or stock to cover the meat. Cover the pan and cook in a slow oven for 1 hour.

During this time, boil all the other vegetables in separate pans. Drain them when done and, at the end of the hour, add them to the meat, cover it again and cook on for a further 20 minutes.

Remove the bouquet, taste the gravy and add salt and pepper if necessary. Pour in about ½ teacup of cold water and if there seems excessive fat, mop it off with absorbent paper. Bring the *navarin* just back to the boil and serve very hot.

PRUE LEITH 1977

Pack into a casserole, in whatever proportions you like, new potatoes (halved), chunks of spring lamb (middle neck or scrag), peeled, sliced young turnips, baby carrots and a few topped and tailed spring onions. Cover with very well-seasoned stock, mixed with 1 teaspoon of chopped fresh mint, and a good dash of Worcestershire sauce. Cover the pot and cook slowly in the oven (Gas Mark 4, 350°F) for 1 hour until the lamb is tender. Twenty minutes before serving, add 1 cup of fresh young peas.

CÔTELETTES D'AGNEAU AU FOUR

Take two large onions, cut them in thin slices and cook them in butter for a few minutes only. Cut also in thin slices about half a pound of good potatoes (the long yellow kind being in this case preferable to the large white floury ones). Put the potatoes and onions in a well buttered fireproof dish; add salt and pepper and a claret glass of beef stock. Cook the vegetables for about one hour in a moderate oven.

Take six lamb cutlets, well trimmed, and brown them in butter on both sides. Bury them in the bed of potatoes and onions, adding here and there a few small pieces of butter. Finish cooking in the oven. You must put in the cutlets just at the right moment, so that they are nicely done just when the potatoes are getting a golden brown colour. It is also essential to put in the correct amount of beef stock, which should have entirely disappeared when the dish is ready: if you put too little, the potatoes will probably 'catch': if you put too much they will be sodden instead of being in that state which is an agreeable mixture of softness and crispness.

BOULESTIN 1923

ÉPAULE DE MOUTON AUX NAVETS

Take a shoulder of mutton, bone it, tie it neatly and brown it on all sides in butter or fat. Remove it from the pan. Add to the butter or fat in the saucepan a tablespoon of flour, and let it get brown (see that it does not become lumpy). Add three glasses of stock (or stock mixed with water if you want to be economical), salt and pepper, a bouquet and spices. Put back the meat and cook it slowly for about two and a half hours, according to size.

Meanwhile, fry in butter a few turnips cut in pieces. When they are pleasantly

Roger de Lavererie 1929

golden and soft, remove them and add them to the saucepan; but they should be added only just half an hour before the meal is ready, so that they do not come to pieces. When the whole thing is ready, remove the mutton, place it in a dish, dispose the turnips round it, and pour the sauce over it through a fine colander.

BOULESTIN 1925

SELLE D'AGNEAU FARCIE

Take a saddle of lamb and put it in a deep iron cocotte, with a piece of butter the size of an egg. Cook it a few minutes only, just enough to seize the meat, then put in the cocotte a few carrots, a bouquet and about half a pound of onions. Season well. Cook slowly.

Meanwhile, cook half a pound of mushrooms, and when ready mash them through a fine sieve. Do the same to the onions, which have cooked with the lamb. Mix the two purées together: the mixture should be very smooth and fairly stiff.

Remove the saddle from the pan before it is quite done. Cut it lengthways in the ordinary way and remodel it on the bone, putting between each slice a layer of the purée.

Pour over the saddle a little of the gravy, sprinkle with breadcrumbs, finish cooking, and brown in the oven. Afterwards, put in the serving dish whatever gravy you have left in the cocotte, after having carefully removed the fat.

BOULESTIN 1928

LANCASHIRE HOT-POT

2 lb best neck of lamb
12 oysters
1 small Spanish onion
2 lb potatoes, sliced
3 sheep's kidneys, skinned and sliced
salt and pepper
½ pt hot stock
1 oz butter

Divide the meat into neat cutlets, trimming off the skin and most of the fat. Put the short rib bones, the trimmings of the meat, the beards of the oysters, and a small onion into a cooking pan. Cover them with cold water and boil down to make ½ pint of gravy. Grease a baking dish and put in a deep layer of sliced potatoes. Arrange on top of this a layer of cutlets so that they overlap each other slightly, and on each place 1 or 2 slices of kidney and an oyster. Season well, add the remainder of the potatoes, and let the top layer consist of small potatoes cut in half and uniformly arranged to improve the appearance of the dish. Pour down the side of the dish the strained hot stock. Season with salt and pepper. Brush the upper part of the potatoes on the top layer with warm butter, cover with a butter paper, and bake for 2 hours. The paper must be removed during the latter part of the baking to allow the potatoes to become crisp and brown. When ready to serve, pour in a little gravy and send the rest to the table in a tureen. The hot-pot must be served in the dish in which it is baked.

CHEF OF THE CARLTON HOTEL 1934

A MODIFIED CASSOULET

I don't dare call this a cassoulet because my French friends would object strenuously, but it is a very good bean dish just the same. Order a little shoulder of lamb weighing about 2½ pounds and ask the butcher to bone and roll it. Peel and chop finely 2 or 3 little white onions and 2 or 3 shallots with 1 clove of garlic. Tuck another piece of garlic into the lamb. Brown the lamb in a little butter or, better still, chicken fat, in an iron cocotte on top of the stove, and don't let it burn. Add the chopped onions, shallots and garlic; salt and pepper the meat, and add the bones from the roast. Cover and put the cocotte in a moderate oven to continue cooking for about 1½ hours. At this stage, add a tin of tomato purée, ½ cup of tomato ketchup and ½ cup of consommé. Cover and put back in the oven for 30 minutes longer.

In the meantime, open a 12-ounce tin of cooked ham. Put it in an enamel pan with 1 cup of consommé and 1 bay leaf and simmer gently. Now remove the lamb from the cocotte and put the gravy through a fine sieve. Remove the strings from the lamb and slice it. Pour the remaining juice from the ham into the strained gravy and slice the ham. Now open an 8-ounce tin of little cocktail sausages and brown lightly in butter.

Open 4 large tins of oven-baked beans with pork and tomato sauce. Put the contents of one in the bottom of a large earthenware casserole and add a layer of lamb, add another tin of beans and then the ham, more beans and then the sausages, and last of all the last tin of beans. Now add enough tomato juice to the sauce to make 1 pint in all and pour it over the beans. Cover the top with a few strips of bacon and bake with a cover for 30 minutes, then remove the cover and bake slowly 30 minutes longer or until brown on top. Serve directly from the casserole.

JUNE PLATT 1936

TRADER VIC'S INDONESIAN LAMB

4 racks of lamb, giving 4 ribs each

JAVANESE SATÉ SAUCE
1 tbsp clear honey
8 fl oz fresh lemon juice
1 tsp turmeric powder
1 teacup chopped onion
3 teacups water

PEANUT BUTTER SAUCE
6 oz peanut butter
6 oz coconut cream
1 fl oz lemon juice
1½ fl oz soy sauce
1½ tsp Worcestershire sauce
1 dash Tabasco
½ tsp salt

Trim off all fat from the lamb. Mix together all the Javanese saté sauce ingredients and leave the lamb to marinate overnight. Cook *à la broche* or on a very slow grill, preferably charcoal. Serve with sliced peaches filled with mango chutney on rice, with a green vegetable or salad and peanut butter sauce, made by thoroughly mixing together all the ingredients. Serves 4.

GAYLE HUNNICUTT 1974

ROAST RACK OF LAMB WITH GARLIC SAUCE

a rack of lamb (or *carré d'agneau*), with 8 bones
15 cloves garlic, unpeeled
⅛ pt dry white wine
¼ pt beef or chicken stock
½ tsp flour
⅛ pt sour cream
sea salt and black pepper

Lay the lamb in a roasting tin with the whole cloves of garlic, unpeeled, all around it. Roast for 20-25 minutes in the hottest possible oven. (Allow 20 minutes for a 4-bone *carré* for 2 people.) Remove the meat and keep warm while you make the sauce.

Pour off the fat in the roasting tin,

leaving the meat juices. Deglaze the pan on top of the stove, adding the wine and stock. Scrape all the residue together and let it boil together for a moment or two. Push the garlic through a food mill and add to the sauce, stirring until smooth. Add the flour to the sour cream, mixing until it is amalgamated, then add to the pan. Stir until blended, then simmer gently for 3 minutes, adding salt and pepper. Serve with the lamb.

ARABELLA BOXER 1983

LAMB TAGINE

1½ lb boneless lamb (½ small boned leg or shoulder)
2 tbsp seasoned flour
3 tbsp olive oil
2 medium onions, sliced
2 green peppers, cut in strips
1 head fennel, sliced
½ tsp ground ginger
1 pt chicken stock
1 packet saffron
sea salt and black pepper
4 oz dried apricots, chopped
1½ tbsp lemon juice

Cut the lamb in cubes, trimming off all the fat. Toss in seasoned flour, then heat the oil in a casserole and brown the lamb lightly. Once it has coloured, remove it and put the sliced vegetables into the pot. Cook gently for 4-5 minutes, stirring often, adding the ginger towards the end. Put back the meat, and pour in the heated stock, adding saffron, sea salt and black pepper. Bring to the boil, cover, and simmer gently for 1 hour, then add the dried apricots. (These do not need soaking, if good quality ones.) Cook for another 15 minutes, then add the lemon juice, and serve. This casserole is best served with a grain like couscous, buckwheat or brown rice, and a green salad. Serves 4.

ARABELLA BOXER 1985

Tessa Traeger 1975

VEAU AU CITRON

Take a good piece of veal, trim it well and put it in a casserole with salt, pepper, a little chopped parsley, and no more than a pudding-spoon of water. Add a sprinkling of cinnamon and nutmeg, keep covered and cook slowly. One hour afterwards add the juice of several lemons (about two lemons to each pound of veal) and go on cooking slowly with the lid on till it is ready.

BOULESTIN 1923

RÔTI DE VEAU BRAISÉ

Get a good piece of veal, preferably from the ribs, but see that the butcher does not cut it into chops. Bone it and trim it carefully and flatten it. If there is a kidney place it in the middle, and, having sprinkled the whole thing both sides with salt and pepper, roll it like a galantine and tie it well. Brown it in butter.

At the same time prepare in a buttered fireproof dish a bed of vegetables: carrots, onions cut in small pieces, a little bacon, and parsley finely chopped. Add a glass of dry white wine and a drop of vinegar and let your veal rest on this. Bake in a moderate oven, basting often.

Before serving, squash the vegetables and pass the gravy obtained through a sieve; remove the string and serve the veal, covered with the gravy.

BOULESTIN 1923

'Heaven sends us good meat, but the Devil sends cooks.'
DAVID GARRICK

ESCALOPES DE VEAU TZARINE

Take some thin escalopes of veal, flatten them well and cook them in butter; they should be well browned. Remove them and keep them hot. Put in the pan about a glass of cream and mix well. Add a tablespoon of good chicken stock, a few pieces of butter and let all this reduce. Squeeze this sauce through a muslin, add to it a little fennel chopped and previously poached, pour it on the escalopes and serve with slices of cucumber *à la crème*. The cucumber for this dish should be cooked slowly in butter till soft, after which you add a little cream, salt and pepper and a very little grated nutmeg — and arranged around the escalopes of veal in the serving dish.

BOULESTIN 1925

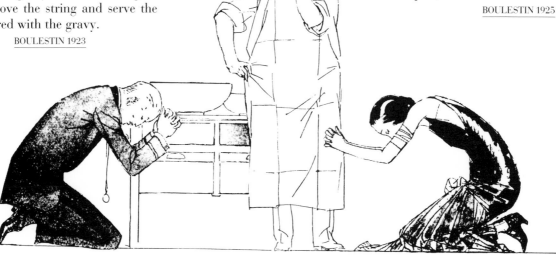

André Marty 1923

CÔTES DE VEAU PAILLARD

Take some nice veal cutlets, thin, white and tender, season them both sides with salt and pepper and brown them in butter. Put them in a fireproof dish, sprinkle them with a mixture of grated cheese and breadcrumbs and finish cooking them (well *gratinées*) in an oven or under the grill.

For the sauce, put in a small saucepan one truffle, finely chopped, and a port glass of Madeira wine. Let it reduce by half, add a little good stock and butter and pour the sauce over the cutlets in the dish in which they have been cooked. See that they have been kept very hot.

BOULESTIN 1925

RAGOÛT DE VEAU

Cut the veal in thickish squares as you would do for a *blanquette*, and brown them in butter in the saucepan, turning them several times. Sprinkle them with flour and stir well, and cook again for a few minutes. When the flour is getting brown, add a glass of water, a glass of claret, salt and pepper, a bouquet of thyme, parsley and bay leaf, a few button onions and little mushrooms. Cook slowly. When ready, remove the bouquet, skim off the fat and serve.

BOULESTIN 1925

COTELETTES À LA MILANAISE

4 veal chops
melted butter
½ small cup flour for dusting
1 small cup grated Parmesan cheese
1 egg, beaten

Trim the chops: dip them in hot butter, flour and Parmesan cheese. Let them remain thus until they are well soaked. Then dip them in beaten egg: once more in flour and cheese: and let them soak again for 2 hours. Sauté them quickly in hot butter and serve them with boiled macaroni that has been richly sprinkled with Parmesan cheese and butter.

COUNTESS BENIGNI 1935

BRAISED VEAL CHOPS EN GELÉE

Brown neatly trimmed veal chops in a little sizzling hot clarified butter. so that they are a golden brown all over. Salt and pepper them and pour over them about ¾ cup of hot stock. Cover them tightly and let them simmer for about 1 hour. Put the chops on a dish and pour the juice left in the bottom of the pan over them through a fine strainer. Let them get cold.

Make a pint of aspic. Pour out some of it on a shallow dish and place it in the refrigerator to set. Lay the chops on this bed when they are perfectly cold. and decorate them with plenty of fresh tarragon leaves and truffles. if you like. dipping the leaves first in the cold aspic. Place in the refrigerator until the aspic on the leaves has set. Then carefully pour the rest of the aspic over the chops and place in the refrigerator to set firm. Serve accompanied by a delicious crisp green salad.

JUNE PLATT 1938

VEAL CHOPS WITH MUSTARD SAUCE

First cook slowly. without browning. 3 or 4 tablespoons of finely chopped onions in 2 ounces of fresh butter. Wipe the surface of ¾-inch veal chops clean with a damp cloth. Sprinkle both sides very lightly with flour. Heat a little less than 4 ounces of butter (previously clarified if possible) in a heavy. not too large. frying pan. and when sizzling hot. add the chops and sauté them quickly to a golden brown on both sides. Then reduce the heat and continue cooking slowly for about 10 minutes.

When the chops are cooked. salt and pepper them well. then place them in a hot. small. covered earthenware or ovenproof baking dish. and add to the butter in which they were cooked about ½ cup of dry white wine. Stir while it reduces to a syrupy consistency. then pour this over the chops. and place round the chops the cooked onions. Cover the lid of the dish tightly with a well-buttered paper. and continue cooking in the oven (Gas Regulo 5. 375°F) for about 20 minutes or until the chops are very tender. Remove the chops temporarily while you add about 4 tablespoons of thick cream to the onions. Bring to the boil for a second. then add a heaped teaspoon of mustard to the cream and stir well. but do not let it boil. Replace the chops and serve at once.

JUNE PLATT 1938

ESCALOPES DE VEAU

Dip paper-thin veal slices in seasoned egg and breadcrumbs: then sauté them quickly in hot butter or a mixture of oil and margarine. Drain on soft paper and keep hot. Have ready a few washed and dried thin leeks: egg and crumb them also and fry for a few minutes in the same pan until pale golden. Garnish with lemon slices and chopped parsley.

DORIS LYTTON-TOYE 1951

John Barbour 1923

GRENADIN DE VEAU ELIZABETH

A recipe created for the coronation of Queen Elizabeth II.

4 oz mushrooms
butter for frying
a little stock
4 small escalopes of veal
salt and pepper
flour for dredging
½ measure dry sherry
4 tbsp cream
finely chopped parsley to garnish

Fry the mushrooms in butter and when they are partly cooked add a little stock: bring to the boil and remove from the pan. Take the escalopes of veal. season them and dredge in flour. Toss them in foaming butter. bringing them quickly to a golden brown on both sides. Add the dry sherry. which will flare immediately. then the previously prepared mushrooms and the cream. This will all blend into a pleasant creamy sauce. Sprinkle over a little finely chopped parsley before serving. This is cooked at table.

QUEEN'S RESTAURANT 1953

CHULETAS DE TERNERA A LA CATALONIA

4 fillets of veal, thinly cut
salt and pepper
flour for dredging
2 tbsp olive oil
2 large onions, sliced
I clove garlic, chopped
3 tbsp chilli sauce or I tbsp Worcestershire
sauce and 2 tbsp tomato sauce
2 oz cheese, grated
chopped parsley to garnish

Season the fillets highly and dredge them with flour. Fry till light brown in the very hot olive oil. Spread the onions and garlic over the veal. Pour in the sauce and just cover with boiling water. Cover the pan closely and simmer for 30 minutes. Sprinkle in the grated cheese, and cook gently until it melts. Serve with chopped parsley on top.

BERYL GOULD-MARKS 1954

ROAST VEAL

A traditional Norwegian recipe for a family lunch.

Mrs Roald Nerdrum, the wife of a Norwegian business man, has two small children. She laments that they have become so far Anglicized as to share with many English children the craze for tinned peas, preferring them to almost any other form of nourishment – but she does roast veal in the traditional Norwegian way to make a good family lunch.

Put the veal joint in the baking tin with 1 or 2 ounces of butter. After 30 minutes add 1 cup of milk and water – mixed half and half – and baste the meat frequently until done. For the sauce, add the liquid from the pan to a foundation of butter and flour. Cook for 20 minutes, then add 1 cup of sour cream (yoghurt will do) or fresh cream and the juice of a lemon. Do not let the sauce boil again.

MRS ROALD NERDRUM 1955

> **'If you make any pretence of catering to the masculine taste, keep to broiled and roast dishes, vegetables cooked without sauces, salads with French dressing, and desserts of the fruit pie variety. In other words, simple straightforward fare.'**
> LEONE B. MOATS

AUBERGINE MOUSSAKA

2½ lb aubergines
salt and pepper
olive oil for frying
½ lb minced veal
3 oz butter
I medium onion
I lb tinned peeled tomatoes
I tbsp sugar
béchamel sauce
½ lb grated cheese (Parmesan, Gruyère or Cheddar)

Cut the aubergines in ¼-inch slices, sprinkle them with salt and leave overnight in a colander. Press the aubergines in a dry cloth to remove liquid and fry them in hot olive oil till lightly golden. Put the minced meat in a frying pan with the butter. Grate the onion, mash the tomatoes and mix them well with the meat, adding the sugar, salt and pepper to taste. Cook till the meat is tender and only a little liquid is left.

Arrange half the aubergines in layers in a deep fireproof dish. Cover them with the meat mixture. Arrange the remaining aubergines in layers to cover the meat. Pour over the béchamel sauce, sprinkle the cheese on top and brown under a hot grill. Serves 8.

LADY FLEMING 1961

VITELLO TONNATO

rolled roast of veal
8 oz tin tuna fish, without the oil
I large onion, chopped
2 carrots, chopped
2 sticks celery, chopped
2 large cloves garlic, finely minced
I tin anchovies, without the oil
I cup dry white wine
2 bay leaves
I sprig parsley
salt and freshly ground black pepper
I cup mayonnaise
lemon juice
cooked rice to serve
capers to garnish

This is one of the best summer luncheon dishes in the world, but a much abused one as many disastrous imitations are served under its name. I got this recipe from a gourmet friend in Geneva, who got it from a famous Italian restaurateur in New York, and I think it is the nearest to the real thing that can be eaten outside Italy.

Brown a rolled roast of veal in a very little oil, not too dark a colour because of the sauce, in a very heavy cast-iron pan, so that it cooks slowly. Add to it the tuna fish, onion, carrots, celery sticks, garlic, anchovies, white wine, bay leaves, parsley, and salt and black pepper. Cook slowly in a moderate oven for 2 hours, closely covered.

Remove the meat and chill it. Reduce the sauce by half by boiling fast. Remove the parsley and bay leaves; all the other ingredients will have infused. Put the sauce in a blender. When chilled, mix this sauce with the mayonnaise, and season with lemon juice. Arrange cold rice on a serving dish. Cover with finely sliced veal. Spread the sauce carefully over the veal and sprinkle with capers.

VERONICA MACLEAN 1969

OXTAIL RAGOUT

Cut into sections an oxtail that has been well washed. Fry it in butter, then add small whole carrots, turnips and onions, and fry again. Season with pepper, salt, 1 clove of garlic and a bouquet of thyme, parsley and bay leaf. Add enough water to cover, and braise for 3 hours. Take out the oxtail and vegetables. Strain the stock to remove the herbs, and return the meat and vegetables to the pan. Replace the strained stock, bring it to a boil and serve in a casserole.

LADY PORTARLINGTON 1934

CALVES' LIVER IN CREAM

Dip both sides of 8 small slices of calves' liver, cut about ½-inch thick, in flour into which you have mixed salt and pepper. Melt at least 4 ounces of butter in a frying pan. When it is hot, add the liver and cook it, not too fast, for 5 minutes on both sides. Place the meat on a hot platter and pour into the pan 1 cup of thick cream. Stir very well until it is heated through. Taste and season with salt and freshly ground pepper. Pour over the liver, sprinkle with chopped parsley and serve at once, accompanied by plain boiled potatoes, peeled and buttered.

JUNE PLATT 1939

KIDNEY PANCAKES

In 1943 in the UK a kidney was a rare treat. This was a way of making one into a whole course.

Chop the kidney up into small pieces. Brown a sliced onion or leek in fat, add the kidney and cook it for 2 minutes. Add a pinch of lemon thyme and 1 heaped teaspoon of flour, stirring all the time. Cook a little more and add 1 cup of stock. Let this simmer for 10 minutes or so while you make the pancakes. These are made from ordinary pancake batter to which you have added 1 cup of finely chopped or sieved spinach or freshly

Anton Bruehl 1940

chopped watercress. When they are ready, fill the pancakes with the kidney mixture and roll them up. Serve at once. *Note:* To serve these pancakes as a delicious savoury, make them very small and sprinkle with grated cheese. Roll up, cover thickly with more grated cheese and brown well under the grill.

BEATRICE DAWSON 1943

KIDNEYS SAUTÉD IN WHITE WINE

Skin the kidneys and cut them into very thin slices. Sauté them over a hot fire in very hot melted butter. As soon as they are cooked, put them in individual dishes. Cool the frying pan with some white wine and a shallot chopped very finely. Reduce the wine by half and add several spoons of brown sauce, a generous piece of butter, and several chopped cooked mushrooms. Let it start boiling and then pour over the kidneys, which should not boil. Sprinkle with parsley and *croûtons* fried in butter.

MRS DAVID BRUCE 1952

RUTILIO'S ROGNONCINI TRIFOLATI

12-15 lambs' kidneys
1½ oz butter
4 tbsp good cooking oil (not olive oil)
1 small glass cognac
finely chopped garlic
1½ tbsp finely chopped parsley
2 tbsp lemon juice
salt and pepper
a little cayenne pepper

Remove the membranes which cover the kidneys and cut out the buttons of fat from their undersides. Use a large and heavy sauté pan and melt the butter and oil in it over a moderately high heat. As soon as the foam from the butter subsides, toss in the whole kidneys and sauté them for 2 minutes only, turning them frequently. Meanwhile have the brandy warming in a small pan by your side. Now pour the brandy over the kidneys and ignite it, averting your face and holding the pan at arm's length. Shake the pan roughly and baste the kidneys while the flame is dying until it finally goes out. Then remove them to a warm serving dish.

Scrape the juices of the sauté pan together, add the garlic and parsley, and

'The French not only despise waste: they regard it with contempt as being a clumsiness of mind . . .'

BOULESTIN

simmer for a little without letting the butter burn; slice the kidneys as finely as possible and return them to the sauté pan for another 2 minutes. Pour on the lemon juice, let the sauce boil up once more and then remove the pan from the heat. Correct the seasoning, adding a little cayenne pepper, and serve at once.

VERONICA MACLEAN 1970

LANGUE DE BOEUF À LA ROMAINE

First, simmer the fresh or salted tongue in water, with an assortment of vegetables to add flavour, until a knitting needle will go in easily. Put aside and make the sauce. Cook 2 tablespoons of sugar and 3 tablespoons of vinegar until the sugar browns and the liquid has reduced to one third. Add ½ pint of strong brown stock and simmer for 15 minutes. Now add 3 ounces of sultanas, previously soaked in hot water, and a handful of roasted almond slivers. Cut the tongue into slices, pour over the sauce, and serve with creamed potatoes.

BERYL GOULD-MARKS 1954

MARINA'S OSSO BUCO

Osso buco is familiar to anyone who has sampled Milanese cooking. In the 10 years which I have spent in Italy I have encountered many varieties, but none to equal the receipt given me by Marina.

Brown 4 marrow bones in a little butter, tilt the pan, and add flour to make a roux. When the flour has cooked for a few minutes, add 1½ wine glasses of white wine; cook hard for a few minutes to allow the alcohol in the wine to

evaporate; then add gradually, stirring all the time, 1 large cup of good white stock. Cover, and leave the *ossi buchi* to simmer over a slow fire for 2 hours, adding a little stock if necessary. Move them as little as possible, so as to keep the marrow in its place in the bone. I usually employ a fairly deep frying pan with a cover, and turn them once, carefully, using a palette knife. Twenty minutes before serving, stir into the liquid a little grated lemon rind, and 2 filleted anchovies chopped up with a piece of garlic and several sprigs of parsley. Serve with boiled rice.

GEORGINA MASSON 1954

RIS DE VEAU AU CITRON VERT

1½ lb veal sweetbreads
6 limes (3 for juice, 3 for zest and segments)
butter for frying
sugar
5 fl oz veal stock (brown)
½ pt cream
salt

Blanch the sweetbreads. Remove all the fat, excess tissue and sinew. Leave to soak in cold water for 1 hour. Blanch the zest of 3 limes and leave it aside. Slice the soaked sweetbreads into ¼-inch slices. Sauté them in hot butter for 2-3 minutes, colouring slightly on both sides. Remove the sweetbreads from the sauté pan and keep them warm while the sauce is prepared.

Pour away the excess fat from the pan. Add the juice of 3 limes, and enough sugar to remove acidity. Bring the liquid to the boil to make a glaze. Add the veal stock and boil the mixture to reduce it by half. Add the cream; continue to boil until the sauce has a coating consistency. Finally, add the blanched zest and segments of limes with sugar and salt to taste. Serve the sweetbreads and sauce on a bed of fresh noodles.

PETER CHANDLER 1984

BRAISED OXTAIL

FIRST DAY
2 oxtails, cut in 2-inch sections
salt and black pepper
2½ tbsp flour
2 tbsp olive oil
1 oz butter
2 cloves garlic, crushed
2 tbsp tomatoe purée
1 large onion, halved
1 large carrot, halved
1 stick celery, halved
1 bay leaf
3 stalks parsley
1¼ pts beef stock
¼ pt red wine
SECOND DAY
1 leek
2 medium carrots
2 small turnips
2 sticks celery
1 parsnip
1 oz butter
1 tbsp olive oil
2 tbsp chopped parsley to garnish

Start a day in advance. Trim excess fat from the oxtail. Add salt and pepper to season the flour, and use it to coat the pieces of oxtail. Heat the oil and butter in a large casserole and brown the pieces of oxtail on all sides, a few at a time, removing them once they are done.

Add the crushed garlic and the tomato purée to the empty casserole, then replace the meat, adding the halved vegetables, bay leaf and parsley. Heat the stock and wine together, then pour over the meat. Add salt and pepper and bring to the boil, then cover the casserole and cook for 4 hours at Gas Mark 4, 350°F. Remove from the oven and leave to cool overnight.

Next day remove all fat from the surface and lift the meat into a shallow earthenware serving dish. It does not need a lid. Discard the flavouring vegetables and herbs. Cut the fresh vegetables into thick strips, like fat matchsticks. Heat the butter and oil in a sauté pan

Tessa Traeger 1983

and add the vegetable strips, cooking them gently in the fat for about 8 minutes. Then heat ½ pint of the oxtail liquid, pour it over the vegetables and cook for another 15 minutes. When the time is up, pour all the liquid from the stew over the oxtail, and scatter the vegetable strips over the surface of the dish. Cook for 1 hour, uncovered, at Gas Mark 4, 350°F, basting from time to time with the juices, but without stirring. The vegetables should become slightly caramelized, brown and crisp, during the course of the cooking. Sprinkle with chopped parsley before serving with potatoes boiled in their skins and a green salad. Serves 6.

ARABELLA BOXER 1987

POULTRY AND GAME

Furred or feathered, game was the natural daily sustenance of our robust primitive ancestors. In the fourteenth century an amazing array of different kinds of game was served to King Charles V of France: boar, chicken, hare and goose for the first courses; swan, heron, pheasant, peacock and partridge during the second courses; followed by capon, blackbird and pigeon for the third courses. They were obviously men of enormous appetite and during the King's reign one of the earliest cookery books was written by his chef, Guillaume Tirel, in 1392.

It was not until the seventeenth century that the presentation of food became more civilized, although appetites continued to be gigantic by our standards. Louis XIV, according to reports, was feeling so ill one evening in June 1708 that all he could manage was 'a few *croûtes*, a pigeon soup and three roast chicken, out of which he had four wings, the breasts and one leg'.

'Does any game bird possess, I wonder, more exquisite a flavour than young, tender grouse?' asked Doris Lytton-Toye in October 1951. Because they herald the arrival of the game season, grouse get all the publicity surrounding 'the glorious twelfth' – though many knowledgeable holders of licences to sell game ignore August 12 and wait to produce the birds when they are good and ready. Mid-September to mid-October is the best time to eat grouse born that year. The older birds of the year before do not compare in flavour or tenderness.

Above: Douglas 1933
Opposite: Lester Bookbinder 1966

November is the highlight of the game-lover's year, with pheasant, partridge, wild duck, woodcock, snipe, rabbit and hare at the top of their form. All foods to warm and stimulate with appetizing smells and visual appeal – the dinner table compensating for the fog and damp outside. Remember that the smaller game birds like woodcock and snipe are at their best after the first frosts.

Mrs Beeton, writing of the pheasant in 1861, said, 'The cock bird is generally reckoned the best, except when the hen is with egg. They should hang some time before they are dressed as, if they are cooked fresh, the flesh will be exceedingly dry and tasteless.' Once plucked and drawn, all game birds are best cooked as soon as possible for they quickly acquire a musty taste which is ineradicable.

COQ AU VIN

Boulestin and June Platt add a glass of brandy to this robust Burgundian dish, while Mirth Moore offers a 'slimming' version with white wine.

BOULESTIN 1926

Take a young chicken and cut it in six pieces. Put in a casserole three rashers of streaky bacon cut in dice, a good piece of butter and a dozen button onions – all this to melt slowly over the fire; then, the classical bouquet, a tiny piece of chopped garlic, a few sliced mushrooms and the chicken well seasoned. Cook on a quick fire with the lid on, so that the chicken is a nice golden colour; shake occasionally. See that it is well cooked and, when ready, season the pieces of chicken and keep them hot. Skim off from the gravy the excess fat and prepare a small brown roux, just enough to 'bind' the gravy (it should not be thickened too much); mix well together, add a glass of brandy and a tumblerful of claret or burgundy; put back the pieces of chicken and let the whole thing reduce over a slow fire.

JUNE PLATT 1936

I suppose to be really authentic about this dish we should order a cock, but I'm sure any 5½-6-pound roasting chicken, cut up as for fricassée, will do. First clean and singe the pieces of chicken nicely, then prepare the following ingredients. Peel and leave whole 12 little white onions. Chop finely 1 clove of garlic with 1 shallot. Prepare 1 cup of cold boiled ham cut in ½-inch squares. Peel and slice finely 2 carrots. Make 1 bouquet of parsley or, better still, chervil with 1 good pinch of thyme and 1 tiny piece of bay leaf. Melt 2 tablespoons of beef extract in ½ cup of boiling water. Peel, wash and slice ¼ pound of mushrooms. Now put the onions in a heavy frying pan with ¼ pound of butter and add the ham. Cook these slowly, stirring frequently, until the onions are a golden brown, but don't let the butter burn during the process or the dish will be ruined. Now add the bouquet, garlic and shallot, carrots and mushrooms. In a minute or two add the dissolved beef extract, stirring well to loosen all the brown on the bottom of the pan. Add salt and pepper, cover the pan and barely simmer for a few minutes.

Brown the pieces of chicken in plenty of butter in an iron cocotte, being equally careful not to burn them. When brown, add ¼ cup of cold water and stir to loosen all the brown in the bottom of the pot; then add the onion and ham mixture with every bit of juice. Cover tightly and cook slowly until the chicken is very tender, stirring at intervals so that it doesn't stick.

Make a roux by cooking 1 tablespoon of flour with 1 tablespoon of butter slowly on a low fire, stirring constantly, until a golden brown. Pour off most of the juice from the chicken and gradually add it to the roux, stirring with a wooden spoon until perfectly smooth. Now put 1 small glass of cognac in an enamel saucepan with 1 generous cup of burgundy and add the thickened gravy to it gradually. Pour the whole back over the chicken, taste and adjust the seasoning, cover tightly and simmer very slowly for at least 20 minutes longer. Before serving, skim off every bit of fat. Put the chicken pieces into a hot earthenware casserole and pour the sauce with the vegetables and ham over them, discarding the bouquet. Serve at once with plenty of crisp French bread and a bottle of burgundy. Serves 6.

MARY BROMFIELD 1953

1 chicken
3 tbsp oil
1½ oz flour
1½ oz tomato purée
1 wine glass red wine
salt and pepper
½ lb bacon, diced
1 large onion, sliced
6½ oz mushrooms, sliced
a little butter for frying

Cut the chicken into pieces while still raw. Heat the oil in a casserole, dip the pieces of chicken in it, sprinkle with flour, then add the tomato purée. Pour the red wine in slowly and season with salt and pepper to taste. Simmer for 2 hours, then leave to cool.

Before serving, cook the bacon and onion until the onion is soft and the bacon beginning to crisp. Add the mushrooms with a little butter, if necessary, and cook gently for a further 5 minutes. Reheat the chicken and add the cooked bacon, onion and mushrooms.
Note: Two hours is the time required for a 3-pound chicken; for a larger chicken, cook proportionately longer.

MIRTH MOORE 1953

Cut a 4-pound chicken into serving pieces and, with 6 small onions, brown in 1 tablespoon of olive oil. Add 4 ounces of mushrooms and 8 carrots, cleaned and cubed. Pour over the chicken and vegetables 2 cups of white wine (or sherry), salt, pepper, ½ teaspoon of marjoram and 2 sprigs of thyme. Cover and simmer gently for about 1 hour or until tender. Remove to a hot dish and sprinkle with chopped parsley.

Ray Williams 1962

OKRA GUMBO

Take a tender chicken, cut it in eight pieces and cut a quarter of a pound of ham in small cubes. Skin six tomatoes and chop them together with one red pepper, one onion, parsley and thyme. (Reserve the juice from the tomatoes.) Wash the okra, cut it in thin slices. Put a good piece of butter (or lard) in a saucepan and, when hot, add the chicken and the ham; cook slowly, with the lid on the pan, for about ten minutes; then add the chopped onions and tomatoes, stirring frequently. Add the okra and, when well browned, the juice of the tomatoes. (The okra, being very delicate and easy to scorch, is sometimes cooked separately by some Creole cooks, and added to the fried chicken.) Add seasoning and a quart of stock, and let it simmer for two hours. Serve, of course, with rice.

BOULESTIN 1926

POULET BONNE FEMME

5 oz butter
2 carrots, sliced
4 white onions, sliced in circles
1 chicken, cut up into pieces
salt and pepper
2 tsp flour
1 pt good chicken stock
2 small tomatoes, peeled and chopped
12 oz small mushrooms, quartered
1 tsp chopped parsley
1 cup red wine

Put most of the butter in a large iron frying pan. When it is melted, add the carrots and onions. Let them cook for 10 minutes, stirring meanwhile. Add the pieces of fowl with more butter, if necessary, and a little salt and pepper. Cook for another 10 minutes, turning the chicken to brown on all sides. Sprinkle with the flour, then add the hot stock and the cut-up tomatoes. Stir until it boils, then let it simmer for 20 or 30 minutes. Add the quartered mushrooms and the chopped parsley. When the chicken is quite tender, add the red wine and let it simmer a while longer. Season again to taste and serve in a hot earthenware casserole.

JUNE PLATT 1935

POULET PORTUGAISE

Joint a young bird, separating it into 8 portions. Sauté them in hot fat in a flat pan till nicely coloured. Remove the chicken pieces from the pan. Reheat the fat; fry in it a finely chopped onion, then add a few sliced tomatoes, a crushed clove of garlic and some sliced mushrooms. Simmer all together for a few minutes. Season well, then lay the pieces of bird on top. Cover with a lid and simmer gently till tender. Add a little stock or water if it shows signs of becoming dry.

DORIS LYTTON-TOYE 1947

Charles Martin 1926

TRUFFLED CHICKEN MOUSSE

A delicious and luxurious dish for a mellow, late summer evening.

12 oz cooked chicken meat
1 cup béchamel sauce
½ cup cream or top of the milk
2 eggs, beaten
2 egg yolks
salt and pepper
grated nutmeg
1 small tin truffles

Pass the chicken meat through a mincer, stir in the béchamel sauce, cream, well-beaten eggs and yolks, salt, pepper and a pinch of nutmeg. Pass the whole mixture through a sieve. Arrange small slices of truffle on the bottom of a buttered pudding basin and pour in the mixture.

Cover and steam until well set. Alternatively, the mixture can be divided into several small moulds and cooked in the oven in a baking dish filled with water.

PETER PIRBRIGHT AND GRETEL BEER 1950

CHICKEN FLAMBÉ

6 pieces of chicken
salt and pepper
lemon juice
flour
6 tablespoons butter
1 onion, chopped
1 cup evaporated milk
1 cup brandy

Remove the skin from the pieces of chicken. Rub salt, pepper and a few drops of lemon juice on each piece and then dip them in flour so that each piece is 'dusted' rather than coated with flour. Melt the butter in a frying pan and cook the onion until soft and just turning colour, then add the chicken, cooking until it has browned (over a low flame).

Transfer the chicken pieces to a casserole and thicken the butter and onion mixture with flour – starting with 1 tablespoon, which should be adequate.

Georges Lepape 1931

Stir in the evaporated milk, and add seasoning as needed, starting with ½ teaspoon salt. Pour the sauce over the chicken and cover the casserole, letting the chicken simmer gently for about 45 minutes. Just before serving, pour the brandy over the fowl and light it. These quantities are enough for 6.

ROSEMARY KORNFELD 1953

CHICKEN WITH PIQUANT TUNNY FISH SAUCE

Take a tender chicken, weighing about 2 pounds, and place it in a deep covered pan in water which you have previously brought to the boil, with the usual bouquet, carrot, and onion. Simmer fairly briskly for about 45 minutes. When the chicken is cooked, joint, skin, bone and slice it, and sprinkle the flesh with a little salt, freshly ground black pepper and a few drops of its own broth.

To prepare the sauce, take 3 ounces of tinned tunny fish, 1½ ounces of capers (squeezed dry of their vinegar), 8 fillets of anchovy and a good bunch of parsley. Chop the parsley finely on a board, then add the rest of the ingredients and chop them together. Transfer the mixture to a mortar and pound it until it is reduced to a paste, then add gradually 2 or 3 tablespoons of good olive oil, stirring all the time. The original receipt directed that the sauce should be further diluted with oil, but I find this too heavy for modern stomachs, and have replaced it satisfactorily with 1 or 2 tablespoons of very

thin cream. When ready, the sauce should have the consistency of a good béchamel. Place the chicken on a flat dish and cover with the sauce. Garnish with slices of hard-boiled egg, tomato and cucumber and serve cold. Though not traditional, sliced avocado makes an excellent addition.

GEORGINA MASSON 1954

STRABANE GROUNDNUT AND CHICKEN CASSEROLE

1 large plump chicken or 2 small ones
2 tbsp butter
2 medium onions, finely chopped
1 jar peanut butter
1 pt chicken stock
salt and pepper
Worcestershire sauce
10 rashers thin streaky bacon, grilled

Cut the chicken(s) into joints. Sauté them in butter with the chopped onions until golden brown. Transfer them to a flameproof casserole and add the contents of a jar of peanut butter and enough chicken stock to make a thick creamy sauce. Have some chicken stock in reserve. Season to taste and add a spoonful of Worcestershire sauce. Simmer until the chicken is tender. If the sauce gets too thick, add more stock. It should take about 35 minutes, depending on the age of the chickens. Before serving, sprinkle with the bacon which you have drained on paper and crumbled. Spinach *en branche* or a green salad goes well with this dish.

VERONICA MACLEAN 1970

'**Cuisine should be taken seriously first of all by the cook (obviously, that is if she is worthy of the name) and also by both hostesses and guests.**'
BOULESTIN

Francis Marshall 1930

POULET BAMAKO

1 big chicken, cut into pieces
juice of 2 lb lemons
powdered bay leaves
a mixture of freshly chopped rosemary, thyme,
sage, tarragon and parsley
salt and pepper
12 slices of bacon, cut very thin
2 tbsp olive oil

Marinate the chicken pieces overnight in the lemon juice which will help to 'cook' the chicken. In the morning leave them to drain. Put all the herbs on a plate and roll each piece of chicken in the mixture. Season with salt and pepper and wrap each chicken piece in 1 or 2 slices of bacon, securing them with a cocktail stick. Lay them on a flat dish and brush each piece with olive oil. Cook in a medium oven for 40-45 minutes.

Remove the sticks and serve the chicken with brown rice and thyme, walnuts, sultanas and sliced bananas (wrapped in foil and warmed in the oven for 15 minutes). Serves 6.

NATHALIE HAMBRO 1974

CHICKEN WITH CHERVIL SAUCE

3½-4 lb chicken
8 thin leeks
2 long thin carrots, plus 1 extra
1 onion
4 sticks celery
1 bay leaf
sea salt and black peppercorns
3 tbsp rice flour or 1½ tbsp potato flour
⅛ pt thin cream
4 branches chervil

Put the chicken in a pressure cooker with the ends of the leeks, 1 carrot, 1 onion and 1 stick celery. Add a bay leaf, salt and black peppercorns, and add enough hot water to cover the legs. Bring to the boil and cook under pressure for 20-25 minutes, depending on the size of the bird. (Or cook in an ordinary pan for 1-1¼ hours.) Lift out the chicken and boil up the contents of the pan for about 5 minutes, to reduce and strengthen the flavour. Cut the white part of the leeks in long thin strips; cut the remaining 2 carrots and 3 sticks of celery likewise. Lay them in a steamer and cook over the boiling chicken stock for 3-4 minutes, until half-way between crisp and tender. Remove immediately and lay them on a shallow serving dish; keep warm. Carve the chicken in neat strips, free from skin and bone, and lay crosswise over the vegetables.

Strain the stock, and cool ¼ pint quickly by stirring in a sink half full of cold water. Pour this slowly on to the rice flour (or potato flour) in a bowl. When a smooth paste, pour it into ½ pint of the remaining stock, heated in a saucepan with the cream. Stir until smooth, and simmer for 4 minutes, stirring constantly. Put in the chervil, after reserving a tablespoonful of the best leaves. Cover and leave for 5 minutes to infuse. Meanwhile, chop the reserved leaves. Remove the branches of chervil and pour the sauce over and around the chicken. Scatter the chopped chervil over all. Serve immediately. Serves 5 to 6, with new potatoes and a green salad.

ARABELLA BOXER 1981

TALKING TURKEY

DORIS LYTTON-TOYE 1950

Around the beautiful bird we always associate with Christmas hovers an air of mystery. Whereas the naturalist tells us the turkey derives from the New World, and not from Turkey, historians write that the Romans deemed it a luxury; moreover, according to an accredited *Dictionnaire de Cuisine*, the Greeks had a word for it about 3000 B.C. To us, however, the essential is that our turkey should be succulent, tender, and cooked just to perfection.

BUYING THE TURKEY. To what avail the valiant basting, the exquisite etceteras, if we have chosen badly in the beginning? What should we look for? Eyes bright and full, smooth black legs, short spurs and supple feet are the signs and portents. Absence of these qualities denotes age and staleness. If the weight needed be up to 14 pounds, then we select a hen; above that weight a cock bird. As a rough guide, a 14-pound bird will be sufficient to feed 12 hungry people amply.

COOKING THE GIBLETS. When the turkey arrives, the giblets should be cooked immediately, as they deteriorate rapidly. Wash in several waters till quite clean. Place in a pan the gizzard, heart and neck, cover with cold water and bring to the boil. Skim carefully. Simmer them with an onion, carrot, 2 cloves and flavouring herbs until the heart can be pierced with a fork. Put in the liver for the last 10 minutes only. Remove the giblets and strain the stock. Store them in the refrigerator for later use.

PREPARATION OF THE TURKEY. The bird must be washed under running water, then drained and well dried. To give it a

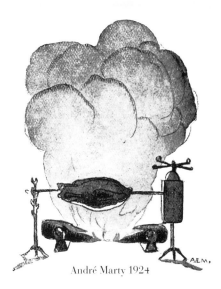

André Marty 1924

fine plump look, place 3-4 folds of cloth over it and bang the breastbone with a rolling-pin in order to flatten it. Rub the outer skin with coarse salt; season the interior with salt and pepper. Fill the cavity with the stuffing of your fancy (see page 121), but lightly – do not pack it in, since the stuffing swells during cooking. Sew up the opening with kitchen string. Brush the bird all over with melted butter or dripping and cover with greased greaseproof paper. Fit a pair of greased paper trousers on to the legs, tying them at the ankles. Or, if you prefer, soak 3 pieces of white cheesecloth in melted fat; drape one over the breast, the remaining two over the legs and baste right through the cheesecloth.

ROASTING THE TURKEY. The saying goes that one is born *rôtisseur*: that's as may be, but following the rules and wielding the basting spoon with a will, who knows, *we* may find we are to the manner born too. Faced with an oversized turkey we may have to put him straight on to the grid, previously greased: otherwise, an average bird can be prepared in the following way.

Line the roasting pan with a layer of sliced onion, carrot and celery, a bay leaf and a little parsley. Set the turkey on this aromatic bed and put in a preheated oven (see below). After it has been cooking for about 30 minutes, pour in ½ pint of the reserved giblet stock and continue to baste with this liquid. About 10 minutes before the finish, remove the papers or cloth and permit the bird to colour well.

ROASTING TIMES AND TEMPERATURES. There are two schools of thought on this subject. One method favours 2 temperatures, the other 1 temperature only. *First method* – hot oven for 20-25 minutes (Gas Regulo 8, 450°F) then reduce to moderate heat (Gas Regulo 3, 325°F). Baste at 20-minute intervals and allow 20-25 minutes per pound for total roasting. *Second method* – moderate oven (Gas Regulo 3-4, 325-350°F) all the time. Baste as above, but allow 25-30 minutes per pound. For turkeys from 15-20 pounds, 18-20 minutes per pound should suffice. To find out whether or not the turkey is cooked, prick the thigh with a thin skewer. When a colourless liquid spurts out, it is ready. Lift the bird from the pan on to a hot dish and replace it in the oven to keep warm while the gravy is being made.

RICH GRAVY. Add to the fat and vegetables in the roasting pan another cup of stock or water. Stir the contents over the flame and bring to the boil. Strain into another saucepan and let it stand for a few minutes. Skim off all the fat from the surface. Dilute a level tablespoon of cornflour with 3 of water. Bring the gravy again to boiling point, stir in the cornflour and boil until clear. Correct the seasoning and serve.

CROQUETTES DE DINDE

One gets tired of everything, even of the best cold turkey; this is a very good way of using up the remnants. Scrape off the white flesh, trim it and cut it in small slices, also cut in the same way some good ham (if you have half a pound of turkey you should use a quarter of a pound of ham). Peel three ounces of mushrooms, chop them finely and cook them in butter; add a cupful of consommé and let it reduce by about half. Put in a little more butter, salt, pepper, chopped parsley and spices; cook slowly for ten minutes, pass through a sieve and bind with a yolk of egg. Then pour the sauce over the pieces of turkey and ham, mixing well. The mixture, when quite cold, should be of such a consistency that you can make croquettes with it, but it must be fairly soft all the same.

Roll the croquettes in beaten egg, then in breadcrumbs, again in egg, and finish by another coating of breadcrumbs. Fry in very hot fat, drain well and serve with a good rich *jus* made with the brown of the turkey or with some other sauce, according to taste. A *sauce madère* with chopped truffles in it would go well with these croquettes, but a tomato sauce would be overpowering.

BOULESTIN 1925

CHRISTMAS GOOSE

salt
1 goose
6 apples
water or stock
chestnut purée to serve
GARNISH
paper frills
6 sprigs parsley

Rub the salt all over the goose, both outside and inside; stuff with the peeled whole apples. Make the roasting pan very hot and fill it with 1 inch of water. Put in the goose, breast down, and roast for 2-2½ hours, basting frequently with its own gravy and, if that is not enough, with water or stock also. A quarter of an hour before serving, baste it well and brown in a very hot oven for 15 minutes. Garnish with paper frills round the neck and legs and with fresh parsley round the dish.

Serve with the baked apples from the inside, and chestnut purée. (An alternative stuffing is chestnuts; if you use these, serve the goose with apple purée.) A tip worth knowing: if the goose is old, put it in the pan with the lid on first and leave it in the oven for 1½ hours, then finish off without the lid.

1940

ROAST DUCK WITH SAUCE ROUENNAISE

Roast 2 Aylesbury ducks in the usual way. In the meantime prepare the sauce in the following manner. Chop finely enough shallots to make 2 teaspoons. Cook these in 2 cups of excellent red wine with a pinch of thyme and half a bay leaf until reduced to ½ cup. Add ½ cup of tinned tomato sauce, heat and strain through a very fine sieve. Now rub the 2 raw duck livers through a fine sieve. Drain off every bit of juice from the ducks and skim off this every drop of fat, then add any juice that may be left to the sauce. Carve the ducks and garnish prettily with parsley. Put the purée of livers in an enamel saucepan and add little by little the hot sauce, stirring all the while. The heat of the sauce should be sufficient to cook the livers. Pass the whole through a sieve again and heat very cautiously on a very low flame. Taste, add a drop or two of cognac, a dash of cayenne, salt and freshly ground pepper and stir in a tablespoon of butter bit by bit. Serve the duck, handing round the sauce separately. Serves 6.

JUNE PLATT 1936

CANTON STEAMED DUCK AND PARSNIP

This is one of the simplest Chinese delicacies. Cut 4 parsnips into quarters lengthwise. Place a young duckling weighing about 3 pounds in a large basin. Arrange the pieces of parsnip around it. Sprinkle in a very little salt and add 2 pints of water. Put a lid on the bowl and steam it gently for 3½ hours. Before serving, cut up the duck and serve as a stew-cum-soup. The flavours are complementary to one another.

BERYL GOULD-MARKS 1954

CANARD AUX RAISINS

2 fat young Aylesbury ducks
4-5 oz butter
1 small glass brandy
¾ bottle white wine (Pouilly or Muscadet)
2 carrots
2 small onions, chopped
1 bouquet garni
2 cups good strained broth or *pot-au-feu*
salt and pepper
3 oz sultanas
4 tbsp fresh cream

Sauté the trussed ducks in butter in a large, deep cocotte pan or casserole. When they are golden all over (about 15 minutes) drain away the butter. Heat the brandy in a small saucepan and light it, shaking vigorously, and pour, flaming, over the birds. Now add the wine, vegetables, bouquet garni, and broth. Season well with salt and pepper. Reduce the sauce over a quick fire, then cover the cocotte and cook gently over a slow fire for 30-40 minutes. A moment before serving, add to the sauce the sultanas that you have plumped up by soaking in a little wine, and then the cream.

Serve new potatoes with the duck, accompanied by small green peas, cooked *à la Française*.

VERONICA MACLEAN 1970

BRAISED DUCK

1 large duck
sea salt and black pepper
¼ pt chicken stock
⅛ pt dry white wine
2 cloves garlic
1 inch square piece ginger
3 shallots
6 spring onions

Prick the duck all over with a sharp skewer and lay upside down on a rack in a roasting tin. Roast for 45 minutes at Gas Mark 6, 400°F. Remove from the oven and turn down the heat to Gas

Anthony Denney 1960

Mark 4, 350°F. Take the rack out of the tin and pour off the fat. Replace the duck in the tin, without the rack, standing right side up. Sprinkle it with sea salt and black pepper. Heat the stock and wine together and pour over the bird. Slice the garlic, ginger and shallots, and scatter them over the duck. Cover with a sheet of foil, or a lid, and cook for 45-50 minutes, basting 2 or 3 times.

While it cooks, cut the spring onions into sections 1 inch long, then split each piece into very thin strips. When the time is up, remove the duck and strain the stock into a small bowl. Carve the duck and lay on a serving dish. Remove the fat from the surface of the sauce, and use a little of it to moisten the duck; pour the rest into a sauceboat. Scatter the spring onions over the duck and serve, with noodles and mangetout. Serves 4.

ARABELLA BOXER 1983

PERDREAUX POÊLÉS

Take some partridges (two for four people), singe them well, and fill them with the following mixture: two ounces of butter well worked with salt, pepper, and the juice of a lemon. Wrap the birds with slices of thin fat bacon tied round with fine string. Put some rashers of bacon, a few carrots, and one onion cut in slices in a deep fireproof dish; place the partridges over this, cover them with slices of lemon and more bacon, and cook them for a good half an hour. Then remove the birds from the casserole and the string from the birds; keep them hot.

Squeeze through a sieve the bacon, lemon, vegetables, etc., over which the birds have been cooked. Add a piece of butter, a glass of white wine, a pinch of flour and cook a few minutes more. Put back the partridges in the casserole, and serve a few minutes later. See that the gravy is salt enough and pleasurably spicy. Should you have some bones of any game left over, you can make a sauce, and add it to the gravy in the casserole. Put the bones in a small saucepan with a few slices of carrot, two shallots finely chopped and one clove; add some beefstock, bring to the boil and cook on a slow fire till well reduced. Pour it over the birds through a sieve.

BOULESTIN 1923

PHEASANTS IN CREAM

You will need at least 3 birds. Clean them well, cover their breasts with strips of bacon and tie them up. Brown carefully in an iron cocotte with 3 or 4 tablespoons of butter and 8 shallots. Pour a little cognac over them and light it. When the flames have died down, add salt and pepper and 1½ cups of veal or chicken broth and cook in the oven for 30 minutes, basting frequently with the juice. Then add 2 pints of thick cream and ¼ cup of freshly grated horseradish. Let all this cook for another 20 minutes, continuing to baste with the sauce. Adjust the seasoning to taste. Place the birds on a serving dish, carve them and then pour the juice over all. Serve with green peas in butter. For 12 people.

JUNE PLATT 1935

ROAST GROUSE

2 young grouse
2 tbsp blaeberries or cranberries
salt and pepper
lemon juice
bacon rashers
2 sprigs of heather
flour
butter
slices of toast

Wipe the grouse well with a clean damp cloth, inside and out. Put 1 tablespoon of blaeberries or cranberries into each bird, then rub them with salt, pepper and lemon juice. Wrap them first in bacon rashers, then in greaseproof paper, enclosing a sprig of heather (for tradition as well as luck). Place the birds, breasts down, in a baking tin and roast for about 20-30 minutes (Gas Regulo 7, 425°F), depending on size. Ten minutes before serving, remove the paper, heather and bacon; sprinkle the grouse with flour and return to the oven.

Cook the livers for about 10 minutes, then chop or mince them finely and pound to a paste. If necessary, add a little butter to give a spreading consistency. Add salt and pepper to taste and spread the liver paste on slices of toast. Remove all but a little dripping from the baking tin and place the toast under the birds 2 or 3 minutes before serving.

PETER PIRBRIGHT AND GRETEL BEER 1950

BRAISED PIGEONS

2 pigeons
seasoned flour
fat for frying
½ lb small onions
¾ tumbler still, dry cider
½ tumbler stock
salt and pepper
1 tbsp chopped parsley
4 oz button mushrooms

Quarter the pigeons, dredge them well with seasoned flour and fry them until golden brown. Remove them from the frying pan and keep hot. Cook the onions (whole) in the same fat, adding the cider and stock, and salt and pepper. Place the pigeons in a casserole, add the onions and liquid and also the parsley. Cover and cook in the oven (Gas Regulo 5, 375°F) for 45 minutes, then add the mushrooms and continue cooking until tender (about 20 minutes).

PETER PIRBRIGHT AND GRETEL BEER 1950

GUINEA FOWL WITH MORELS SAUCE

I prepared guinea fowl, including liver
(about 2 lb)
salt and pepper
2 thin slices of truffle
4 oz butter
½ lb morels
2 tbsp Madeira
I small leek, finely chopped
I shallot, finely chopped
I carrot, finely chopped
I cup white wine
½ pt chicken stock
6 tbsp double cream
I bunch watercress

Remove the legs and breasts of the guinea fowl: pull off the skin and cut off all fat and tissue. Bat the legs and breasts lightly, and add seasoning. Cut the liver in half and roll pieces of liver and truffle into each leg. Place the rolled legs on the breasts, form into cigar shapes and wrap tightly in Cellophane. Place each prepared portion in simmering water and cook them for about 20 minutes. Meanwhile, heat 2 ounces of butter in a small *sauteuse*, add the morels and seasoning and simmer. Add the Madeira and cook until nearly all the moisture has evaporated.

Heat the remaining 2 ounces of butter in a large *sauteuse* and brown the carcass with the prepared vegetables. Add the wine, stock and salt and pepper, and simmer for 20 minutes, then remove the carcass. Add the cream and reduce to a coating consistency. Pass the sauce through a *chinois*, then add the morels and adjust the seasoning.

Slice the guinea fowl thinly and arrange on a plate with each slice overlapping slightly. Surround with the sauce and garnish with watercress. We serve this dish with a potato basket filled with two quails' eggs. Serves 2.

JACK DICK 1985

1928

SALMIS OF GAME WITH CELERY AND TARRAGON

This is an unusual game dish, in that it is steamed over game stock, and served lying on a bed of celery, with a sauce made from its stock. It goes well with freshly made noodles.

2 grouse or 4 partridge or squab
1½ tbsp sunflower oil
1½ lb chicken wings or jointed rabbit (if using
partridge or squab)
I onion, halved
I carrot, halved
½ bay leaf
sea salt and 8 black peppercorns
¼ pt dry white wine or ⅛ pt vermouth
6 sticks celery
2 tsp cornflour
2 tbsp *fromage blanc*
2 tbsp chopped tarragon

If using grouse, cut the breasts and wings off the carcasses to make 4 pieces. Use the carcasses to make a stock with the onion, carrot, bay leaf, seasonings, wine or vermouth, and 1¼ pints of water. If using partridge or squab, simply cut them in half and make a stock with rabbit or chicken wings. Strain the stock after making, cool quickly, and remove any fat from the surface. Put it in the bottom part of a steamer and bring to the boil. Cut the celery into strips about 3 inches long by ¼ inch wide; lay them in the top part of the steamer with the cut-up birds lying on them. Cover and cook over the boiling stock for 15 minutes, then set aside, covered, to keep warm. Measure about 12 fluid ounces of the stock, and reheat in a small pan. Mix the cornflour in a cup with 1 tablespoon of cold water, then stir into the measured stock. Boil gently for 2-3 minutes, stirring, then remove from the heat and cool slightly. Pour into a food processor, add the *fromage blanc* and tarragon, and process briefly until smooth. Tip back into the pan and reheat gently, without allowing it to boil. To serve, lay the celery strips in a shallow dish with the game lying on them. Spoon a little of the sauce over, and serve the rest in a jug. Fresh noodles make an excellent accompaniment to this delicate game dish. Serves 4.

ARABELLA BOXER 1986

'An infallible sign of youth in a pheasant is a pointed last large wing feather; a rounded one denotes age.'

DORIS LYTTON-TOYE

FRESH PASTA WITH GAME SAUCE AND WILD MUSHROOMS

I love this dish, finding it full of character and flavour, but it is only worth making with fresh wild mushrooms, and delicate fresh pasta.

1 grouse or ½ pheasant
1 medium onion, coarsely chopped
4 tbsp sunflower oil
1 medium carrot, coarsely chopped
1 stick celery, coarsely chopped
1 tsp flour
2 shallots, finely chopped
1 large clove garlic, finely chopped
½ lb wild mushrooms: *girolles, cèpes* or oyster mushrooms, when available
3 tbsp flat parsley, chopped
1 lb fresh tagliatelle
FOR THE STOCK
½ onion, sliced
1 small carrot, halved
½ stick celery
¼ bay leaf
sea salt and 6 black peppercorns
4 tbsp vermouth

Cut all the flesh off the bird and cut it in cubes. Make a stock with the carcass, flavouring with vegetables and bay leaf, seasonings and vermouth, and ¾ pint of water. Strain and cool, then remove any fat on the surface.

Cook the coarsely chopped onion in half the sunflower oil for 6-8 minutes until it has started to soften. Meanwhile, parboil the carrot and celery in the stock for 5 minutes, then drain them, and add to the onion. Cook for 2-3 minutes, then add the chopped game. Stir until lightly coloured and cook for another 2-3 minutes. Then stir in the flour and cook for another minute, stirring. Pour on 8 fluid ounces of the hot stock and stir until blended. Simmer gently for 5 minutes, then set aside in a warm place.

Shortly before serving, bring a large pan of lightly salted water to the boil. Stew the shallots gently in the remaining 2 tablespoons of sunflower oil in a sauté pan, adding the garlic after 1 minute. After another minute, add the wild mushrooms, cut in large pieces, and cook for 6-8 minutes, stirring now and then until they have softened, adding the parsley towards the end. Cook the pasta for 2-3 minutes and drain in a colander. Tip into a large shallow bowl and pour the game sauce over it. Lift lightly to distribute the sauce, then spread the wild mushrooms over the top. Serve immediately, with a green salad. Serves 4.

ARABELLA BOXER 1986

ROASTED SQUAB WITH GARLIC

This is an adaptation of the recipe from The Nouvelle Cuisine *by Jean and Pierre Troisgros. Try to get the livers with the squab, if you can, otherwise substitute chicken livers.*

4 squab, with livers
(2 oz chicken liver, if no squab livers)
1 oz butter
3 tbsp sunflower oil
15 cloves garlic, unpeeled
¼ pt dry white wine
3 sprigs fresh thyme
1 shallot, chopped
2 tbsp *crème fraîche*
2 oz *mâche* (lamb's lettuce) to garnish

Brown the birds all over in the butter and 2 tablespoons of oil in a casserole. Remove them and put in the whole cloves of garlic. Brown the garlic gently in the butter and oil for 1-2 minutes, pour on the wine and add the thyme. Bring to the boil, lay the squabs on the garlic and cover. Cook in the oven for 35-40 minutes at Gas Mark 5, 375°F.

Heat the remaining tablespoon of oil in a frying pan and cook the chopped shallot gently for 1-2 minutes. Add the livers and cook briefly, until they are no longer pink. When the birds are cooked, transfer to a serving dish and keep warm. Push the garlic cloves through a food mill, with the livers and shallot. Mix with the juices from the casserole, stir in the *crème fraîche*, and reheat, adding salt and pepper if required. Serve the birds on a bed of *mâche*, with the sauce in a separate jug. Accompany them with fresh noodles, and wild mushrooms, when available. Serves 4.

ARABELLA BOXER 1987

Roger de Lavererie 1933

106

RECIPES FOR RABBIT

BOULESTIN 1925

LAPEREAU À LA MINUTE

Having cleaned the rabbit and wiped it well with a cloth, cut it in pieces. Put a quarter of a pound of butter in a saucepan: when it has melted put in the pieces of meat together with salt and pepper, spices and grated nutmeg. Cook on a quick fire: ten minutes will do. Two minutes before it is ready, throw in the saucepan two or three shallots and parsley finely chopped. Shake well, see that it is well seasoned, and serve.

LAPEREAU SAUTÉ AU CHABLIS

Cook the rabbit in the same way as directed above. When it is ready, remove the saucepan from the fire, sprinkle the meat with flour (not more than a pudding-spoonful) and add a good glass of Chablis (or Graves or any dry French white wine – not sherry or Madeira, which are too full flavoured and would change the character of the dish). Shake and stir well, put on a slow fire to cook a few minutes. See that the sauce is well *liée* and smooth, also that it does not reach the boiling point.

CUISSES DE LAPEREAU EN PAPILLOTES

The legs of rabbit can be utilized in this pleasant way. First make some *lardons* the size of your larding needle, roll them well in salt, pepper and spices and insert them in the legs. Put these in a saucepan with butter and cook them for about half an hour, turning them once or twice. Sprinkle them with *fines herbes à papillotes* (see below): cook slowly for ten minutes; then dispose your legs of rabbit on a board well coated with the *fines herbes* and let them grow cold.

Meanwhile prepare the paper for the *papillotes*. Take a sheet of paper large enough, and paint it with melted butter or oil: put in the middle of it a thin rasher of streaky bacon, on the top of it one leg of rabbit with its *fines herbes*: fold the paper over, pleat the ends together, gather and tie them well so that the butter and the gravy cannot escape. Cook in a slow oven for about half an hour, turning the *papillotes* once (the original recipe, of course, says grill on charcoals). The heat of the oven should be well regulated, so that the paper does not burn. Serve if you like with a *sauce diable* or sharp sauce of some kind.

FINES HERBES À PAPILLOTES

The *fines herbes* should be prepared as follows: chop very finely three rashers of streaky bacon and four mushrooms, and cook these for a few minutes in a small saucepan with butter. Add two or three shallots also finely chopped, cook two minutes more and add a tablespoonful of chopped parsley, salt, pepper, spices and grated nutmeg. Mix well. Your *fines herbes* are ready for your *papillotes*. Veal cutlets are also very good treated and cooked *en papillotes* and you can, if you like, add a little tomato *purée* to the preparation.

There are many other ways of cooking rabbit or leveret: it is delicious *en purée* as a *gibelotte* or *en filets sautés* with mushrooms and a well-flavoured cream sauce, but the thing to remember is that it must be well seasoned as the flesh is rather tasteless. Rabbit indifferently cooked is not worth eating.

JUGGED HARE

Skin, clean, and cut a hare in neat pieces not larger than an egg. Season with pepper and salt, and fry over the fire with 2 ounces of butter and 2 ounces of chopped bacon. When it is a good brown colour, remove it and put it into a wide-mouthed jar with 4 good wine glasses of port wine or claret. Cover the jar and put it in the oven for 20 or 30 minutes. Remove the jar and add a pint of strong game stock, a tablespoon of strained lemon juice and a herb bag composed of the following: a piece of cinnamon, 4 cloves, 4 bay leaves, a blade of mace, a sprig of fresh thyme, 12 peppercorns, 2 Jamaica peppers, a sprig of marjoram and a sprig of parsley. Cover the jar, put it in the oven in a pan containing boiling water and cook for 3 hours.

When the meat is cooked, strain off the gravy and thicken it with 1½ tablespoons of flour and butter mixed together. Boil this and pour it back on the meat and heat again. Serve with forcemeat balls around the base of the dish. This dish is excellent for lunch or dinner. *Note:* Forcemeat balls are made with equal quantities of breadcrumbs, suet and chopped parsley – all mixed well and rolled into balls, dusted with egg and breadcrumbs, and fried in deep fat.

MRS CHARLES CARTWRIGHT 1935

> **'When you have a good hare, jug the paws and forequarter, but let the back and hindquarters pickle for 3 or 4 days (wine, vinegar, carrots, onions) before roasting.'**
> MARCEL ROUFF

> **'Furred or feathered, game is the daily food of robust, primitive peoples who do not know where their liver is or even if they have such a thing.'**
>
> MARCEL ROUFF

HARE IN CREAM SAUCE

I hare
strips of bacon fat
salt and pepper
fat for roasting
I carton natural yoghurt
pinch of sugar
flour (optional)
MARINADE
I tumbler red wine
½ tumbler vinegar
I tsp pickling spice
2 bay leaves
2 carrots, sliced
2 onions, sliced
salt
I stick celery, sliced
handful of parsley

Skin the hare carefully, removing the flaps, and cut off the legs. If possible, keep the saddle in one piece. Put all the ingredients for the marinade into a saucepan and bring to the boil with 1½ pints water. Simmer for 20 minutes, then pour it boiling over the hare, which should be completely covered by the liquid. Leave for 24 hours.

Take out the hare and dry it well; strain the marinade. Cut the bacon fat into thin strips and lard the saddle and legs neatly. Rub with pepper and salt and place in a baking dish with the melted fat. Roast at Gas Regulo 4, 350°F, basting with liberal helpings of the marinade. Before serving, stir in the yoghurt and a pinch of sugar, and bring to the boil. If a thicker sauce is required, also add some flour slaked with water.

PETER PIRBRIGHT AND GRETEL BEER 1950

Roger de Laveveerie 1933

REHBRATEN

Cover 4 pounds of shoulder of venison in this marinade: equal quantities of vinegar and water, with peppercorns, bay leaves, thyme leaves, sloes, cloves and salt to taste. Leave to soak for 3 days. Remove the venison, lard it with fat bacon, and bake in a moderate oven with a little butter. Mix a glass of sour cream with the gravy from the meat; pour the sauce over the meat and decorate with slices of orange. Serve with macaroni or potatoes, and cranberry preserve.

MARGARETE HAMERSCHLAG 1937

VENISON CASSEROLE

Venison, properly hung and cooked, is a dish with regal attributes. The chef of a hunting lodge serves venison in a casserole that deserves more than passing mention. He rolls bite-sized portions of venison steak in flour lightly seasoned with powdered sage, rosemary and marjoram, and fries them slowly in butter until brown. He lines a large casserole with thin slices of fat, country-cured ham, and in goes part of the venison, a layer of small potato balls, a layer of onion rings, then more venison, and the process is repeated, ending up with venison. Then comes enough claret to fill the casserole. In a medium oven the claret soon cooks away and is replaced by sweet cream. This is a good one-dish meal in itself. The chef serves with it a salad of sliced cucumbers and raw button mushrooms in a garlic dressing.

HARRY BOTSFORD 1953

VENISON À LA NORMANDE

Venison must be hung for at least 2 or 3 days before eating, and it is always better if it is marinated before cooking, although some cuts can be grilled or fried like steak. This dish should be made with the haunch for preference.

Make a marinade with 1 pint of cider, ¼ pint of wine vinegar, a sprig of parsley and thyme, 1 bay leaf, 2 crushed cloves of garlic, 2 carrots and 2 onions, cut in rounds and fried in olive oil until golden, salt and pepper. Mix the marinade and leave the venison in it for at least 4 days. If you are only using a small quantity of meat, reduce the marinade, but keep the same proportions of cider to vinegar.

Drain the joint, cover it with a few rashers of fat bacon and roast it in a hot oven, allowing 10-15 minutes per pound (more for a very small joint). Half-way through the cooking time, baste with a wine glass of calvados or brandy, mixed with the juice of half a lemon and 6 tablespoons of the cider marinade. While the meat is cooking, make a purée of cooking apples with a little of the marinade; add no sugar, it should be sharp. Make a gravy with the juices from the meat, a little of the marinade and 5 tablespoons of fresh cream. Serve surrounded with the apple purée, a fluffy purée of potatoes, and the first tiny button Brussels sprouts.

BERYL GOULD-MARKS 1954

Tessa Traeger 1986

SAUCES
AND STUFFINGS

'It is the duty of a good sauce,' wrote the editor of the *Almanach des Gourmands*, 'to insinuate itself all round and about the maxillary glands and imperceptibly awaken into activity each ramification of the Organ of Taste; if not sufficiently savoury, it cannot produce this effect, and if too piquant it will paralyse instead of exciting those delicious titillations of tongue and vibrations of palate that only the most accomplished Philosophers of the Mouth can produce on the highly educated palates of thrice happy Grands Gourmands.'

Boulestin admitted that not many people could make the marvellous sauces and dishes which thrilled this epicurean editor: 'a light hand is required, as it is for making pastry – also that mysterious gift which Nature sometimes gives to cooks, professional or otherwise. Apart from great chefs, some well-known people have it bestowed on them extravagantly, and are natural cooks who can create things of a distinction that no training, however perfect, can ever hope to produce.'

Monsieur Momo, the friend and biographer of Henri de Toulouse-Lautrec, provided *Vogue* with a delicious roster of sauces in 1961 but insisted that they should not be given names. 'Our cookbooks

Above: Pierre Brissaud 1934
Opposite: von Alvensleben 1983

mention a number of sauces,' he wrote. 'Hundreds of them. What good is it to cram the heads of illiterate cooks with noble titles which will only perplex them?' Monsieur Momo's nameless recipes – which *Vogue* entitled 'The rainbow sauces of Toulouse-Lautrec' – are on page 115.

The famous Mrs Beeton naturally appreciated the value of a good sauce: 'The preparation and appearance of sauces and gravies are of the highest consequence, and in nothing does the talent and taste of the cook more display itself. Their special adaptability to the various viands they are to accompany cannot be too much studied, in order that they may harmonize and blend with them as perfectly, so to speak, as does a pianoforte accompaniment with the voice of the singer.'

A hundred years later Elizabeth David was telling her *Vogue* readers: 'Like skirts, sauces may be either long or short. Though the short sauces have the more immediate appeal, the long ones are important in good cooking.' On the following pages there are recipes for sauces both long and short, brown and white, sweet and savoury – but the remark made by Miguel de Cervantes still applies: 'Hunger is the best sauce in the world.'

SAUCE BÉCHAMEL

Béchamel sauce should be made as follows: put in a saucepan on a slow fire a piece of butter the size of a small egg and a tablespoonful of flour; cook for a few minutes and add a little beef stock, stirring all the time. Then add a glass of milk, salt, pepper and a little nutmeg. Mix well and cook for a quarter of an hour, stirring occasionally, after which you add a few pieces of butter and pass through a sieve.

BOULESTIN 1923

SAUCE FLAMANDE

Melt some butter in a saucepan and put in four onions finely chopped, two cloves, a little nutmeg, a bay leaf and the liver, heart and blood from a hare. Add about a pint and a half of wine vinegar and water mixed in equal parts. Boil it very slowly for five hours, then pass it through a sieve. Add to it a tumblerful of good claret and a pinch of sugar; bring to the boil again, and add a little potato flour. Cook for a few minutes more.

BOULESTIN 1923

SAUCE BORDELAISE

There are many sauces often served in France with *grillades*: one of the best is the *sauce bordelaise* which comes from Bordeaux.

Put in a small saucepan a chopped shallot and half a glass of white wine. Cook it so that it reduces to a spoonful. Poach the marrow of a bone and cut it in small cubes; add these to the sauce with a little piece of butter, seasoning and chopped parsley. Cook for a minute or so and either pour it over your grilled *entrecôte* or serve it in a small (and very hot) sauceboat.

BOULESTIN 1925

SAUCE HOLLANDAISE

This is the simplest way of making a good *sauce hollandaise*: put in a small saucepan two tablespoonsful of wine vinegar and a little pepper and reduce it by three-quarters. Put in a basin the yolks of four eggs, mix them well with about one ounce of butter, and pour over the mixture the hot vinegar you have reduced. Stir all the time on a slow fire while the butter melts; the mixture should be very smooth. Squeeze through a muslin into another saucepan and cook *au bain marie*, whipping all the time and adding, occasionally, small pieces of butter till the sauce is thick enough and well 'bound'. The butter used should be absolutely fresh and really the best.

BOULESTIN 1928

SAUCE ESPAGNOLE

All good cooks keep this sauce on hand as it is the chief brown foundation sauce and forms the basis of a number of other sauces. The following recipe produces 4 pints: 6 pints of rich stock, 4 ounces of lean veal, 4 ounces of raw ham or lean bacon, 1 bouquet garni, 12 peppercorns, 4 ounces of butter, 4 ounces of sifted flour, 1 carrot, 1 turnip, 1 onion, 2 cloves, ½ pint of tomato pulp, ¼ pint of claret, 1 glass of sherry and some mushrooms. Peel the carrot, turnip and onion. Cut them up small and put them in a stewpan with the bouquet, peppercorns, cloves, veal and ham (both cut up in small pieces). Add 1 ounce of butter and stir them over the fire until they are a rich brown. Pour off the fat, and add the stock, claret, sherry, mushrooms and tomato pulp. Boil slowly for 1 hour, skimming from time to time.

Meanwhile prepare a brown roux by melting the remaining butter in a saucepan. Stir in the flour and cook slowly over a moderate fire, stirring until the roux is a rich brown. Allow it to cool and

'To the epicure who looks on cooking as one of the fine arts and a perfectly planned meal as an achievement, there is a certain joy in merely reading of food and drink, even when not partaking.'

pour in gradually the prepared stock with all its flavourings. Stir the sauce over the fire until it boils. Let it simmer for 1 hour, skim it well and pass it through a fine sieve. In order to prevent a thick crust forming on the top, stir occasionally until cool.

LEONE B. MOATS 1933

SAUCE MOUSSELINE

Squeeze and strain the juice of half a lemon. Put 4 tablespoons of vinegar in an enamel pan, with a big pinch of salt and a little white pepper. Reduce it by simmering until only 2 teaspoons are left. Add 2 tablespoons of cold water and the yolks of 4 eggs, being sure not to include any of the white. Also add 2 pieces of butter the size of walnuts. Place the pan directly on a very low flame and beat incessantly with a wire whisk until the mixture thickens slightly. Remove the pan from the fire. Place it over hot water in a double boiler and add little by little (beating continuously with the whisk), 1¼ cups butter (not melted), and from time to time add a tablespoon of cold water. When the sauce is thick, stir in the lemon juice. Season to taste with salt and white pepper. Remove from the fire and fold in 6 tablespoons of cream, beaten stiff. Continue beating for a second or two with the whisk. Serve in a warm, not hot, bowl.

JUNE PLATT 1937

PARSLEY SAUCE

bunch of parsley
3 oz margarine
pinch of salt and black pepper

Clean the parsley. Chop it finely and put it into a saucepan with the margarine, salt and pepper. When the margarine is melted, the sauce is ready to serve — it must not boil.

Note: This is very good with such white fish as whiting, hake, halibut, or plaice, which are also improved by the addition of a bay or tarragon leaf to the water in which they are steamed.

BETTY MARIE LONGDEN 1942

NORWEGIAN SAUCE

2 tbsp French mustard
3 oz margarine
a few capers
½ glass fish liquid

This sauce adds piquancy to rock cod, salt cod or any kind of coarser fish: put the mustard, margarine and capers into a saucepan with the hot liquid strained off from a poached fish. Stir well to blend. Take off the heat and serve as soon as the margarine is melted.

BETTY MARIE LONGDEN 1942

SIMPLE WHITE SAUCE

Use white sauce as a base for parsley, shrimp, anchovy sauce, etc. For 1 pint of liquid, milk or milk and water, you will need 1½ ounces of margarine and 1½ ounces of flour. Melt the fat in a saucepan: add the flour: stir over a flame for a few seconds till the mixture looks honeycombed. Away from the fire, add the liquid gradually, stirring, till the sauce is smooth. Stir briskly over the heat till it is boiling: simmer for 5 minutes gently. Season with salt and pepper.

DORIS LYTTON-TOYE 1947

SAUCE BÂTARDE

This is very quick and economical. With a wooden spoon, cream ½ ounce of margarine or butter and ½ ounce of flour (1 level tablespoon) in a small pan. Add ½ pint of milk. Place the pan over the fire. Bring the milk to the boil without stirring. When it boils, remove from the heat, whisk briskly — no, there won't be any lumps — and season to taste. Simmer for 5 minutes.

DORIS LYTTON-TOYE 1947

Rudy Muller 1964

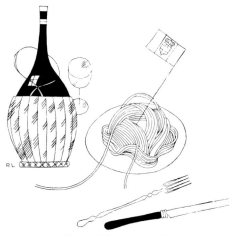

Roger de Lavererie 1933

OYSTER CREAM SAUCE

For poached turbot, halibut or brill – a lovely fish now neglected.

Melt 1 ounce of butter or margarine and stir in ¾ ounce of flour. Cook over the fire for a few seconds then moisten with ½ pint of scalded milk. Whisk until perfectly smooth and permit the sauce to simmer for 10 minutes. Season with salt, paprika and a generous dash of lemon juice. Just before serving, bring the sauce to boiling point and add ½ dozen chopped oysters with a tablespoon of chopped parsley and the liquor from the oysters. It goes without saying that a spoonful of cream added at the finish is a real improvement.

DORIS LYTTON-TOYE 1951

SIGNOR PARMIGIANI'S SPAGHETTI SAUCE

1 medium onion, chopped
½ cup olive oil
1 small tin tomato purée
1 small tin peeled tomatoes
salt and pepper
2 oz Italian salami
Parmesan and Gruyère cheese, grated

Fry the onion in olive oil and add the tomato purée and peeled tomatoes. Season with salt and pepper to taste. Finally add the finely chopped salami, cover with a lid and cook gently for 15 minutes. Serve with freshly cooked and drained spaghetti, sprinkled with a mixture of grated Parmesan and Gruyère cheese.

PETER PIRBRIGHT AND GRETEL BEER 1952

TUNNY FISH AND TRUFFLE SAUCE FOR SPAGHETTI

Take 2 ounces of tinned tunny fish, 1 ounce of fillets of anchovy, a piece of garlic, several sprigs of parsley, and a walnut of black truffle. Chop the garlic and fry it in a wine glass of olive oil; just as it is beginning to colour, add the rest of the ingredients, roughly chopped, with some freshly ground black pepper. Cook fairly quickly, until the fish is beginning to brown, then stir in 4 peeled and sliced tomatoes of medium size, and add 1½ cups of water. Cover, and simmer for about 45 minutes, adding more water if required. Toss the spaghetti in this sauce, and serve piping hot.

GEORGINA MASSON 1954

EGG SAUCE

2 eggs
½ pt milk
½ bay leaf
1 slice onion
1 clove
2 oz butter
1½ tbsp flour
pinch of mace or nutmeg
sea salt and black pepper
2 tbsp chopped parsley

Hard-boil the eggs and shell. Heat the milk in a small pan with the bay leaf, onion and clove. When simmering point is reached, turn off the heat, cover the pan and leave to infuse for 20 minutes. Melt the butter, stir in the flour and cook for 1 minute. Discard the bay leaf, onion and clove, and pour on the heated milk. Stir until blended, add a pinch of mace or nutmeg, some sea salt and black pepper and simmer for about 4 minutes. Chop the eggs and stir in, adding the chopped parsley also.

This sauce can be enriched by the addition of cream but I prefer it without. It is delicious with poached white fish – turbot, halibut, haddock or cod – also with hot boiled bacon, cauliflower or broccoli. Serves 4.

ARABELLA BOXER 1977

MUSHROOM SAUCE

1 packet dried mushrooms
¾ pt chicken stock, heated
½ lb round mushrooms
sea salt and black pepper
⅛ pt *crème fraîche* or sour cream
3-4 tbsp coarsely chopped parsley

Pick over the dried mushrooms carefully, looking out for small stones. Put them in a bowl and pour over ¼ pint of the heated stock. Leave to stand for 15 minutes and drain, reserving the stock for another dish. (The stock is useful for making gravy after roasting birds or meat; simply add to the pan juices, stir well, and reduce.)

Wipe the fresh mushrooms and trim the stalks. Cut the caps in quarters and the stalks in thick slices. Put them in a pan with the remaining ½ pint of stock. Bring to the boil and simmer gently, half covered, for 10 minutes. Chop the drained, dried mushrooms and add when the time is up. Simmer for another 5 minutes. Add sea salt and black pepper to taste, then stir in the cream and the chopped parsley.

This can be served as it is, or processed until the desired consistency is reached in a food processor. If serving with roast game, poultry, or meat, it is probably best puréed; left as it is, it makes a good side dish to eat with brown rice, buckwheat, or other grains. Serves 6 as a sauce, or 3 to 4 as a side dish.

ARABELLA BOXER 1983

THE RAINBOW SAUCES OF TOULOUSE-LAUTREC

1961

A sauce should not have a proper name, according to Monsieur Momo, friend and biographer of Toulouse-Lautrec: 'Just like the rainbow, it is blond, rosy, red, russet, yellow, green, and ought to be good, anonymous, and discreet. Matching the shade of her dress to the dish itself, she is a good, pretty girl who passes without a name, be she gentle or piquant.' Here are some of M. Momo's recipes.

WHITE SAUCE

3 tbsp unsalted butter
2 hard-boiled egg yolks
I tbsp minced shallots
I cup veal or chicken stock
3 egg yolks
I tbsp minced parsley
4 oz white mushrooms, sliced
I cup heavy cream
juice of I lemon
salt and freshly ground white pepper

Cook together in a casserole 2 tablespoons of butter, the mashed egg yolks, the shallots, and the stock. Bind them with the raw egg yolks and add the parsley, the mushrooms previously sautéd in the remaining butter, and the cream. Stirring constantly, cook the sauce until it is thick and smooth. At the last moment, add the juice of the lemon and salt and pepper to taste.

Serve lamb, veal, or other white meat in this sauce. It is also delicious poured over slices of mild pink ham, but for this omit the salt and pepper.

Henri de Toulouse-Lautrec 1961

GREEN AND WHITE SAUCE

3 tbsp butter
3 tbsp flour
¾ cup fish stock
¾ cup heavy cream
salt and freshly ground black and white pepper
2 tbsp capers
juice of I lemon
I tbsp finely minced dill

Put the butter and flour in a casserole over a low flame. Blend together to make a roux. Gradually add the fish stock and cream, stirring and cooking until the sauce is thick and smooth. Remove from the flame and add the salt and pepper, capers, the juice of the lemon, and the dill. Serve with poached fish.

YELLOW AND GREEN SAUCE

4 egg yolks
unsalted butter
tarragon
I tbsp wine vinegar
salt and freshly ground white pepper

Put the egg yolks and a piece of butter the size of an egg in a small bowl, and

stir gently with a wooden spoon over hot water until the mixture thickens. Remove from the heat and add another egg-sized lump of butter, stirring while it melts. Add a good handful of chopped fresh tarragon with the vinegar and let the sauce thicken. Season with salt and fresh white pepper.

Serve with all charcoal-grilled meats, kid, mutton, venison or beefsteak.

YELLOW-ORANGE SAUCE

6 egg yolks
6 Madeira glasses of white bordeaux, port, or cherry liqueur
6 heaped tbsp powdered sugar

Put the egg yolks in a 4-pint mixing bowl and beat them over hot water on the stove until light lemon-coloured. Add the 6 glasses of wine one at a time, beating constantly, then the sugar. Beat until thick and frothy, pile in dessert glasses, and serve at once.

DEEP ORANGE-YELLOW SAUCE

4 tbsp butter
I onion, finely minced
bouquet of parsley
I tbsp finely chopped raw ham
I tbsp flour
I tsp curry powder
I thread saffron
I cup chicken bouillon
2 egg yolks

Place 2 tablespoons of butter, the onion, parsley and ham in a saucepan and cook until the onion is blanched. Add the flour, curry powder, saffron and bouillon, and cook for 15 minutes. Strain. Heat the sauce again and then, removing the casserole from the fire, bind it with the egg yolks and remaining butter. Serve over hard-boiled eggs, shrimps, chicken or lamb.

Julie Brown 1984

AÏOLI

This sauce is given here *à titre de curiosité* or for the few English people who are not afraid of a strong smell of garlic. It is a classical sauce in Provence and really delicious. Take four cloves of garlic, pound them in a mortar and add the yolks of two eggs, then olive oil (the very best) drop by drop, stirring meanwhile with the pestle as you would do for a mayonnaise sauce with a spoon. Stop occasionally to squeeze a little lemon juice into the sauce. When you have used about four tablespoonsful of oil, put in a pudding-spoonful of warm water, which ought to give the sauce the right consistency, which must be that of a stiff, smooth mayonnaise. Serve with fish and with plain boiled potatoes, and retire from your most British friends for a day or so. The taste is marvellous, but the bouquet, so to speak, quite strong and persistent.

BOULESTIN 1925

THOUSAND ISLAND DRESSING

Mix 2 tablespoons of mayonnaise, 1 of chilli sauce and 1 of French dressing, then stir in 1 tablespoon of chopped red pimiento and 1 dessertspoon of chopped olives. Add salt and pepper. Place in a screw-top bottle and shake well.

DORIS LYTTON-TOYE 1948

Lester Bookbinder 1966

RICH TOMATO SAUCE

2 cloves garlic
salt and pepper
12 oz onions
4 lb tomatoes
2 large green peppers
2 tbsp sugar
1½ pts vinegar

Crush the garlic with salt under the blade of a knife. Slice the onions and tomatoes and cut the peppers into thin strips. Place all the ingredients in a large saucepan and cook for 2-2½ hours. Taste for seasoning. Strain the sauce, pour it into bottles and sterilize in a water bath for 10 minutes (165°F). Seal and store.

PETER PIRBRIGHT AND GRETEL BEER 1950

CUMBERLAND SAUCE

1 shallot or small onion
2 oranges
1 lemon
½ lb red currant jelly
1 tsp *moutarde de Dijon*
¼ pt port
2 tsp arrowroot

Mince the shallot or the onion and put in a small saucepan. Pare the rind of 1 orange and the lemon, cut in very thin strips and add to the shallot in the pan. Cover with cold water, bring to the boil, and cook for 5 minutes. Drain, throwing away the water.

Put the jelly in a small china bowl set over a saucepan of hot water. Boil the water in the pan and stir the jelly until it has melted. If there are still lumps, put it through a strainer and return it to the clean bowl over simmering water. Stir in the mustard, the port, the juice of the oranges and the lemon, the blanched rind and the minced shallot. Cook for 5 minutes, then add the arrowroot which you have mixed to a paste with a tablespoon of water. Simmer for 2-3 minutes, then pour into a sterilized jar and cool.

Close the jar tightly and do not eat for a week, if possible. It will keep for about 2 months, but should be kept in the refrigerator once opened. The best of all accompaniments to cold meats of all sorts, especially ham, game, or pâté.

ARABELLA BOXER 1975

PLUM SAUCE

12 oz plums
¼ pt red wine
2 tbsp brandy
1 orange
1 lemon
¼ tsp ground cinnamon (optional)
¼ tsp ground cloves (optional)
3 tbsp red currant jelly
1 tbsp *moutarde de Dijon*
sugar to taste (optional)

Cut the plums in half and remove the stones. Cut the fruit in pieces and put in a pan with the red wine and brandy. Pare the rind off the orange and half the lemon with a potato peeler. Cut it in thin strips and add to the pan. Bring to the boil and simmer for 10 minutes, covered. For a spicy sauce, add ground cinnamon and ground cloves during cooking.

Melt the jelly in a small china bowl over a pan of boiling water, and stir in the mustard to form a smooth paste. Add 2 tablespoons of lemon juice and 2 tablespoons of orange juice. Put the cooked plums in a blender with the jelly and fruit juice mixture. Blend very briefly, stopping before it is completely smooth. Taste and add a little sugar if necessary — it should be quite tart. (Another version can be made with damsons, but in this case add 1 tablespoon of sugar during the cooking.)

Leave to cool, and serve with hot or cold game, duck, goose or hot or cold ham. This sauce can be made in double quantities and kept in airtight jars in a cool place for 2 to 3 weeks.

ARABELLA BOXER 1977

MAYONNAISE

Included in the four mayonnaise recipes is a wartime version without oil, and a recipe from Robert Carrier with a watercress and herb variation.

OLD FRENCH COOK 1933

A great deal has been written about mayonnaise, which, however, is quite easy to make if you follow a few simple rules. To make the oil and egg emulsion, the one necessary thing is to have both at the same moderate temperature; what so often causes mayonnaise to go wrong in hot weather is that the cook has used ingredients fresh from the refrigerator and they are too cold to combine well.

To mix it, put the yolks in a basin that can be clamped to the table or stand the basin on a cloth so that it will not slide about. Add the oil, drop by drop, always stirring in the same direction, either with a wooden spoon, or with one of the various beaters sold for the purpose. When the mayonnaise thickens, add more oil, then salt, pepper and vinegar. If, in spite of precautions, the mayonnaise curdles during the mixing process, throw in a spoonful of warm water – this will make it right again.

NELL HEATON 1944

Mix well together in a pan a dessertspoon each of sugar, mustard, cornflour, 1 teaspoon of salt, ¼ teaspoon of pepper and a chopping of chives. Add 2 beaten eggs, 4 tablespoons of vinegar and 3 tablespoons of water. Cook till thick, stirring the whole time. Just before removing from the heat, add 1 ounce of margarine and stir till melted. When the mixture is well chilled and just before serving, add a little whipped cream or thick tomato purée, if desired.

ROBERT CARRIER 1966

2 eggs
¾ pt olive oil
4 tbsp lemon juice or vinegar
½ level tsp dry mustard
½ level tsp salt
freshly ground black pepper

Combine the eggs, ¼ pint of olive oil, lemon juice or vinegar, dry mustard, salt and freshly ground pepper, to taste, in an electric blender. Cover the container and turn the motor to high. When blended, remove the cover and add the remaining olive oil in a thin steady trickle, blending continuously. Correct the seasoning and use as desired.
Variation: To prepare Green Mayonnaise, wash sprigs of watercress, parsley and chervil; pick them over carefully and put them in a saucepan with a little salted boiling water. Allow the greens to boil for 6-7 minutes; drain and press as dry as possible. Pound them in a mortar; rub through a fine sieve and add the green purée to plain mayonnaise. Whirl in a blender or blend well with a whisk; add lemon juice, salt and black pepper to taste. Chill before serving.

ALISON PRICE 1984

2 egg yolks
2 tsp wholegrain mustard
juice of 1 lemon
½ pt olive oil
salt and pepper to taste

Place the egg yolks in a blender or Magimix bowl with the mustard and lemon juice. Process for 2 minutes. Slowly add the oil. When all the oil is incorporated, season with salt and pepper to taste. Serves 2.

FOAMY YELLOW SAUCE

1 egg
pinch of salt
1 tsp Dijon mustard
¼ pt sunflower seed oil or nut oil
3 tsp white wine vinegar
2 tbsp yoghurt

Separate the egg and put the yolk in a china bowl. Stir hard with a wooden spoon, adding the salt and the mustard. Start adding the oil, drop by drop, until an emulsion is formed, then more quickly. If it gets too thick, add a teaspoon of vinegar. When all the oil is absorbed, add the remaining vinegar. Beat the egg white until stiff and fold in 2 tablespoons together with 2 tablespoons of yoghurt.

This light sauce is delicious with all aspic dishes, whether they are based on fish, eggs, chicken or simply vegetables. Serves 4 to 5, but is easily made in double quantities.

ARABELLA BOXER 1980

MUSTARD AND DILL SAUCE

1 egg yolk
1 tsp Dijon mustard
pinch of salt
¼ pt olive oil
2-3 tsp white wine vinegar
¼ pt *crème fraîche*
2-3 tbsp chopped dill

Make a mayonnaise with the egg yolk, mustard, salt, olive oil and vinegar (see method Foamy Yellow Sauce above). Fold in the *crème fraîche*, and stir in the chopped dill.

Serve at room temperature, with cold poached salmon, salmon trout, shellfish, cold poached chicken, or new potatoes, boiled and served warm.

ARABELLA BOXER 1983

Tessa Traeger 1980

SWEET SAUCES FOR ICE CREAM

DORIS LYTTON-TOYE 1951

CHOCOLATE SAUCE

Melt together ¼ pint of water with 4 ounces of chocolate, cut up. Stir till quite smooth and add a tiny bit of butter and a pinch of salt. Flavour with rum, almond essence, peppermint essence or cinnamon according to the ice it is to go with. Strong coffee instead of water is excellent in this sauce for chocolate or coffee ice. Serve hot.

CREAMY CHOCOLATE SAUCE

Melt 1 ounce of bitter chocolate in 6 fluid ounces of milk; then beat it smooth. In a basin, combine 1 level dessertspoon of flour, 2 ounces of sugar and a pinch of salt; pour in gradually the chocolate mixture, stirring. Cook for 5 minutes until it becomes thickened. Remove from the heat, add 1 ounce of butter and flavour with vanilla. Serve hot or cold.

PLAIN SYRUP

Boil ½ pound of sugar and ½ pint of water together for 10 minutes. Cool and store in the refrigerator in a covered jar. Most useful for sweetening fruit to be served with ices; or to use, flavoured, as a quick sauce.

A QUICK CHOCOLATE PEPPERMINT SAUCE

Melt some chocolate peppermint creams with a little cream over hot water.

CARAMEL SAUCE

In a strong pan, slowly melt 8 ounces of sugar with very little water, without stirring. When every grain is dissolved, increase the heat and allow the liquid to boil till it turns a light brown. Add 4-6 fluid ounces of hot water (it will splutter) and boil and stir for 5-6 minutes. A dash of brandy, though extravagant, enhances a caramel sauce. It may be served hot or cold.

QUICK CARAMEL SAUCE

Put 4 ounces of caramels in a basin placed over hot water. Add 8 tablespoons of cream and let them melt slowly. When they have blended, beat in a nut of butter. Serve hot or cold.

MARSHMALLOW SAUCE

Put 4 ounces of marshmallows, cut in pieces with floured scissors, in the top of a double boiler with ¼ pint of evaporated milk until they melt. Stir well. To make chocolate marshmallow, add 2 ounces of chocolate.

HOT JELLY SAUCE

In a saucepan, melt slowly ½ pound of red currant jelly with ¼ pint of hot water and 1 dessertspoon of finely chopped candied orange peel.

CREAMY CUSTARD SAUCE

I know one English country house where they serve a choice of home-made custard and a jug of thick cream with the pudding. As we all seem to end up eating both together, I thought I would simplify things by combining them – this works wonderfully well.

2 egg yolks
2½ tbsp vanilla sugar or 2½ tbsp caster sugar
and ½ vanilla pod
½ pt milk
¼ pt double cream

Have the egg yolks in a bowl and beat them very well, using an electric beater if you have one. When pale yellow and creamy, start adding the vanilla sugar, as you continue beating. (If you do not have any home-made vanilla sugar, use caster sugar and infuse the milk with ½ vanilla pod. Bring the milk slowly to boiling point with the pod in it, then remove from the heat, cover, and leave to infuse for 20 minutes, before removing the pod and reheating.) If using vanilla sugar, simply heat the milk until almost boiling, then pour on to the eggs, continuing to beat well for a couple of minutes. Stand the bowl over a saucepan of simmering water and stir with a wooden spoon until it has thickened very slightly. Remove from the heat, and stand in a sink half full of cold water to cool quickly, stirring often to prevent a skin forming.

When cooled to the desired temperature – you may serve it hot if you prefer, but I like it best warm – whip the cream lightly and fold in. Serve in a jug, with hot or cold puddings, or compotes of fruit. Serves 4 to 6.

ARABELLA BOXER 1985

FARCE AUX MARRONS

This stuffing is remarkably good for roast goose or duck. Take a quarter of a pound of onions, cut them in thin slices and cook them slowly in pork fat or butter till golden brown. Peel about a pound of chestnuts (both skins should be carefully removed) and add them to the onions with salt, pepper and a little more fat or butter. Cook very slowly till the chestnuts are reduced to a pulp, and stir well before stuffing the bird.

BOULESTIN 1924

BREAD AND CELERY STUFFING

3½ cups stale breadcrumbs
1 cup boiling water
1 tbsp stock made from turkey giblets
½ tsp salt
½ tsp pepper
¾ cup finely chopped celery
½ cup melted butter

Soak the crumbs in the water for 20 minutes. Squeeze out all the liquid and add the rest of the ingredients; mix well together.

1938

POULTRY AND GAME STUFFING

For turkeys and fowls
Add to breadcrumbs a little shredded bacon or ham, chopped onion, a good chopping of parsley, a grating of nutmeg, a little melted margarine to help bind the mixture and a seasoning of salt and pepper.

For ducks and geese
Chop fresh sage leaves and onions together; place them in a pan with only enough water to prevent them catching and just bring it to the boil. Strain. Mix with breadcrumbs and a little melted margarine, and season with salt and freshly ground black pepper.

Edward McKnight-Kauffer 1926

For partridges and pheasants
Take 4 ounces of suet or melted margarine, 1 pound of breadcrumbs, a grating of nutmeg, a little thyme, a good chopping of parsley and the chopped livers of the birds. Season with salt and pepper and bind with beaten egg.

For hares and rabbits
Add to breadcrumbs the chopped liver, a chopped rasher of fat bacon, a tablespoon of anchovy essence, a little grated onion, 2 ounces of suet or melted margarine and salt, pepper and a grating of nutmeg to season. Bind with an egg.

NELL HEATON 1943

CORN BREAD STUFFING

1 medium onion
2 oz butter
½ lb pure pork sausage meat
1 turkey liver
½ lb corn breadcrumbs (see recipe for Corn Bread page 188)
sea salt and black pepper
3-4 tbsp chopped parsley

Chop the onion and sauté in the butter until pale golden. Lift it out with a slotted spoon, leaving the fat in the pan, and transfer to a large mixing bowl. Fry the sausage meat in the same pan, breaking it up as it cooks with 2 wooden spoons. When half cooked, add the chopped liver and fry all together. Add the meat mixture to the onion and mix well. Add the breadcrumbs and stir until well mixed, adding sea salt and black pepper to taste, and the chopped parsley. Allow to cool completely before using to stuff a medium-sized turkey – 10-14 pounds.

ARABELLA BOXER 1978

NUT STUFFING

1 oz onion
½ oz butter
2 oz minced veal
2 oz shredded suet
1 oz chopped apple
1 oz chopped almonds
1 oz chopped pistachio nuts
pinch of sugar
sea salt and black pepper
pinch of mace
pinch of ground coriander
1 egg

Chop the onion and brown slowly in the butter. Add the minced veal and stir until browned evenly all over. Remove from the heat and cool slightly. Stir in the shredded suet, chopped apple, nuts and seasonings. Beat the egg and stir in. Cool, and use to stuff a 3½-4 pound chicken.

Poach the chicken as usual, allowing an extra 20 minutes, with the usual flavouring vegetables. (Alternatively, roast as usual, remembering to allow an extra 15-20 minutes cooking time for the stuffing.)

This unusual and delicious stuffing is especially good with a poached chicken, served with boiled rice and a cream sauce made with some of the stock. Serves 5.

ARABELLA BOXER 1979

SALADS

According to Boulestin, the world's best salad is green, plain, fresh, crisp, seasoned with some wine vinegar, olive oil, freshly ground pepper, sea salt, and *fines herbes*. 'All the other mixtures, whatever and however good they may be, are not *une salade* but salads of this or salads of that, standing as separate dishes (or falling) on their own merits.'

He also warned that, 'a salad is one of those things that is either beautifully right or desperately wrong. There are no in-betweens. It can of course include any and every fresh green thing that grows in a garden, and that is why it is at its triumphant best in spring and summer. To begin at the very beginning, the greens are first washed, then every bit of moisture is shaken from them in a *panier de salade* or they are dried with a cloth and put in the refrigerator to chill. This matter of drying is important. Strong men have been known to rise up in wrath at a bowl of greens glistening with water, knowing that this spells ruination to any dressing. When the salad is served, it is heaped into its bowl. French dressing is poured over it, and the whole is well marinated, the leaves being turned over and over again in the dressing with a fork and spoon.'

Above: June Platt 1935
Opposite: Tessa Traeger 1981

After this precise lesson in salad-making Boulestin exhorted his readers to become more adventurous: 'There is a real embarrassment of choice. Why insist on having silly little lettuces – heartless, green and tasteless – grown at great expense? There are now endives, chicory, *mâche* or corn salad, celery, even dandelion if you know how to find it. There is no end to the combinations, the subtle chords, the harmonizations, the dissonances one can create when making a salad.'

The thirties ended with *Vogue* asking, 'If your cook does not make a good salad, why not let the guests make their own?' Mary Bromfield, wife of the American novelist Louis Bromfield, took this do-it-yourself idea a stage further: 'Have your oil, vinegar, salt and pepper on the table and let the guests make their own dressing, they love to argue about it.' She also suggested, 'Have two salads – people love them. For instance, a cold vegetable salad, or one of tunny fish, or apples and nuts.'

In the forties Doris Lytton-Toye, always an advocate of healthy eating, said, 'A salad a day should be your housekeeping motto through all four seasons of the year.' It is a motto that is just as appropriate nearly 50 years on.

Keith Vaughan

MACÉDOINE VEGETABLE SALAD

Cut some new potatoes, young carrots, beetroots and cauliflower (all previously cooked and thoroughly drained) into dice, also a few slices of apple. Season with salt and black pepper. Mix this thoroughly with a good French dressing, and arrange in a salad bowl over crisp lettuce leaves; then put an edging of cress and some crossed strips of filleted anchovy on the top and, finally, sprinkle over it some finely minced parsley.

1911

APPLE AND CELERY SALAD

A dainty salad for a simple luncheon is as follows: take 2 good-sized apples, 4 sticks of celery and half a cup of broken walnuts and stoned olives, very finely chopped. Mix everything well together, adding a pinch of salt and pepper. Serve on individual salad plates with mayonnaise dressing.

1911

SALADE RHÉNANE

This salad is usually served as an hors d'oeuvre. Chop together two smoked fillets of herring, two cold boiled potatoes, one apple, a slice of roast veal or the wing of a roast chicken (also cold), a piece of beetroot, the heart of a lettuce, two or three gherkins and a few capers. Season with olive oil, red wine vinegar, salt and freshly ground pepper.

BOULESTIN 1923

SALADE DE CONCOMBRES AUX OEUFS DURS

Take a good-sized cucumber, peel it, cut it in very thin slices and put them in a flat dish. Sprinkle with a good deal of salt and let it rest for about one hour and a half. The salt draws the moisture out of the cucumber, making it tender and more digestible. Throw away the water which has come out and wash the slices of cucumber in water, otherwise they are likely to be too salty. Then dry them carefully.

By then your hard-boiled eggs should be ready; that is, cooked and cold. Cut them in quarters and put aside two-thirds of the yolks. Crush these with a fork and add them to the salad dressing, which should be made as follows: dissolve the salt in the vinegar (red wine vinegar, of course), add pepper, oil (the best olive oil, of course) in the proportion of three tablespoons of oil to two of vinegar. Beat all this well with the cucumber and hard-boiled eggs. Put the mixture in a salad bowl and dispose round it the white leaves from the hearts of several lettuces, over which you squeeze a little juice out of a lemon.

BOULESTIN 1923

SALADE ALGÉRIENNE

Take some tomatoes and some sweet peppers, either green or red, cut them in two, remove the seeds and grill them. Then cut them in very fine slices, add 2 small onions, 1 shallot and parsley finely chopped. Season with pepper, salt, oil and vinegar.

BOULESTIN 1925

SALADE AUX TRUFFES

This salad is prepared with celery cut very thinly, slices of boiled potatoes and a sprinkling of fresh truffles cut *en julienne*. Quite plain seasoning and not too much vinegar.

I would, once more, remind my reader that for this, as well as for all salads, the olive oil must be the very best, and the vinegar wine vinegar, either made with red or white wine.

BOULESTIN 1926

SALADE AU LARD

The chauffeur who was gathering dandelions while we were poetically admiring the bluebells told me he often ate his salad in the following manner: season it with less oil than usual and add to it little cubes of bacon crisply fried in fresh butter. Stir quickly and serve at once. It is specially good with a long kind of lettuce – and served on hot plates.

BOULESTIN 1926

SALADE DE COEURS DE LAITUES AUX POINTES D'ASPERGES

Take some lettuce. Remove all the outside leaves. keeping only the nice white ones, and wash these carefully in cold water. Dry them well and put them in a salad bowl together with asparagus tops. cold and well drained. Season simply with salt and pepper. oil and vinegar.

As I am on the subject of salad. it must be remembered that it is a great mistake to let chicory. endive and especially lettuce. which has tender leaves. remain in water for long: ten minutes are quite enough to refresh the leaves; if you leave them in water longer they will get soft and sodden. They must be. of course. well shaken in a wire basket. and if you have to keep them for an hour or two. it is a good plan to wrap them loosely in a thin cloth; they will remain perfectly white and crisp.

The other important thing to remember about salads – besides the ingredients – is that a large salad bowl is absolutely necessary for mixing the salad well and lightly without bruising the leaves. Those used in England. when any. are usually the size of a finger bowl and the depth of a soup plate.

BOULESTIN 1926

SALADE CARMEN

This salad is a mixture of endives. celery and beetroot. The sauce is to be prepared with very little oil. some salt and pepper. fresh cream. lemon instead of vinegar. and tomato ketchup. which gives it a pleasant pink colour and a peculiar taste. also pleasant if you like it.

BOULESTIN 1926

SALADE LORRAINE

Cut in thin slices some cold boiled potatoes (the yellow Dutch kind which are not floury). Season them with oil. vinegar and a little claret. Add chopped beetroot. chopped gherkins and *fines herbes*.

BOULESTIN 1926

Norman Parkinson 1951

SALADE PARISIENNE

Mix in equal parts watercress, batavia and beetroot. Season with salt, pepper, oil and vinegar. Add parsley, chervil and tarragon, finely chopped together.

BOULESTIN 1926

JELLIED SPINACH SALAD

To 1½ cups of lemon jelly that has been made very tart by leaving out most of the sugar, are added 4 tablespoons of minced green peppers, 2 cups of chopped, cooked spinach, and ½ teaspoon of salt. Individual moulds, rubbed with salad oil, are packed with the salad mixture, and, when cold and stiffened, it is turned out on lettuce leaves and served with mayonnaise seasoned with 2 tablespoons of chilli sauce.

1927

THE WORLD'S BEST SALAD

There is only one – the green salad; plain, fresh, crisp, seasoned with wine vinegar, olive oil, freshly ground pepper, sea salt and *fines herbes*. All the other mixtures, whatever and however good they may be, are not *une salade*, but salads of this or salads of that, standing as separate dishes (or falling) on their own merits.

BOULESTIN 1928

PALM BEACH SALAD

A large, crisp leaf of lettuce forms the foundation of this salad. On this are placed a few perfect sections of orange and grapefruit, topped by a mixture of crisp green salad consisting of chicory, endive, and *julienne* of celery. This may be decorated with strips of pimiento. It is served with French dressing – olive oil and wine vinegar for choice, with a sprinkling of black pepper.

1930

BEETROOT SALAD

Diced cooked beets are mixed with shredded red cabbage and cold cooked flaked fish which has been marinated in wine vinegar. This is served on lettuce with French dressing, seasoned highly with cayenne and garnished with sliced hard-boiled eggs.

1931

1944

SALADE ALONZO

A salad bowl is filled with crisp white lettuce, on which are placed quarter slices of freshly cooked, cooled pears and watercress. The French salad dressing that is poured over this is varied with the addition of the juice of 1 lemon and 2 tablespoons of tomato ketchup.

LEONE B. MOATS 1933

SALADE DUFOUR

Four small beetroots and 3 potatoes are cooked and marinated well in French dressing. Just before serving, the dressing in which they have been marinated is mixed thoroughly with a few shreds of cooked ham, several anchovies, cut into bits, 1 tablespoon each of chopped parsley, gherkins and onions. Toss lightly. This salad is served on a bed of small lettuce leaves.

1933

CELERIAC SALAD

This very crisp salad is generally served as an hors d'oeuvre. Take a clean root and peel and cut it into thin slices. Mix with mayonnaise or oil and vinegar. The celeriac can be cooked, if preferred, and is more digestible that way. Before preparing, boil it, either whole or cut into quarters, for 15 minutes.

OLD FRENCH COOK 1933

WILTED SALAD

Lettuce, sorrel or dandelion may be used for this. Prepare the greens and put them in a hot bowl. Sprinkle with salt and freshly ground pepper and use this dressing: cut 6 slices of fat bacon in little squares and fry in a hot pan until crisp. Pour the hot fat and the bacon directly on the greens. Quickly put a teaspoon or so of vinegar in the hot pan, and then pour it over the salad. Mix well and then eat at once. The salad will wilt slightly, but it is quite delectable.

JUNE PLATT 1935

CELERY SALAD WITH MUSTARD DRESSING

Use 1 piece of celery for each person. Remove all the tough outer stalks – use only the tender stalks and take off as many strings as possible. Cut in 2-inch pieces and split each piece several times, almost to the end. Curl them by putting them in iced water for several hours. Shake or wipe thoroughly dry. Then pile in a cold bowl and treat with the following dressing: put a small soup-spoon of German mustard in a bowl. Add some freshly ground pepper and salt to taste and the juice of 1 small lemon. Stir well and then add ¾ cup of thin cream.

JUNE PLATT 1935

Tessa Traeger 1985

STRING BEAN SALAD

Cut the sides and ends off 3 pounds of string beans. This will be much easier if you soak the beans for 1 hour in very cold water before preparing them. Tie the beans in 8 or 10 bunches, as you would asparagus. Boil them in plenty of furiously boiling, salted water. Cook until just tender, not floppy. Drain them well and lay them neatly in a row on a platter. Untie the strings and place the beans in a refrigerator to chill well. Make some good tart French dressing, using red wine vinegar; put in it a small white onion, finely grated. Pour this over the beans 15 minutes before serving. Serves 8.

JUNE PLATT 1935

ROMAINE SALAD WITH HARD-BOILED EGG DRESSING

Prepare the romaine (cos) lettuce in the usual manner. Hard boil 3 eggs. Pass the yolks through a fine sieve and put them in the bottom of a cold salad bowl. Add 1 teaspoon of French mustard, freshly ground pepper and salt. Then add 3 tablespoons of olive oil, and 1 of tarragon vinegar. Stir well to blend the ingredients. Add the romaine, broken in small pieces, and sprinkle with a teaspoon of freshly chopped tarragon. Mix well. Sprinkle the top of the salad with the whites of the eggs, which have been chopped up finely.

JUNE PLATT 1935

Irving Penn 1948

CUCUMBER, TOMATO AND RADISH SALAD

Peel 1 cucumber and slice it finely. Soak the slices in iced water without salt. Peel 6 ripe, juicy tomatoes and chill them thoroughly. Wash 12 baby radishes and put them to soak in iced water. Remove the slices of cucumber and wipe them dry on a linen cloth. Put them in a bowl containing French dressing and mix well. Lift out the cucumber slices and place them in a shallow, cold dish. Slice the tomatoes in thin circles with a sharp knife and arrange them in a wreath round the cucumber. Pour the dressing left from the cucumber over all — then slice the radishes very thinly and sprinkle them over the cucumber and tomatoes in the dish.

JUNE PLATT 1935

POTATO SALAD

A dozen or more recipes for potato salad have appeared in *Vogue* over six decades. It can be, as an old French cook says, 'either quite delicious or very bad'; here are five good recipes, including a warm version from Arabella Boxer.

1931

Six or 8 large potatoes should be pared and boiled, then sliced thinly while hot. A white onion is then peeled, cut into small bits, and mixed with the potatoes. Some breakfast bacon cut into small bits, sufficient to fill a teacup, is fried a light brown and the meat removed; then 3 tablespoons of vinegar are stirred in, making a sour gravy, which, with the bacon, is poured over the potatoes and onions. The ingredients are mixed lightly, and the salad is eaten while hot.

OLD FRENCH COOK 1933

Some people make it with left-over boiled potatoes; it cannot be too much insisted on that this is the worst method. Follow this recipe and you will have the best.

Choose potatoes of equal size. Many people like firm and waxy potatoes for salad; choose the kidney varieties for this or, if you grow your own, you can have special yellow-fleshed salad varieties. On the other hand, the floury kinds can be used to make a very good salad. Steam the potatoes in their skins, then peel them and cut into slices while still warm. Moisten them with a little warm stock if you have it and then mix either with mayonnaise or with oil and vinegar, adding some chopped fresh herbs and a little onion, if liked.

DORIS LYTTON-TOYE 1946

Steam the potatoes in their jackets. Peel them while they are still hot, then slice them into a basin containing vinegar, pepper and salt. Use 2 or 3 tablespoons of dressing to a pound of potatoes. Let them marinate in this till cold. Lift out the potatoes carefully so as not to break them and fold them into mayonnaise with chopped chives for flavour.

DORIS LYTTON-TOYE 1951

Boil in their skins 1 pound of new potatoes, then peel and cut them in cubes. Fry 4 thin slices of bacon until they are crisp enough to break in bits. Sprinkle the bacon over the potatoes. Keep the bacon fat hot; add pepper, French mustard and vinegar, and salt if the bacon is not salty. Pour this dressing over the potatoes. Leave them to cool, then garnish with the sieved yolk of 1 hard-boiled egg.

ARABELLA BOXER 1980

1½ lb new potatoes
3 tbsp olive oil
4 shallots
sea salt and black pepper
1 tbsp white wine vinegar
⅛ pt thin cream
4 tbsp chopped chives

Boil the potatoes in their skins; drain, and leave to cool for a few moments. Skin them and cut in thick slices. (If tiny, they can be left whole.) Put them in a bowl and, while still hot, stir in the olive oil. Chop the shallots and mix with the potato, season well, and add the white wine vinegar. Leave for about 45 minutes, then stir in the cream and the chopped chives. Serve immediately. Serves 5 to 6.

> **'Chopped fried bacon, well crisped, is a comfortable addition to a potato salad.'**
> DORIS LYTTON-TOYE

POTATO AND TRUFFLE SALAD

For a surprisingly good salad for a picnic, first wash and boil in salted water 3 pounds of new potatoes. Peel them when they are cold and slice finely. In the meantime, boil as many truffles as you can afford in white wine for 5 minutes, then peel them carefully and slice very thinly. Sprinkle some finely chopped chervil over the potatoes, and pour over it all some good French dressing. Add the truffles and mix very lightly so as not to break the truffles or the potatoes. Put the salad in a big jar, and pack it in a hamper. Also take a little lettuce and a bowl. When you are ready to serve, make a nest of the lettuce and pile the potato and truffle salad in the middle.

JUNE PLATT 1935

SALADE AUX FINES HERBES

Pull apart and wash carefully 2 or 3 heads of young lettuce. Use only the tender leaves. Dry each leaf carefully. Chop finely a small bunch of chervil and a few leaves of tarragon. Make a good French dressing to your liking, using lemon juice and red wine vinegar, and plenty of oil. Pour the dressing over the salad. Toss it lightly but thoroughly. Sprinkle with the chopped herbs. Give it one more little toss, and serve at once. The salad plates should be as cold as ice – place them in the refrigerator for several hours before using.

JUNE PLATT 1937

GRAPEFRUIT, ORANGE AND AVOCADO SALAD

Americans, whose summer is one long heatwave, know all about salads. This is a favourite recipe.

Place in a glass dish a layer of orange sections, a layer of grapefruit sections and a layer of sliced avocado pear. Repeat these layers until the dish is full. Pour over all a well-seasoned French dressing and garnish with crisp young lettuce leaves.

1939

MACARONI SALAD LUCULLUS

Cook some macaroni in salted water, and take it off the flame while the macaroni is still firm; drain it and keep it warm. Prepare some highly seasoned mayonnaise. Mix in a salad dish the macaroni, mayonnaise, some very thick tomato purée, and, in season, some cooked *fonds d'artichauts* (artichoke hearts), very finely chopped. Add, if you wish, a chopped hard-boiled egg and a little lean ham cut in thin slivers; finish off with a sprinkling of chopped parsley.

1940

DANDELION SALAD

This is an unusual and most appetizing dish. Use well-washed, very young dandelion leaves soaked in French dressing. Add cold diced potatoes, carrots, green beans, a very little garlic and some cold minced cooked bacon. Sprinkle lavishly with grated cheese. This is best served in a wooden bowl.

1942

Denton Welch 1946

KOHLRABI SALAD

This vegetable can be prepared in many ways; but only the young roots should be used, as otherwise it is apt to be tough. To make an unusual salad, chop some kohlrabi very finely, add some chopped parsley and serve with a dressing made of oil, vinegar and seasoning.

1942

SUNSHINE SALAD

A salad that is full of precious vitamins: place some coarsely cut lettuce leaves in a well-oiled wooden bowl, and add celery stalks, grated carrot, shredded cabbage heart, green peas, endives, cooked dried prunes and apricots. Mix all the ingredients together well and serve with French dressing made with oil, lemon juice and chives.

1942

COWSLIP SALAD

As soon as cowslips appear in the fields, send the children to pick them and make this delicate luncheon treat. It's good for a sandwich filling, too. Use only the petals of the freshly gathered flowers, removing them carefully from the calyx. Drop them lightly on to hearts of lettuce and serve with mayonnaise.

NELL HEATON 1944

CAULIFLOWER SALAD

If February frost clamps down on tender greenstuff, try this for a change. I am sure you will like it.

Choose a firm young cauliflower, wash it thoroughly and break off a few florets for garnishing. Grate the rest of the head and place in a bowl. Dress with mayonnaise and season with salt and pepper. Garnish with the florets, grated radish and a few sprigs of watercress or mustard and cress.

NELL HEATON 1944

WATERCRESS SALAD

Wash the cress and pick it over, removing any bruised and discoloured leaves. Throw it into a bowl and dress with an oil and vinegar dressing. Sprinkle on a little salt, but do not add any mustard or pepper. Garnish with hard-boiled egg and shrimps or prawns.

NELL HEATON 1944

YOUNG RAW SALAD

Choose the really young, baby vegetables that start about April — carrots, turnips and parsnips. Grate them finely and make into a design on a dish. Garnish the grated vegetables with shredded spinach and grated radish.

NELL HEATON 1944

GREEN WALNUT SALAD

As soon as the walnuts have formed, but are still young enough to pierce with a pin, make this unusual and luscious dish. Peel the nuts carefully, toss the kernels in French dressing and garnish the salad bowl with cress.

NELL HEATON 1944

von Alvensleben 1983

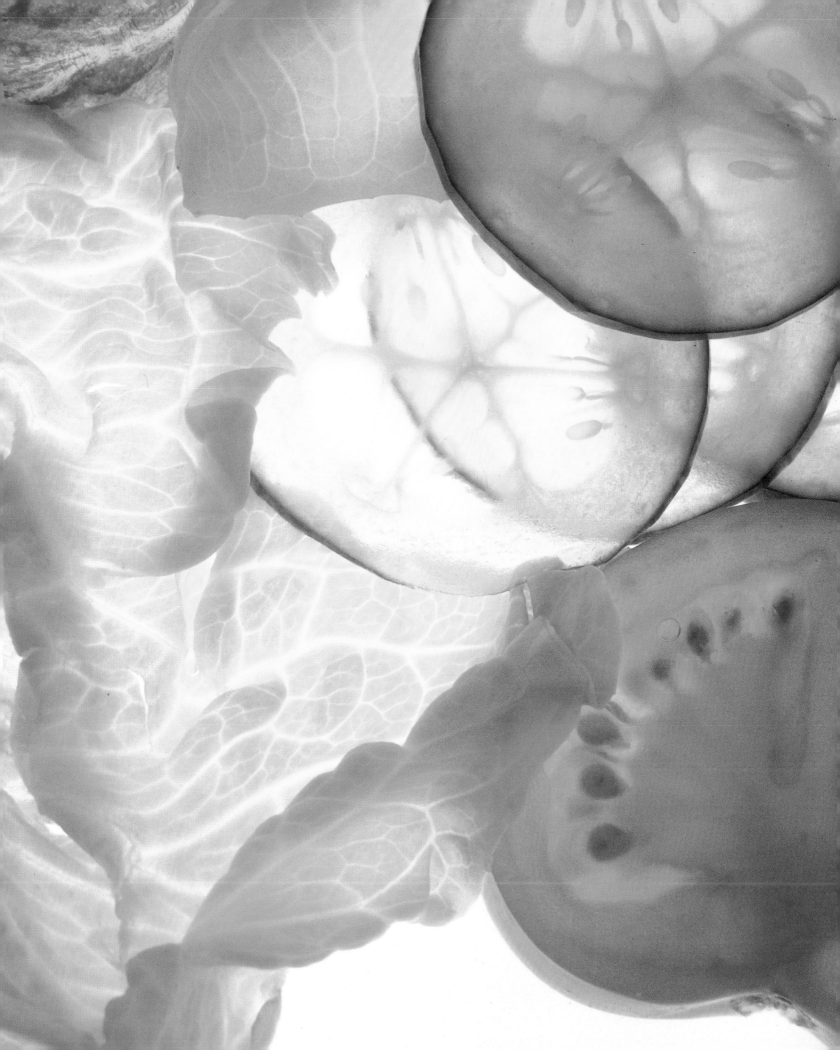

Libis 1933

APPLE AND CHESTNUT SALAD

Boil and skin some chestnuts and break them into pieces. Peel and cut an equal amount of apples into dice. Mix the 2 ingredients in a bowl and marinate with French dressing. Serve individual helpings on the outer leaves of lettuce, or in fruit cups made by scooping out the pulp from halved apples. In either case, garnish with mayonnaise or cream cheese and chopped parsley.

NELL HEATON 1944

OYSTER SALAD

Use this recipe for mussels, too. Take 1 pint of oysters, shell them and boil them in their own juice till they are tender. Drain and skin them and season with a sprinkling of salt and pepper, 1 tablespoon of vinegar and a squeezing of lemon juice or essence. Dice, or shred into thin pieces, the tender heart of a head of celery. Mix this with the oysters, add ¼ cup of mayonnaise and garnish with the top celery leaves and a dusting of red pepper.

NELL HEATON 1944

WINTER SALAD

The great thing about this salad is that you can serve it hot or cold.

Prepare and cook all the vegetables separately, allowing equal proportions of carrots, turnips, potatoes, celery and – from your store cupboard – broad beans and French beans. The last two are nice, but not necessary. The carrots and turnips should be diced, the potato scooped into balls.

Take a large flat dish and arrange the cooked vegetables in sections. Garnish with a border of peas and bunches of watercress and sprinkle the centre with chopped parsley.

NELL HEATON 1944

ICED CHEESE SALAD

Mash about 4 ounces of cottage cheese with half a cup of evaporated milk till it is as smooth as velvet. Season with salt and pepper and a pinch of cayenne; then mix in some finely chopped pickle. Turn into a refrigerator tray and freeze till firm. Cut the cheese in slices and arrange on lettuce leaves. Serve with a tomato mayonnaise and a hot salted biscuit.

DORIS LYTTON-TOYE 1946

HADDOCK SALAD

To cooked green peas add an equal amount of diced cooked carrot and potato. Marinate the vegetables awhile in a dressing of oil and vinegar with seasoning. Fold into them some cooked and flaked smoked haddock, having as much fish as vegetable; also a stalk or so of chopped celery. Turn into a bowl and decorate with sprays of watercress.

DORIS LYTTON-TOYE 1948

AUBERGINE SALAD

6 aubergines
olive oil
I clove garlic
salt and pepper
I small onion
I tsp French mustard
I tbsp chopped parsley
vinegar

Peel, slice and fry the aubergines lightly in oil. Crush the garlic well with a little salt. Chop the onion finely. Mix together all the ingredients (using liberal portions of oil and vinegar). Chill in the refrigerator before serving.

PETER PIRBRIGHT AND GRETEL BEER 1949

'Outside leaves of lettuce, cabbage, etc, are richer in vitamins than the hearts.'
PAMELA PAIN

MEAT SALAD

1 lb cold cooked beef
4 anchovy fillets
4 small pickled gherkins
3 hard-boiled eggs
2 tbsp oil
1 tbsp vinegar
1 dessertspoon finely chopped shallot
2 tsp chopped capers
1 tbsp chopped parsley
mustard
salt and pepper

This quickly served luncheon dish has a tempting piquancy for jaded appetites.

Cut the meat into cubes, and slice the anchovies and gherkins into strips. Remove the yolks from the eggs and mash them well with a fork. Gradually stir in the oil and vinegar, chopped shallot, capers, parsley, and mustard, salt and pepper to taste. Garnish with the finely chopped whites of the eggs.

PETER PIRBRIGHT AND GRETEL BEER 1950

WALDORF SALAD

Mix together 2 cups of diced sweet apple, which has previously been dropped into salted water, drained and dried (this keeps it white), 1 cup of chopped celery, ½ cup of broken walnuts and ½ cup of seedless raisins (optional). Make 1 cup of creamy salad dressing or mayonnaise and blend the ingredients with it until well coated. Line the salad bowl with crisp lettuce and pile the mixture in the centre.

DORIS LYTTON-TOYE 1953

TOMATO AND CABBAGE SLAW

Mix 1 cup of finely shredded white cabbage with the flesh of 2 skinned, seeded and diced tomatoes, and add a little chopped spring onion or shallot. Add salt, pepper and a pinch of sugar. Use a simple dressing such as 3 tablespoons of cream mixed with 1 tablespoon of wine vinegar, and mix thoroughly with all the ingredients in a salad bowl.

DORIS LYTTON-TOYE 1953

BURMESE SALAD

Peel and dice a small pineapple, or use a tin of pineapples which has been well drained. Put the pieces in a salad bowl. Chop finely a peeled and cored sour apple; slice into wafer-thin slivers half a head of celery and a small pimiento. Add them to the pineapple, season well, and dress with fresh lime or lemon juice and sesame or peanut oil. Mix thoroughly. This is good with chicken.

BERYL GOULD-MARKS 1954

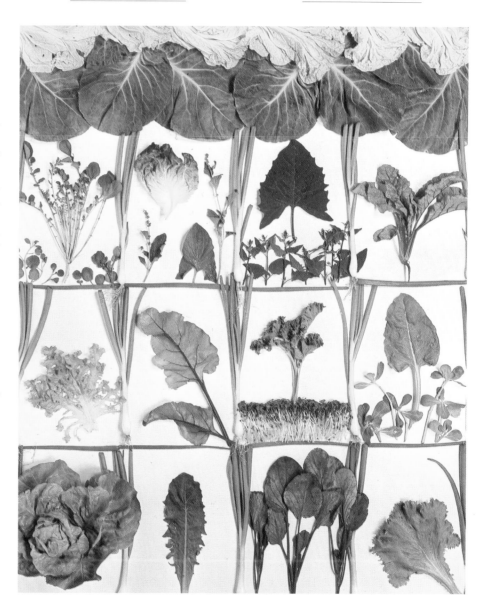

Tessa Traeger 1977

MUSHROOM AND SWEET PEPPER SALAD

Take 3 pounds of button mushrooms, 3 large sweet peppers (1 each red, green and yellow if possible) and ½ pint (about) of well-seasoned vinaigrette dressing, which should be made at least 3 hours before the salad is wanted so that the mushrooms can marinate in it.

The mushroom stalks are not used in this salad, so cut them off level with the caps. Do not peel the mushrooms but wash them under running water, then halve or quarter them according to their size. Blanch them in salted water, drain quickly and put them into the vinaigrette. Toss them gently but thoroughly and leave for as long as possible.

In the meantime, cut the stalk-end off the peppers, quarter them and remove all the seeds. Cut them into small slices or dice and add them to the mushrooms.

CHRIS HASKETT-SMITH 1961

BEAN SHOOT SALAD

1 lb bean shoots
4 oz Gruyère cheese, cut into cubes
1 tbsp currants
a few pumpkin seeds
4 slices of bacon, cut very thin
1 avocado pear
DRESSING
olive oil
lemon juice
French mustard
salt and freshly ground black pepper

Make the dressing by combining all the ingredients well. In a salad bowl put the bean shoots, Gruyère, currants, pumpkin seeds and the bacon cut into tiny pieces and fried. Toss in the dressing and decorate with the avocado, cut into long slices and arranged like a star.

NATHALIE HAMBRO 1974

Tessa Traeger 1985

June Platt 1935

RICE SALAD

Cook some rice in chicken stock until it is quite dry. Mix into it cooked peas, blanched almonds, walnuts, currants, chopped green peppers and chopped cucumbers. Make a French dressing, add garlic and chives and mix them with the rice.

LADY VICTORIA YORKE 1974

TUNA AND FLAGEOLET SALAD

1 cup shell-shaped pasta
1 large can flageolet beans
1 onion, finely sliced
2 small or 1 large tin tuna fish
1 tsp chopped basil
1 dessertspoon chopped parsley
French dressing of 3 tbsp oil and 1 tbsp wine vinegar
salt and black pepper
1 box mustard and cress
6 black olives, stoned

Cook the pasta in plenty of boiling salted water until it is just tender (about 10 minutes). Rinse it under cold water and drain well. Rinse the starchy liquid off the flageolets and drain them. Gently mix the sliced onion, beans, tuna fish (and the liquid in the can), pasta and chopped herbs in just enough French dressing to moisten the salad. Add salt and pepper if needed. Care should be taken not to over-mix, or an unattractive soggy salad will result. Decorate with the snipped cress and the black olives. Serves 6.
Note: If you prefer, substitute lightly cooked French green beans for the tinned flageolets.

PRUE LEITH 1977

JERUSALEM ARTICHOKE AND WATERCRESS SALAD

1 lb Jerusalem artichokes
1 celery heart, with leaves
1 bunch watercress
DRESSING
sea salt and black pepper
1 tbsp white wine vinegar
3 tbsp olive oil

Peel the artichokes and cook in lightly salted boiling water until just tender; drain well. Leave to cool a little, then put them in a bowl with the chopped celery heart and its leaves (left whole). Add the leaves only of the watercress. Mix the dressing, pour over all and toss gently so as not to break the artichokes. This delicious and unusual dish serves 4. If you have plenty of celery leaves you can omit the watercress altogether.

ARABELLA BOXER 1981

'The mellowing influence of good food on civilized beings cannot be underrated, or its importance exaggerated. It is conducive to success and, which is more important, to happiness.'
BOULESTIN

'A fine filling for avocados: finely chop an onion and hard-boiled egg and mix with French dressing. Fill the avocados and serve extra in a sauceboat.'

TOMATO, AVOCADO AND MOZZARELLA SALAD

1 lb tomatoes, skinned
1 large ripe avocado
1 mozzarella cheese
sea salt and black pepper
3 tbsp olive oil
½ tbsp white wine vinegar

Slice the tomatoes, avocado and mozzarella cheese, keeping them separate. Arrange them on a large flat dish and sprinkle with black pepper. (Only add salt just before serving.) Dribble over the olive oil and vinegar, and stand for 1 hour before serving. At the last moment, sprinkle with a little sea salt and serve as a first course. Serves 3 to 4.

ARABELLA BOXER 1983

ORANGE, LETTUCE AND PEPPER SALAD

3 small oranges
1 cos lettuce
1 green pepper
¼ Spanish onion
10 black olives
2 tbsp lemon juice
2 tbsp olive oil
sea salt and black pepper
1 clove garlic

Peel the oranges, removing all the white pith, and cut in thick slices, reserving half an orange for juice. Discard all but the pale inner leaves of the lettuce; break into halves or quarters and lay in a salad bowl. Cut the pepper into rings, discarding the inner membrane and seeds, and lay over the lettuce. Arrange the sliced orange over and among the pepper. Slice the onion and scatter over the salad together with the whole olives.

Mix 2 tablespoons of the orange juice with the lemon juice and the olive oil, adding sea salt and black pepper and a whole clove of garlic. Just before serving, discard the garlic and pour the dressing over the salad. Toss gently; serve with cold roast duck. Serves 4 to 6.

ARABELLA BOXER 1983

CARROT, FENNEL AND CELERY SALAD

This salad of grated raw vegetables is so good as to become at times almost addictive. It has a terrific sharp juicy taste, very refreshing, and is also quite sustaining.

½ lb carrots
4-5 oz fennel, trimmed (inner leaves only)
4-5 oz celery, trimmed (tender stalks only)
2 tbsp sunflower seed oil
1 tbsp sesame oil
2 tbsp lemon juice
2 tbsp toasted sesame seeds (see note) or chopped almonds or hazelnuts, or chopped celery leaves

Grate the 3 vegetables fairly coarsely; the medium grating disc of the Magimix is just right. Mix them in a large bowl, and stir in the oils and lemon juice. Lastly, stir in half the toasted sesame seeds, or chopped nuts, or celery leaves. Turn into a serving dish and scatter the remaining seeds, nuts, or leaves over the top. Serves 4 as a vegetable accompaniment or 2 to 3 by itself. If serving alone, use seeds or nuts; if serving with meat, use celery leaves. This goes well with the Poached Sirloin Steak (see page 79).
Note: Cook the sesame seeds in a dry frying pan over low heat, stirring, until lightly coloured.

ARABELLA BOXER 1984

Opposite: Lester Bookbinder 1966

COOKED MIXED VEGETABLE SALAD

1 lb new potatoes
6 oz young carrots
4 oz shelled peas, fresh or frozen
DRESSING
⅛ pt single cream
⅛ pt yoghurt
4 tbsp sunflower seed oil
1 tbsp white wine vinegar
sea salt and black pepper
2 tbsp chopped chervil, dill, chives, or parsley

Boil the potatoes in their skins, then peel and cut in thick slices, or in quarters, if they are small. Slice the small carrots thickly and cook till tender in lightly salted boiling water; drain and add to the potatoes. Cook the peas as usual; drain and add to the other vegetables.

Mix the cream and yoghurt in a jug, and stir in the oil gradually, beating with a small whisk. Then add the vinegar slowly. When thoroughly mixed, add salt and pepper to taste. Stir most of the sauce into the salad while the vegetables are still hot, mixing gently. Add most of the herbs, reserving a few. Serve within the hour, if possible, while the vegetables are still warm. Just before serving, spoon the remaining sauce over the top. Sprinkle with the reserved herbs, and serve as a side dish. Serves 4.

ARABELLA BOXER 1984

LAMB'S LETTUCE AND TOMATO SALAD

½ lb lamb's lettuce
4 tomatoes
lemon juice
olive oil
sea salt

Wash the salad leaves and remove the base stalks. Peel, seed and chop the tomatoes and put them into a bowl with the lamb's lettuce. Dress with a little lemon juice, olive oil and salt.

JANE LONGMAN 1986

VEGETABLES

'Why must we endure the tyranny of so much food snobbery?' wrote Cecil Beaton in 1932. 'Why turn up the nose at a turnip or a parsnip?'

Boulestin was prepared to be patient and satisfied with the old winter vegetables and even decided that there are many enjoyable ways of preparing the 'beastly old things'. His recipes 'to help you along through Lent' included Choux à la Crème and Purée de Navets. Lent, he thought, was a time of mortification, therefore the season for economy, but he warned: 'It is never pleasant to economize, for economizing is, as a rule, conducive to bad temper, domestic discussions and indifferent food. But what a triumph if we can manage to reduce the household bills and, at the same time, enjoy the results of this measure; we have then the double satisfaction of having done our duty and well deserved our happiness.

'Winter vegetables are plentiful and varied, white cabbage, celery, celeriac, salsify, spinach, so "why shriek for peas, haricot beans and asparagus?" A delicious purée of carrots and beetroot will be devoured as readily as the first green peas at many times the price.'

Above: Jesse Collins 1940
Opposite: Tessa Traeger 1988

This, of course, was long before the advent of frozen vegetables. In 1937 Smedley's introduced frozen food to the British housewife; some 30 tons of 'frosted' peas packed in waxed milk cartons were sold, and these were followed by broad beans, spinach and Brussels sprouts.

It is difficult to imagine life without the convenience of frozen food today but still there is nothing like freshly picked home-grown vegetables. We eagerly look forward, as June Platt did in the fifties, to June and the arrival of 'green peas, broad beans, French beans, asparagus, cucumber, carrots, baby turnips, new potatoes, crisp lettuce and all the herbs of green and white magic'. She warned that 'young vegetables are so fragile, timing can be tricky. But little mounds of them served as a first course just when they are cooked make a splendid start to a meal.'

The delicate vegetables of summer are replaced by the richly colourful Mediterranean aubergines, peppers and marrows which the Greeks know how to cook so well. Many of their national dishes make main meals to suit the ever-growing preference for vegetarian dishes – as do Arabella Boxer's recipes for Mexican Beans and Vegetable Couscous.

ARTICHAUTS À LA BARIGOULE

Take some artichokes, cut off three quarters of the leaves and remove the smaller ones which are near the stalk. Put them in boiling water and cook them for about ten minutes. Remove them and dip them in cold water. Then remove all the inside, leaving only the heart and outer circles of leaves, and fill with a mixture prepared as follows.

Put in a saucepan one onion, one shallot and a few mushrooms very finely chopped, a piece of butter the size of a small egg and a little olive oil. Cook on a moderate fire for about ten minutes: then add parsley and a rasher of bacon chopped together, salt and pepper, a drop of white wine, a tablespoonful of beefstock and a teaspoonful of purée of tomatoes.

Fill the artichokes with this mixture; place over each a very thin rasher of bacon and tie them with some thread.

Put in a fireproof dish pieces of carrots and onions, one bay leaf, and whatever scraps of meat and small bones you have by you; add a tablespoonful of beef stock. Place your artichokes on this bed and bring to the boil, keeping the dish covered. Put it aside a few minutes, remove the lid, baste the artichokes, cover them with oiled paper and finish cooking in a moderate oven, basting occasionally.

When ready, remove the strings and bacon. Serve the artichokes covered with a gravy obtained by squashing through a sieve all the ingredients in which they have cooked.

I should like to add that this dish – which dates from the end of the eighteenth century – is far more complicated to describe than to make; in any case, it is well worth the trouble.

BOULESTIN 1923

Denton Welch 1946

ARTICHOKES À LA POLITA

24 small onions or shallots
carrots cut into 1½-inch pieces
12 large tinned *fonds d'artichauts*
24 small cubes of potatoes (about ½ inch square)
½ cup olive oil
1 tsp flour
juice of 2 lemons
salt to taste
dill leaves, chopped

Tinned *fonds d'artichauts* are a little less tasty than the fresh ones but make much less work as the preparation of the fresh artichokes takes some time.

Partly cook the onions and the carrots in a little water (because the artichokes are already cooked; but with fresh artichokes this is not necessary). Place the *fonds d'artichauts* in a saucepan, being careful not to break them. Then add the partly cooked onions and carrots with their water, and all the remaining ingredients, thickening with a little flour. Place a plate on them to keep still. Cook on a strong heat till onions are tender. Do not disturb until cold. Serves 6.

LADY FLEMING 1961

ARTICHOKES WITH GREEN MAYONNAISE

4 artichokes
salt
juice of ½ lemon
GREEN MAYONNAISE
½ pt well-flavoured mayonnaise
1 tbsp finely chopped watercress leaves
1 tbsp finely chopped chervil
2 tbsp finely chopped parsley
1 tbsp finely chopped tarragon leaves
lemon juice
salt and freshly ground black pepper

Remove the tough outer leaves of the artichokes and trim the tops of the inner leaves. Trim the base and stem of each artichoke with a sharp knife. Cook until tender (30-40 minutes) in a large quantity of salted boiling water to which you have added the juice of ½ lemon. Artichokes are ready when a leaf pulls out easily. When they are cooked, turn the artichokes upside down to drain. Serve cold with Green Mayonnaise, made by combining the basic mayonnaise with herbs, lemon juice and seasoning.

Pull off a leaf at a time and eat the tender base, then remove the 'choke' (fuzzy centre) and eat the artichoke heart. Serves 4.

ROBERT CARRIER 1966

ASPARAGUS

Scrape or peel, and wash thoroughly, 3 or 4 bunches of green asparagus. Cut off the tough part. Tie the spears in bunches. Soak them a little while in cold water, heads down, to be sure they are perfectly clean. Cook in the usual way in salted boiling water, until tender but not floppy. Drain carefully. Serve at once, with Sauce Mousseline (see page 112).

JUNE PLATT 1937

von Alvensleben 1986

ASPARAGUS TIPS À LA FRANÇAISE

Wash thoroughly 2 bunches of tender green asparagus, and soak them heads down in cold water for 1 hour. Cut them in uniform pieces the size of a pea. Put in boiling, salted water and let boil for just a few seconds, or until barely tender when crushed between the fingers. Drain and place in cold water. Fifteen minutes before serving, drain them well. Put 2 good tablespoons of butter in a saucepan, add the asparagus, salt and freshly ground pepper and warm in the butter. Sprinkle with 2 teaspoons of flour, ½ cup of meat stock and 1 teaspoon of sugar. Bring to a boil and simmer a minute or two; bind with the yolks of 3 eggs. Serve with fried *croûtons*.

JUNE PLATT 1936

AUBERGINES SAUTÉES

Take some aubergines (eggplant is, I am told, the correct English name), cut them in thin slices, sprinkle them with salt and leave them on a plate for an hour or so. This will bring out the water they contain. Drain them well, fry them in a mixture of oil and pork fat, and keep them hot. Then cut a few tomatoes in quarters and fry them in a very little of the same mixture, till soft. Pass through a sieve and pour the sauce thus obtained over your aubergines. Cook the whole a few minutes longer, add pepper (more salt will not be necessary) and serve hot.

BOULESTIN 1924

von Alvensleben 1983

GUACAMOLE

3 ripe avocado pears
2 thimble-sized, dried green chillies
1 sweet red pimiento (preferably canned)
2 scallions (a species of onion)
1 large ripe tomato, peeled
juice of 1 lemon
1 tbsp olive oil
¼ tsp salt
1 head of crisp lettuce, well washed

Peel the pears. Soak the dried green chillies in boiling water and discard the seeds before adding them to the recipe. Canned pimientos are already prepared. Save 2 narrow strips for a garnish. Chop the pimientos, chillies, scallions and the peeled tomato very finely. Add the flesh of the pears. Beat to a smooth paste, stir in the lemon juice and olive oil, and salt to taste. Be sparing with the salt. This should be prepared not more than 5 minutes before it is to be served, as the avocado pear turns dark when it stands long. To prevent this, the Mexicans leave two of the pear pits in the mixture. Serve on crisp lettuce leaves.

MARIAN 1936

FÈVES MAÎTRE D'HÔTEL

Take some broad beans (they should be young and tender) and throw them in salted boiling water, to which you add a bouquet composed of the heart of a lettuce, parsley and one small onion. Cook on a quick fire and drain well. Put in a saucepan a good piece of butter, a tablespoonful of the water in which the beans have cooked, and salt and pepper; bring to the boil, put in the beans and go on cooking for a few minutes. Just before serving add a little more butter, a teaspoonful of cream and chopped parsley.

BOULESTIN 1923

GRATIN DE HARICOTS VERTS

3 lb French beans
½ lb button mushrooms
3 oz butter
½ pt cream
salt and pepper

Throw the beans into plenty of boiling salted water and cook them, uncovered, until they are about three-quarters done – some varieties take longer than others so bite into one to test it. While the beans are cooking, wash and dry the mushrooms and chop them. Sauté them for 2 minutes in about 1 ounce of the butter.

When the beans are ready, tip them into a colander and drain thoroughly. Put them back into a pan with the cream, a very little salt and pepper and finish off their cooking over very low heat. Turn the beans and cream into a buttered ovenproof dish and spoon the mushrooms over the top; melt the rest of the butter and pour it over. Add salt and pepper and set in a hot oven for 10 minutes. Serve these beans as a course on their own or with any roast meat.

MAPIE DE TOULOUSE-LAUTREC 1961

CHINESE GREEN BEANS

1 lb green beans
2 tbsp peanut oil or lard
1 level tsp salt
¼ pt water
1 tbsp soy sauce, sake, or dry sherry

Wash and trim the beans; break them into sections about 1 inch long. Heat the oil or lard in a wok (or frying pan); add the beans and cook over medium heat for 1 minute, stirring constantly.

Add salt and water; cover the pan and cook the beans for 3 minutes; remove the cover and simmer, stirring from time to time, until all the water has evaporated (about 5 minutes). Add soy sauce, sake or dry sherry, to taste.

ROBERT CARRIER 1965

June Platt 1936

HARICOTS MANGETOUT

Take some fresh haricot beans of the kind called mangetout, the pod of which is still tender, although the bean has reached its normal size. Break off the ends, removing at the same time any stringy parts, then break them in two and wash them well. Prepare a saucepan of boiling water (with salt and a bouquet of parsley and thyme), throw your haricots in this and add to it the juice of some ripe tomatoes (four to a pound of mangetout), cooked in very little water and squeezed through a sieve. Let it reduce a good deal, and just before serving add a piece of fresh butter.

In the South of France, instead of adding butter they add a small amount of bacon, fresh parsley and garlic finely chopped together. The taste is delicious. But it must be remembered, if trying this Southern way, that the garlic which grows in the North is much more powerful than the one from the South, and very little of it is sufficient to give it the right taste.

BOULESTIN 1923

PURÉE DE HARICOTS BLANCS

You can use either the small or the large variety of *haricots*. Wash them well in running water, and soak them for twelve hours, then put them in a saucepan with lots of salted water, coarsely broken pepper, one onion, one carrot and the usual bouquet of thyme, bay leaf and parsley. Start them on a quick fire, skim well, let them simmer till perfectly tender and mash them through a sieve. Add seasoning and fresh butter just before serving. The consistency should be that of a potato purée.

BOULESTIN 1924

HARICOTS ROUGES BOURGUIGNONNE

Wash the beans well in running water. Soak them for twelve hours. Put in a saucepan one carrot, one onion, a piece of streaky pickled pork, and a good piece of butter. Brown well on a moderate fire, then add a good glass of claret,

a teacupful of beef stock, salt, pepper, bouquet, the haricot beans and just enough water to cover them if necessary. Bring to the boil, and let it simmer actually for hours. Before serving, cut the pork in small pieces and remove the bouquet, carrot and onion. Some people let this cook slowly (with the lid on) in the oven for a whole day.

BOULESTIN 1924

HOPPING JOHN

1 cup brown haricot beans
2 strips white salt pork
1 cup uncooked rice
large lump of butter

Soak the beans, then drain them and add to the salt pork with 1 pint of water and boil for 4 hours. Add the rice to the beans, adding more water to cover. Cook for 1 hour, stirring occasionally. Add butter and stir just before serving. *Note:* This dish is typical of Charleston and is delicious served as an accompaniment to steak and a green salad.

1938

BOSTON BAKED BEANS

Wash 2 pints of small haricot beans and soak them overnight in cold water. In the morning, drain and cook in fresh water until the skins begin to break. Drain and turn into the bean pot (a casserole with a lid). Cut up ½ pound of salt pork (bacon will do) and press into the beans. Add 2 teaspoons of salt, ¼ cup of treacle, 1 tablespoon of brown sugar and ½ teaspoon of dry mustard. Pour on boiling water to cover. Put on the lid of the casserole and bake in a very cool oven (Gas Mark ½, 250°F) for 6-8 hours, putting in more water as needed to keep the beans covered. Remove the lid during the last 30 minutes so that the beans and pork may brown.

DORIS LYTTON-TOYE 1953

MEXICAN BEANS

The combination of citrus fruit and fresh coriander with the bland taste of red or black kidney beans sounds surprising, but works amazingly well.

½ lb red or black kidney beans, pink borlotti
or pinto beans
½ medium onion, chopped
2 cloves garlic, chopped
1 small bay leaf, crumbled
1 green chilli, fresh or tinned
sea salt and black pepper
GARNISH
¼ pt *fromage blanc*
2 limes (or lemons), halved
6 tbsp roughly chopped coriander

Soak the beans overnight, then drain off the water. Put them in a heavy pan and add 1½ pints fresh cold water. Put them over a moderate flame and as they heat, add the chopped onion and garlic, crumbled bay leaf and chopped chilli. Don't add salt yet. Let the water boil hard for 10 minutes, then reduce the heat so that it simmers gently. Cook in this way, half covered, for 1½ hours, or until the beans are tender, testing them with a fork every 15 minutes after the first hour is up.

When they are ready, tip the beans into a colander standing over a bowl and discard the bay leaf. Then take ½ pint of the beans and put them in a food processor with ¼ pint of the liquid. Add sea salt and black pepper and process until roughly puréed. Put the whole beans back in their pan over low heat and stir in the puréed beans, adding more salt and pepper as needed. Cook gently, stirring often, for 3 or 4 minutes, then pour into a serving dish.

Serve in bowls, and set the *fromage blanc*, halved limes (or lemons) and chopped coriander on the table so that each guest can add them as they wish. If you prefer, you can add them just before serving, so that the garnishes do not have time to lose their fresh sharp taste.

Tessa Traeger 1976

The only accompaniment required is a green salad. Serves 3 to 4.
Note: In Mexico, bean dishes of this sort are often served as fillings for tortillas. These are difficult to make without a tortilla press, but I find the beans are just as good served inside wholemeal pancakes, with their garnishes.

ARABELLA BOXER 1988

CHARTREUSE OF BEETROOT

Make an aspic by boiling 1 pint of water with a sliced onion, a scant tablespoon of tarragon vinegar, 2 cloves, 3 pepper-corns, 1 bay leaf, 1 spray of parsley, 1 sprig of thyme and a pinch of sugar and salt. Soften 4 level teaspoons of gelatine in a little water. Add the gelatine to the pan when the water is boiling. Simmer for 15 minutes, stirring from time to time. Strain through fine muslin. Fill a flat dish with sliced beetroot, pour over the aspic gently to cover completely. Turn out when cold, and cut in wedges.

DORIS LYTTON-TOYE 1946

HARVARD BEETS

Blend 2 teaspoons of cornflour, $\frac{1}{3}$ cup of dry white wine, 2 tablespoons of sugar, 2 teaspoons of lemon juice and $\frac{1}{2}$ teaspoon of salt in a double boiler. Cook over boiling water till transparent. Add 2 cups of peeled, diced, cooked beets and allow them to get hot without boiling. Finish off with 1 ounce of butter, and pepper to taste. Done in this manner, the beetroot looks like glistening rubies; it goes well with ham or bacon.

DORIS LYTTON-TOYE 1953

CHOUX DE BRUXELLES À L'ITALIENNE

Wash and clean some Brussels sprouts, drain them well and cook them in boiling salted water on a quick fire for about a quarter of an hour. Meanwhile, put in a small saucepan a piece of butter the size of an egg and a spoonful of flour and cook this for five minutes, stirring and mixing well; add about a pint of milk, bring to the boil and let it thicken; it is then time to add the seasoning, a little grated nutmeg, the juice of a lemon and grated cheese. Then put your sprouts (well drained once more) in the sauce and cook a little more on a slow fire,

---

'Cook finely shredded cabbage – about a breakfast cup – with half a grated apple; finish with a nut of butter, pepper, salt and a grating of nutmeg.'

DORIS LYTTON-TOYE

---

bringing to the boil. Needless to say, it is no use being mean about the sauce, and the quantities given above, which would only do for a small quantity of sprouts, should be increased accordingly.

BOULESTIN 1924

BRUSSELS SPROUTS APPETIZER

1 lb small Brussels sprouts
$\frac{1}{4}$ pt well-flavoured vinaigrette dressing
lettuce leaves
2 tbsp finely chopped onion
4 tbsp finely chopped parsley

Prepare and cook Brussels sprouts in the usual way. Place them in a bowl; pour over the vinaigrette dressing, toss well and leave to marinate in this mixture for at least 2 hours.

To serve, line a salad bowl or hors d'oeuvre dish with lettuce leaves and arrange the marinated Brussels sprouts in the centre. Sprinkle them with finely chopped onion and parsley and serve. Serves 4.

ROBERT CARRIER 1965

CHOUX À LA CRÈME

Choose a good-sized Savoy cabbage, remove the coarse outer leaves and cut the cabbage into four pieces; wash them well and cook them in boiling salted water till quite tender. Then remove the cabbage, drain off all the water, season it and put it in a serving dish with the following sauce poured over: put a tablespoonful of flour in a small sauce-

---

pan with a good piece of butter and cook it a little, then add a little milk, salt and pepper. Bring to the boil, stirring constantly, add a little more butter, and if too thick more milk; also, just before serving, some fresh cream.

BOULESTIN 1924

SAVOY CABBAGE

Wash and soak 2 savoy cabbages, cut in quarters, in cold salted water for 30 minutes. Then cook in salted boiling water for 10 minutes. Drain well and chop finely. Put 1 little onion (chopped finely) in a frying pan with 2 table-spoons of butter. Brown until a light golden colour. Sprinkle lightly with 1 tablespoon of flour. Add the chopped cabbage and $\frac{1}{4}$ cup of meat juice or 1 teaspoon of beef extract dissolved in a little water and thinned with a little of the cabbage juice. Add salt and pepper and a sprinkling of nutmeg. Cook for 10 minutes and serve.

JUNE PLATT 1936

RED CABBAGE

Wash and slice finely 2 tender red cab-bages and put them to soak in 2 table-spoons of vinegar and some water. Then finely chop 1 onion and brown it in 2 tablespoons of bacon fat and 2 table-spoons of butter in a frying pan. Put in the cabbage which has been drained well. Add 1 bay leaf, 3 cloves, 2 pepper-corns and 2 tart, juicy apples, sliced finely. Cook slowly until tender, stirring frequently, as red cabbage burns easily. When it is done, melt 1 tablespoon of butter in a saucepan, add 1 teaspoon of flour, stir and put in the cabbage and its juice. Sprinkle with 1 teaspoon of sugar and the juice of $\frac{1}{2}$ lemon. Simmer for 1 or 2 minutes and serve.

JUNE PLATT 1936

David Edgell 1963

CAROTTES VICHY

Carottes Vichy was one of Boulestin's favourite recipes. Like June Platt, Mrs Lytton-Toye and the Countess de Toulouse-Lautrec he insisted that only young carrots could be used.

BOULESTIN 1926

Take some young carrots, scrape and wash them and cut them in very thin slices. Put a good piece of butter in a saucepan, then your carrots; sprinkle with salt, a little sugar and, if necessary, add later some more butter. Cook on a medium fire till the carrots are soft and nicely browned. The mixture of the salt, the sugar, the butter and the little water left on the carrots combine in the process of cooking to make a really delicious dish; but you must use new carrots.

You can serve them as soon as they come out of the saucepan. There is also another way which is another version of *carottes à la crème* or *à la poulette*: having prepared the carrots in the way I have described, remove the saucepan from the fire; add then a glass of cream and the yolks of two eggs previously beaten, a little more seasoning, shake well, warm carefully, and serve at once. Young turnips are also very good treated in the same manner.

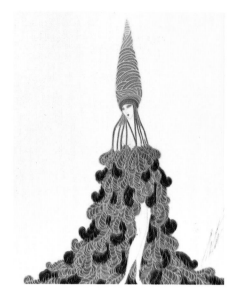

Erté 1926

JUNE PLATT 1936

Peel and wash about 3 bunches of tender young carrots and cut them in tiny thin slices. Melt ½ pound of butter in an ovenproof baking dish and add some salt and a teaspoon of sugar. Mix well. Add the carrots and pour over it all ⅓ cup of cognac. Cover the dish and put into a moderate oven to cook for 1 hour. Do not stir but watch carefully so that they don't cook too long and get hard or brown. Serve with well-browned slices of toast Melba.

DORIS LYTTON-TOYE 1946

Scrub some young carrots well, then slice them across finely. Place in a pan with water to barely cover, a nut of margarine, ½ teaspoon of brown sugar, a good pinch of salt and a little pepper. Bring to the boil, then cover and simmer till the carrots are tender and the liquid is syrupy. Shake them to give them a shiny coat, without breaking. Turn into a hot dish and sprinkle with chopped parsley or mint.

MAPIE DE TOULOUSE-LAUTREC 1961

3½ lb young carrots
3 oz butter
1 dessertspoon caster sugar
salt

Peel the carrots and slice them across as thinly as possible. Put them in a pan with just enough water to cover them. Add the butter, sugar and a very little salt. Simmer, uncovered, over a very low heat until practically all the water has evaporated and the liquid is the consistency of syrup. Let the carrots sauté gently in this until they glaze and are just beginning to brown.

CARROT RING MOULD

2-3 lb new carrots
butter for frying
¼ pt chicken stock
1 tbsp sugar
salt and freshly ground black pepper
2 eggs
4 tbsp softened butter
6-8 tbsp grated cheese
cooked peas and button onions

Wash the carrots; slice them thickly and place in a saucepan. Cover with cold water and cook over a high heat until the water boils. Drain.

Simmer the blanched carrots in some butter, chicken stock, sugar and salt to taste, until they have absorbed all the liquid and are tender. Combine the mixture with the eggs, softened butter, cheese, salt and black pepper to taste in the blender; blend until smooth. Press into a buttered ring mould and heat in a moderate oven (Gas Mark 3, 325°F) for 15 minutes. Turn the carrot ring out on a heated serving dish; fill the centre with cooked peas and onions. Surround with remaining peas and onions. Serves 6.

ROBERT CARRIER 1966

Carl Erickson 1938

CAULIFLOWER WITH CREAM SAUCE AND BUTTERED CRUMBS

Cut away the leaves and part of the thick stem of a firm white cauliflower and put to soak, head down, for 20 minutes in salted water. Plunge it into rapidly boiling water and cook for 15 or 20 minutes. Put it in a round dish, head up, and pour over it some hot cream sauce.

With the cauliflower hand a bowl of buttered crumbs made in the following manner: cut some stale bread in little pieces and fry in butter until crisp and brown. When cold, roll them out and put back in a warm oven until ready for use. Cauliflower so cooked can be served as a separate course or with any roast joint.

<u>JUNE PLATT 1936</u>

SOUFFLÉ OF CAULIFLOWER À LA BARONNE

Trim a cauliflower. Blanch and rinse it, put it in boiling water with a little salt and let it cook until tender. Drain it and cut it in pieces. Place the pieces in a buttered soufflé dish with alternate layers of raw sliced tomatoes. Season with salt and pepper and fill up the dish with a mixture prepared as follows: make a white sauce with 2 ounces of butter, 2 ounces of flour and ½ pint of milk. Add the raw yolks of 2 eggs, a dusting of cayenne pepper and a pinch of salt; stir until it boils. Add 3 ounces of grated Parmesan and 3 egg whites, whipped stiff. Mix all together and pour over the vegetables in the soufflé dish. Bake for 25 minutes (Gas Regulo 6, 400°F).

<u>1938</u>

BEIGNETS DE CHOUFLEUR

Boil the buds of cauliflower in salted water, but do not let them get too soft. Drain very well. Prepare a batter with 4½ ounces of flour, 1 egg yolk, a cup of milk and a little salt. Beat until smooth, then add the whipped egg white. Dip the sprigs of cauliflower in this and fry in hot fat till golden. Drain on absorbent paper, then keep hot in a warm oven. Pile on a hot dish, garnish with a parsley bouquet and hand a tomato or cheese sauce with it.

<u>DORIS LYTTON-TOYE 1946</u>

CURRIED CAULIFLOWER

1 medium onion
¼ oz fresh or well-soaked root ginger
1½ oz ghee
1½ tsp turmeric
½ tsp or more chilli powder or ¼ tsp cayenne pepper (optional)
2 lb cauliflower, weighed after the outside leaves have been removed
1 medium potato
2 tsp salt
1 tsp garam masala

Using a large heavy frying pan, fry gently the sliced onion and ginger in the ghee for 3-4 minutes. Add turmeric and chilli powder and let it sizzle for a little while. Cut the cauliflower into thin 2-inch pieces, keeping some of the stalk with the flower. Wash, drain and put the pieces in the sizzling mixture along with cubes of the potato, which should be scraped, not peeled. Stir with a slice to avoid crushing.

Cook gently, uncovered, for about 10 minutes. Then add salt. Mix and cook for a little while longer, then cover with a loose lid and cook gently until the cauliflower is tender (not broken). Mix in the garam masala and, if the curry is not dry enough, remove the lid and turn the heat a little higher.

<u>SAVITRI CHOWDHARY 1955</u>

BRAISED CELERY

Remove and discard the outer stalks from 16 stalks of celery. Cut off the leaves, making the stalks all the same length. Wash very carefully, pulling the branches slightly apart and letting the cold water run through the heart to remove any sand. Remove as many threads as possible by scraping with a knife. Shake out and dry well on a tea-cloth. Place the stalks side by side in an oblong Pyrex dish that will hold them all and which has been well buttered. Sprinkle with salt and freshly ground pepper and dot well with ½ pound of butter. Squeeze a few drops of lemon juice over all and pour over the celery 3 tins of clear chicken consommé. Now butter copiously on both sides enough white paper completely to cover the dish. Press the paper to the edge of the dish and put in a moderate oven to cook slowly for at least 2 hours. Watch carefully, and when the juice begins to caramelize around the edge of the dish, remove the paper, scrape the brown part down into the remaining juice and with a spoon stir it gently to melt it into the bouillon. Ladle it over the celery, replace the paper and continue to cook until the celery is tender through. If the juice should dry out completely, add a little more bouillon. The celery should be very tender when done and well caramelized, with plenty of rich brown juice still left in the bottom of the dish. Sprinkle lightly with finely chopped parsley and serve at once in the dish in which it was cooked.

1936

Tessa Traeger 1978

CHESTNUT PURÉE WITH BRUSSELS SPROUTS

Wipe 1 pound of chestnuts. Slit them round with a sharp knife. Cover them with water in a pan and bring them to the boil, then drain them and remove the shells carefully, including all inner skin. To make the purée, cook them in boiling water, adding a stick of celery and, if available, some white stock. When quite soft and tender, rub them through a sieve. Reheat with a little butter and seasoning. Cook small Brussels sprouts, keeping them whole and green; press them into a border mould and place in the oven to keep warm. Turn them out upon a hot dish with the chestnut purée piled high in the middle. This is the easiest manner in which to cook chestnuts and is a lovely adjunct to roast turkey or to any game.

DORIS LYTTON-TOYE 1947

BRAISED CHICORY WITH MUSHROOM SAUCE

Remove the outer leaves from 16 pieces of chicory. Wash the heads well, pulling the leaves slightly apart; shake them and dry quickly on a teacloth. Proceed as for Braised Celery (left). To make the sauce, first grate 1 cup of Parmesan or Gruyère cheese. Melt 4 tablespoons of butter in an enamel pan and cook in it until a golden brown 1 white onion and 1 carrot, which have been chopped very finely. When browned lightly add 6 level tablespoons of flour and cook together for a minute or two, then add 2 medium tins of cream of mushroom soup and stir well until thick. Place in a double boiler to continue cooking a while. A small bay leaf may be added if you like the flavour. When you serve the chicory, add the grated cheese to the sauce and stir until well mixed. If the sauce is too thick add a little cream. Serve the chicory from the dish and hand the sauce separately.

1936

GRATIN OF ENDIVES AU JAMBON

8 heads of chicory
juice of 1 lemon
crust of bread
4 large thin slices cooked ham
breadcrumbs
MORNAY SAUCE
1½ oz butter
1 oz flour
1 cup milk
2 oz grated Swiss cheese
salt and pepper
pinch of nutmeg

Wash and clean the chicory, removing any damaged leaves. Cook uncovered in boiling salted water to which you add the juice of a lemon and a crust of bread (to prevent the chicory losing its colour). Do not boil too fast; 25 minutes should be enough but test for tenderness by sticking in a silver fork. Then strain thoroughly and dry carefully on a cloth. Keep ½ cup of the drained-off liquid.

To make the Mornay Sauce, melt 1 ounce of butter in a heavy saucepan over low heat. Blend in the flour and cook slowly for about 2 minutes without colouring. Remove from the heat and pour in the milk and chicory liquid that you have heated to boiling point in a small pan. Beat vigorously with a wire whisk to blend, and then return the pan to the heat and bring to the boil, stirring hard. Boil for a minute or two, stirring, then once more remove from the heat and beat in three-quarters of the cheese, salt and pepper to taste and nutmeg. Wrap each head of chicory in half a slice of ham, lay in a buttered fireproof dish and pour the sauce over. Sprinkle with breadcrumbs and the remaining cheese. Dot with the remaining butter and put in a hot oven for about 10 minutes, until the top is golden brown, or reheat under a moderate grill.

VERONICA MACLEAN 1969

'The root and stems of parsley contain more flavour than the leaves. Use roots when making stock; finely chopped leaves and stems for garnishes, sauces and soups.'

Anthony Denney 1960

CORN BATTER CAKES

Sift ¾ cup of flour with ½ teaspoon of salt and 1 teaspoon of baking powder. Beat in gradually ¼ cup of milk, 1 beaten egg, a dessertspoon of melted margarine and 1 cup of strained sweet-corn. Drop the batter in spoonfuls on to a hot greased griddle or frying pan. Turn when cooked on the underside.

DORIS LYTTON-TOYE 1953

ZUCCHINI FRITTI

Take zucchini (courgettes) the length of a finger and a bit; wash and cut them in slices, lengthways. Remove a little of the seedy centres, salt them lightly. Leave for an hour or so; drain off any liquid. Without completely drying them, dip them in egg and flour, then fry in hot clarified fat. Move them as little as possible till they take colour — they break easily. Season with salt after frying.

DORIS LYTTON-TOYE 1947

ZUCCHINI RIPIENI

Choose even-sized courgettes. Throw them into boiling water for 2-3 minutes. Drain, cut through the centres and hollow them out. Sauté a little onion in hot margarine till gold; put in the chopped pulp of the courgettes and cook for a minute or so. Add any remains of cooked fish or meat, binding all together with a little white sauce. Season well. Fill the courgettes and place them in a buttered ovenproof dish. Scatter breadcrumbs on top, and tiny bits of butter. Pour a tablespoon or so of water into the dish and bake in a moderate oven till tender and delicately browned.

DORIS LYTTON-TOYE 1947

CONCOMBRES FARCIS

Peel some cucumbers, cut them in two or three pieces according to size and scoop out the inside. Fill them with a mixture made of a little cucumber flesh, one onion, one rasher of bacon, a few mushrooms, one tomato, breadcrumbs, salt and pepper, all finely chopped together and cooked in butter. Place the cucumbers on a bed of bacon rind, onions and tomatoes in a fireproof dish, add meat stock, and cook on a moderate fire, finishing in the oven. Serve when the flesh is soft, in an entrée dish, and pour over them the gravy through a sieve.

BOULESTIN 1923

BRAISED FENNEL

3 heads fennel
2 oz beef dripping or butter
⅓ pt game, poultry or beef stock
I tbsp lemon juice
sea salt and black pepper
I tsp butter
I tsp flour

Cut off the roots and tough outer leaves of the fennel, then cut each head in half and wash well. Pat dry and lay in one layer in a broad sauté pan or casserole. Cut the fat in small pieces and scatter over the fennel. Heat the stock and pour over, adding lemon juice, sea salt and black pepper. Cover and then cook very gently for 1½-2 hours, turning them over from time to time. When they are very soft, lift out with a perforated spoon and lay them in a shallow dish – brown earthenware gratin dishes look good with these pale vegetables.

Mix the butter and flour to a smooth paste, and drop by degrees into the liquid remaining in the pan. Simmer gently, stirring constantly, for about 3 minutes, while the flour cooks and thickens the sauce. Adjust the seasoning and pour over the fennel. Serves 3.
Note: This makes a wonderful accompaniment to dishes of brown rice or other grains. In a more traditional meal, it is a delicious vegetable to serve with game: in this case it will serve 6.

ARABELLA BOXER 1984

FENNEL, ONION OR LEEKS WITH CHEESE

2 large heads fennel, washed and trimmed, or
4 medium onions, peeled, or 4 leeks, washed
and trimmed
salt and pepper
4 oz Cheddar cheese, grated
¼ pt cream

Boil the vegetables whole, in salted water, until tender. Drain. If using fennel or onions, cut them in half from top

Hilary Stebbing 1942

to bottom. Lay the vegetables in a buttered ovenproof dish, and season. Cover with cheese and pour the cream over the top. Bake in a preheated oven for 30 minutes at Gas Mark 4, 350°F, or until melted and lightly brown. Serves 4.

MARWOOD YEATMAN 1985

POIREAUX AU GRATIN

Have ready some boiled leeks, well-drained, and potatoes steamed in their jackets. Line a gratin dish with the leeks cut small. When the dish is nearly full, cover with a layer of potatoes, peeled and sliced thickly. Season as you go. Make a cheese sauce from 1 ounce of margarine, 1 ounce of flour (1 heaped tablespoon) and ¾ pint of milk. When the sauce is well cooked, season to taste with salt, pepper from the mill and a little mixed mustard; fold in 2 ounces of grated cheese. Pour sauce over to mask the potatoes and bake in a moderate oven until brown.

DORIS LYTTON-TOYE 1949

LAITUES AU FOUR

Take some lettuces and remove the outside green leaves. Throw them in salted boiling water and cook for just a few minutes. Remove most of the water and finish cooking in a closed dish on a slow fire. Drain well and put them in a buttered ovenproof dish, cover with a béchamel sauce, sprinkle with breadcrumbs and brown in the oven.

BOULESTIN 1923

MARROW GRATINÉE

Peel a marrow thinly, remove the seeds, and cut the flesh in squares or stamp out rounds with a 2-inch cutter. Steam the squares or rounds till almost cooked. Drain them thoroughly. Dispose these pieces overlapping in a well-greased dish. Season with salt and pepper, then dust lavishly with grated cheese and a light sprinkling of paprika. Bake in a moderate oven till golden on top.

DORIS LYTTON-TOYE 1945

MARROW IN CREAM SAUCE

I medium vegetable marrow
salt and pepper
I tbsp margarine
I tbsp self-raising flour
¼ pt natural yoghurt
I tsp paprika
dash of vinegar
2 tsp sugar
I tsp caraway seeds

Peel, slice and core the marrow and cut it into thin strips. Sprinkle with salt, cover and leave for 1 hour. Drain well and toss in hot margarine. Sprinkle with the flour. Continue frying until golden brown. Gradually add to it the yoghurt, paprika, vinegar, pepper, sugar and caraway seeds. Bring to the boil and simmer over a low flame for 30 minutes. Add milk if necessary.

PETER PIRBRIGHT AND GRETEL BEER 1949

'Brillat-Savarin who was not, as some people seem to think, a chef, but an indifferent Government official, a delightful writer and a distinguished gourmet – was in dead earnest about the Things of the Table. To him the kitchen was a temple and the cook a high priestess.'
BOULESTIN

IVANHOE MUSHROOMS

Take large, morning-gathered white mushrooms. Wash them and remove their stalks. Put a small fillet of smoked haddock through the mincer. Chop the mushroom stalks finely, and sauté them in margarine; put in the fish and cook slowly for a few minutes. Add a sprinkle of flour, black pepper and enough milk to bind and make a thick sauce. Use this paste to fill the mushroom caps; sprinkle over melted margarine and cook in a greased pan in the oven till the caps are tender. Set them on toast, very hot, garnished with watercress.

DORIS LYTTON-TOYE 1945

MUSHROOMS À LA GRECQUE

1¼ lb button mushrooms
olive oil
1 tbsp finely chopped onion
¼ pt dry white wine
juice of 2 lemons
1 tsp salt
pinch of pepper
1 tsp mustard
pinch of coriander
chopped fennel
chopped parsley
1 bay leaf

Wash and dry the button (or small field) mushrooms carefully, but do not peel them. Trim the stalks and cut them into 2 or more suitable portions. Heat a generous cup of oil in a large enamel saucepan; add all the ingredients, putting in the mushrooms last of all. Cover and cook for 3-4 minutes. Turn the mixture into an earthenware serving dish and leave to cool in the marinade for at least 6 hours. Serve cold in the same dish. If you wish you can make this dish one day to serve the next.

VERONICA MACLEAN 1970

MUSHROOM PUDDING

PASTRY
½ lb self-raising flour
pinch of salt
4 oz shredded suet
iced water to mix
FILLING
12 oz small button mushrooms
1 oz butter
salt and pepper
juice of ½ lemon
¼ pt game or chicken stock

Sift the flour, add a pinch of salt and mix in the shredded suet. Add enough iced water to make a thick paste. Cut in 2 uneven pieces and roll out the larger one thinly to line a 1½-pint pudding basin. Fill with the mushroom caps, wiped and trimmed, and the butter cut in small pieces. Sprinkle each layer with salt and pepper, then pour over the lemon juice and the stock. Roll out the remaining pastry to form a lid, lay over the top and trim and seal the edges. Cover with a greased piece of aluminium foil and tie with string. Place in a large pan half-full of boiling water and steam for 2½ hours. This unusual suet pudding is absolutely delicious served with stewed beef, carrots and onions. Serves 4.

ARABELLA BOXER 1976

RAGOUT OF OLIVES

Chop 3 peeled shallots very finely and let them simmer in about 2 tablespoons of butter till they are golden brown. Add 2×8-ounce tins of tomato sauce, 1 cup of good dry white wine, and 2 teaspoons of beef extract dissolved in 1 tablespoon of boiling water. Reduce by simmering until quite thick.

In the meantime open and drain a 13-ounce bottle of olives stuffed with pimiento. Pour boiling water over them and let them stand a few minutes, drain again and scald once more and drain well. Now heat 2 good tablespoons of olive oil in a little pan and add the olives and 2 tablespoons of capers. When they have heated through, add them with the oil to the sauce and continue to simmer gently. When ready to serve, make some crisp, lightly buttered toast. Put the ragout in a hot small earthenware casserole and serve at once, accompanied by the hot toast. This is delicious served with roast duck, and in this case add a little of the meat juice from the duck and a few drops of lemon juice.

JUNE PLATT 1936

BAKED ONIONS

Baked onions are best made by peeling and washing the onions and parboiling them. Drain well and sauté in a frying pan with a little butter and a teaspoon of sugar until glazed. Stick 2 whole cloves in each one and arrange them neatly in a small oblong fireproof dish. Make a very thin cream sauce with 1 teaspoon of butter, 1 teaspoon of flour and 1 cup of thin cream, salt and pepper. Add 2 tablespoons of thick cream and pour over the onions. Bake for 15 minutes. Serve hot.

JUNE PLATT 1935

PARSNIP FRITTERS

Wash and boil 4 or 5 parsnips. When they are tender, take off the skins and mash them finely. Add 1 teaspoon of flour, 1 beaten egg and a little salt and pepper. Have some whole shelled walnuts ready and form the parsnip mixture into little balls with 1 walnut in each. Fry to a golden brown in butter in a frying pan. Decorate with parsley and serve on a very hot dish.

JUNE PLATT 1936

Lester Bookbinder 1964

PETITS POIS AU LARD

Cut two rashers of streaky bacon in little cubes; cook them in butter with six small onions and a pinch of flour. Add a tablespoon of beef stock and a tumbler of water, salt, pepper and a bouquet (of parsley, chives and one bay leaf). Bring to the boil; throw in your peas and cook till tender. Remove the bouquet of herbs before serving.

BOULESTIN 1923

PEAS À LA FRANÇAISE

Thaw out a packet of peas. Place them in a saucepan and barely cover with water; add 2 lettuce leaves and a little chopped onion or 6 whole spring onions. Put in a sprinkle of salt, a dust of pepper, a pinch of sugar and a nut of margarine. Cover the pan, bring to the boil and simmer for 20 minutes.

DORIS LYTTON-TOYE 1948

PURÉE ST GERMAIN

2 lb fresh or frozen peas
1 lettuce heart, shredded
12 tiny spring onions or ½ Spanish onion, sliced
3 sprigs parsley
4 oz butter
4 tbsp chicken stock or water
sugar
salt
2 potatoes, cooked until soft and puréed (optional)

Put the peas in a saucepan with the shredded lettuce heart, spring onions, parsley, half the butter, the chicken stock or water, and sugar and salt to taste. Bring to the boil and cook slowly until the peas are tender. When cooked, remove the parsley and drain, reserving the juices. Blend to a fine purée in an electric blender (or press through a fine sieve) and reheat in the top of a double saucepan, adding a little of the strained

John Minton 1946

juices and the remaining butter. If the purée seems too thin, then add puréed potatoes to lend body. Serves 4.

ROBERT CARRIER 1966

GREEN PEPPERS

Pull off the stalk and calyx, and with a sharp knife cut the top off the pepper — just as you would cut the top off a boiled egg. Then, with a knife, scrape out the rows of tiny flat seeds, the core and pith.

Fry a chopped onion in oil, and add a cup of uncooked rice. Fry all together for a few moments and then remove from the fire. Season with chopped parsley, mint or mixed herbs, salt and pepper. Carefully fill the peppers rather more than half full, and put them into a casserole with a little oil and a cup of water. Cover the casserole tightly and cook gently till the rice is tender.

The peppers are often cooked in a

shallow dish in the oven. It is usual then to put with them as many medium-sized ripe tomatoes as there are peppers, stuffed with the same rice mixture. Cut the tops off the tomatoes, and with a teaspoon scoop out some of the pulp. The tops of the peppers and the tops of the tomatoes should be put on again. They must be cooked in a moderately hot oven with a little water and oil poured round them in the dish, so they do not burn.

1939

STUFFED GREEN PEPPERS

6-9 green peppers
1 pt béchamel sauce
1 large tsp curry powder
¼ pt whipped cream
6 hard-boiled eggs, chopped
4 tbsp chopped lean ham
1 tbsp diced cucumber

Roll peppers on a hotplate or under the grill until they blister a little. Cut off the tops and empty them of seeds. Combine the cold béchamel sauce, curry powder and cream. Add the chopped eggs, ham and cucumber. Fill the peppers with this mixture. Take a little slice off the end so that they sit up nicely.

VERONICA MACLEAN 1970

POMMES FRITES PAYSANNE

This way of frying potatoes is, so to speak, against all rules, yet they come out of the pan crisp and delicious. Cut the potatoes in small cubes and fry them in very little fat, so that there is none left at the end of the process (a piece of fat the size of an egg would be enough for a pound and a half of potatoes), shaking them often. When they are nearly done, add chopped parsley, salt and, if you like, a little garlic very finely chopped. Serve at once.

BOULESTIN 1925

SWEET POTATOES

These can be dressed in many different ways – fried, baked, boiled, also in fritters and waffles. They are also very good, if you like them, *au caramel*. Boil the potatoes, then cut them in half lengthways; fry them in butter, and while frying sprinkle them with sugar, which will melt and mix with the butter, forming a kind of caramel. This dish is apparently served as a 'sweet entrée'.

BOULESTIN 1926

PROVINCIAL POTATOES

Wash and boil in their skins 3 pounds of new potatoes. Put 2 ounces of butter in a saucepan. Cut the butter up and pour 3 dessertspoons of olive oil over it. Then add the grated rind of half a lemon and also some chopped parsley and chopped chives, a little freshly grated nutmeg, a pinch of flour and some salt and pepper. When the potatoes are cooked, peel and cut into quarters or eighths and put them into the butter mixture. Heat, but without letting the butter boil. When ready to serve, add the juice of 1 lemon.

JUNE PLATT 1936

POTATO PUFFKINS

Form well-mashed potatoes into balls or small rolls. Dip into a little melted fat and then roll in grated cheese. Season with a sprinkle of mustard, pepper and salt, and brown under the grill or in a hot oven. This dish can be developed into an excellent savoury by adding oysters. Stew the oysters in a little milk: mash the potatoes with this liquid: wrap each oyster in mashed potato, roll in grated cheese and cook as above.

NELL HEATON 1943

'Add a tablespoon of capers to sauté potatoes just before serving.'

POMMES DE TERRE CHÂTEAU

Peel, then pare potatoes into equal-sized barrel shapes. Blanch them quickly (cover with cold water and bring to the boil). Drain them and dry in a cloth. In a flattish pan, melt some clarified fat; roll the potatoes in this and cook over a moderate heat till golden yellow. If the potatoes are not cooked when coloured, season them with salt and finish cooking in the oven with the lid on. Drain off any fat and serve scattered with chopped parsley.

DORIS LYTTON-TOYE 1950

FLORENTINE D'EPINARDS

Pick over 1 pound of spinach, removing the stalks. Wash the leaves in several changes of water. Cook in a large open pan with only the moisture clinging to the leaves: add a pinch of salt and sugar. When the leaves are tender, press them dry in a colander, reserving the liquid. Chop or sieve the spinach. Melt a knob of margarine in a smaller pan: put in the spinach and stir it over a fast flame for a minute or two. Add 1 ounce of flour; cook, stirring, for 2 minutes. Gradually pour in the liquid and enough milk to give a soft creamy mass when it boils up. Season with salt, pepper and a grating of nutmeg, which brings out the flavour. Away from the fire, beat in 2 egg yolks. Whip up the whites and fold them in gently with a little grated cheese. Three-quarters fill a well-greased soufflé dish. Sprinkle grated cheese over the top and bake in a steady oven until risen and browned. Serve without delay or the soufflé will flop.

DORIS LYTTON-TOYE 1949

SPINACH PUDDING

Spinach is sometimes prepared in Italy as a steamed pudding simply bound with thick white sauce and yolk of egg, then turned out on a hot dish and topped by sautéd liver in a brown sauce. If you enjoy spinach, then you should like it prepared this way.

Much more unusual is fresh spinach, chopped and sautéed with some sultanas and anchovies. Perhaps not to everybody's taste, still, out of the common, and definitely for the adventurous.

DORIS LYTTON-TOYE 1949

FRIED TOMATOES IN CREAM

Slice 4 firm tomatoes in ¾-inch slices. Sprinkle both sides with salt and pepper and a very little granulated sugar, then dip them in flour, both sides. Put them one by one into a frying pan containing plenty of hot butter and bacon drippings in equal quantities. Fry quickly to a golden brown, turn and brown the other side and place on a hot platter. Pour 1 cup of cream into the pan and stir until hot; season to taste. Pour over the tomatoes and sprinkle with fresh parsley chopped up finely.

JUNE PLATT 1939

STUFFED TOMATOES

Halve some large firm tomatoes: hollow them out, season and place a small nut of margarine in each. Set in a greased baking dish and cook for about 10-15 minutes in a moderate oven. Fill them with peas tossed in butter, or a *julienne* of carrots and beans.

DORIS LYTTON-TOYE 1946

TOMATOES MIGNONNE

Hollow out some tomatoes, firm and equal in size (save the insides for a sauce). Mix sufficient shrimps with mayonnaise to fill the tomato shells. Arrange them on lettuce leaves and tuck a spray of parsley in each tomato. Serve with good brown rolls, buttered and filled with mustard and cress.

DORIS LYTTON-TOYE 1946

PURÉE DE NAVETS

Peel and wash five or six turnips and cook them in boiling salted water; drain them well first, chop and then mash them well with a fork. Melt a good piece of butter in a frying pan, add the turnips, well seasoned, and fry them for a few minutes, stirring well. You may add a little Devonshire cream just before serving; it gives a pleasant mellow flavour to the turnips.

BOULESTIN 1924

PURÉE OF WATERCRESS

Wash and pick over carefully 10 small bunches of watercress, removing the coarse stems. Do this the day before you wish to serve the dish. Put them into salted boiling water and cook for 12 minutes. Drain and rinse in cold water and put through a sieve. Then leave in the refrigerator until the next day. When ready to use, pour off the juice which has formed. Melt 3 tablespoons of butter in a saucepan and add 1 tablespoon of flour. Cook for a minute without browning, then add the cress and 1¼ cups of cream. Add salt and pepper to taste and heat slowly, stirring meanwhile. When hot and well mixed, serve the purée garnished with crisp *croûtons*.

JUNE PLATT 1936

RAGOÛT LANDAIS

Cut in cubes two small vegetable marrows and two aubergines, season well and toss for a few minutes in butter. A little later add four sweet peppers, two tomatoes (also cut in cubes with seeds removed), and one head of garlic well pounded. Cook them for about twenty minutes, or less, according to the tenderness of the vegetable, and serve very hot.

BOULESTIN 1925

VEGETABLE COUSCOUS

12 oz couscous
2½ pts chicken stock
6 small leeks, cut in 1-inch slices
½ lb small carrots, cut in halves or quarters lengthwise
6 small turnips, quartered
3 sticks celery, cut in 1-inch chunks
½ lb sprouting broccoli, cut into short sprigs
6 small tomatoes, skinned
6 apricots, halved and stoned, or ½ lb dried apricots
6 oz shelled peas, fresh or frozen
1 packet saffron
Hot Sauce (optional – see below)

Place the couscous in a bowl and pour ¾ pint of water over it; stand for 10 minutes, by which time the water will have been absorbed. Put the stock in the bottom part of a *couscousière*, or into a deep pan, adding the leeks, carrots, turnips and celery. Bring to the boil. Put the couscous in the top part of the *couscousière*, or into a strainer lined with muslin, and suspend over the boiling stock, being careful it does not touch it. Cover and cook steadily for 30 minutes. Remove the top part, or strainer, and add the broccoli to the stock. Replace the couscous and cook for another 15 minutes. Add the whole tomatoes, apricots and peas. Replace the couscous and cook for another 5 minutes. Finally, add the saffron to the stock, cover and remove from the heat. Stand for 5 minutes before serving.

To serve, tip the couscous into a dish, breaking up any lumps. Pour the vegetables and their stock into a tureen or deep bowl and serve in soup plates, with soup-spoons and forks. If you like, serve a small bowl of Hot Sauce with it, to sprinkle over the couscous. Serves 4 to 5.

HOT SAUCE

2 tsp tomato purée
1 tsp Maggi Chilli Sauce, or several shakes Tabasco

Mix the tomato purée and the chilli sauce (or Tabasco) in a small bowl, and thin with 1-2 tablespoons of the hot vegetable stock to taste. Serve with the Vegetable Couscous.

ARABELLA BOXER 1983

MIXED ROOT VEGETABLE PURÉE

2 oz butter
12 oz carrots, thinly sliced
12 oz parsnips, thinly sliced
12 oz swedes, thinly sliced
¾ pt beef, game or chicken stock
sea salt and black pepper
3 tbsp chopped parsley

Melt the butter in a broad pan with a lid. Cook the three vegetables all together, stirring often, for 5 minutes. Then pour on the heated stock, adding salt and pepper, and bring to the boil. Cover the pan and simmer gently for 25 minutes, stirring now and then. When the time is up, drain the vegetables, reserving the juice – which is delicious – for a sauce or soup. Push the vegetables through the coarse mesh of a food mill, then reheat for a few moments in a clean pan, adding more salt and pepper as needed, and the chopped parsley. Serves 4.

ARABELLA BOXER 1983

Tessa Traeger 1976

PUDDINGS
AND DESSERTS

'Many a reputation for puddings has been built on recipes from a great-grandmother's cookery book,' according to *Vogue* in 1931. 'Jelly possets, frumities, syllabubs, elderflower fritters suggest themselves.' Today's puddings are more likely to be fruit salads, mousses, tarts and pies, or nursery puddings. 'If you make any pretence of catering to the masculine taste, then keep to simple straightforward fare and desserts of the fruit pie variety,' was the advice *Vogue* gave in 1934. 'No matter how cultured and refined they may become, or how far they've travelled from their football days, men's tastes practically never change.'

Above: John Minton 1947
Opposite: Tessa Traeger 1967

Most countries have a traditional pancake recipe: the French delight in their paper-thin crêpes; the Russians have smaller and fatter buckwheat blinis; the Swedes serve pancakes with thick blackcurrant jam; and the British remain loyal to their Shrove Tuesday variety with sugar and lemon. But Mary Frost Mabon, writing about 'Civilized Sweets' in 1935, warned against them: 'Pancakes are frankly difficult and not worth eating at all unless they are of paper thinness and succulent tenderness.' She continued, 'There have always been two kinds of sweet – good and bad.

Which is a matter for each person to decide. Spotted Dog, the bitterest of many childhood memories, seems to an adult palate the fine flower of a noble line of English puddings. For the purpose of the present-day hostess, sweets can be divided into two types – simple and grand. Among the former, fruit cooked or uncooked is perfect for an elaborate meal; stewed fruit or compote is the best or worst thing in the world. Try stewing whole green pears with honey or adding the end of a bottle of claret or burgundy to an ordinary compote of pears. Peaches certainly gain by being baked (not stewed), either without their skins or in the Italian way, in their skins with their stones replaced by a paste of ground blanched almonds and powdered sugar. Our summer, short as it is, has bequeathed to us the best compote in the world: raspberries and currants cooked separately and then mixed, served with junket, brown sugar and thick cream.'

The fruit compote may be just as delicious as it was 50 years ago – and our summers equally short – but it is closely matched by Arabella Boxer's Cold Mango Mousse with Passion Fruit, which takes advantage of the exotic fruits now found so readily in our markets.

ÎLE FLOTTANTE

Take four eggs, beat the whites to a stiff froth, add four tablespoonful of caster sugar, put this in a tin mould previously coated with caramel and cook in the oven, *au bain marie*, for about twenty minutes. Make a liquid custard by boiling some milk flavoured with vanilla and sweetened, and adding the yolks, cooking on a slow fire till it thickens. Turn the whites out of the mould into a hollow dish, and pour the sweet custard around it.

BOULESTIN 1924

POIRES AU CARAMEL

Get some good sound pears, peel them and leave them whole, put them standing in a saucepan, just covered with water; add sugar, half a vanilla pod and cook till soft on a moderate fire. When cooked, remove the pears carefully, add to the juice a glass of good port wine and let it reduce till it has the consistency of syrup; then remove it from the fire for a few minutes and add a tumblerful of fresh cream. Cook a few minutes, pour it over the pears and serve.

BOULESTIN 1924

CRÊPES SUZETTE

Put in a basin half a pound of flour, make a hole in the middle of the heap, add a pinch of salt, a little sugar, three eggs one after the other, a glass of rum, brandy or Curaçao and mix well. Add warm water little by little till it is very smooth; let this rest for three hours, then add a glass of fresh cream, mix well; it should have the consistency of cream.

Put in a frying pan a very small piece of butter; when it is getting brown put in quickly a tablespoonful of the batter, move the pan so that it covers the bottom (it should be very thin) and cook on a quick fire, tossing once.

Melt in a silver dish over a spirit lamp a piece, the size of a walnut, of the special butter you have prepared beforehand (butter well worked with caster sugar and the juice of an orange). Put in your pancake with a liqueur glassful of brandy and one of Curaçao, set it alight, *flambé* your pancake well, fold it in four and serve at once.

BOULESTIN 1924

PRUNEAUX AU WHISKY

Soak your prunes for at least twelve hours and cook them slowly in water, adding sufficient sugar. When they are quite soft and the water well reduced, add a pinch of cinnamon and a claret glassful of good whisky and cook for about twenty minutes more. The juice, of course, should have the consistency of syrup. This is one of the few sweets in which whisky can be used with great success; the taste of the prunes and the flavour of the whisky blend admirably. Devonshire cream goes well with this.

BOULESTIN 1924

BANANES CRÉOLE

Peel six bananas and put them in a fire-proof dish. Sprinkle over them three tablespoonsful of demerara sugar, the squeezed juice of one lemon and add three tablespoonsful of water. Bake until brown in a slow oven and half-way through the baking add a sherry glassful of Jamaica rum. Should you require more bananas, the other ingredients, including the water, should be increased proportionately. Serve the bananas with cream, whipped and flavoured with either rum or lemon.

BOULESTIN 1925

Alan Cracknell 1967

CRÊPES À L'ANIS

These pancakes are very different from any other pancakes, either French or English, and really delicious. Prepare the batter in a basin in the usual manner, but using for two pints of cold boiled milk, four eggs, and not quite a quarter of a pound of flour. Add the classical pinch of salt and two tablespoonsful of olive oil. As for the flavouring, *anis*, you can use powder of aniseed or, better still, two tablespoonsful of that liqueur called '*anis*' (not *anisette*) which in France has now taken the place of *absinthe*. Have your pan very clean and put in it very little oil and butter mixed, then some of the batter, which must be fairly liquid. Cook in the ordinary way but on one side only, sprinkling caster sugar meanwhile on the pancake. Then roll it in the pan and serve immediately. The result is a rich *crêpe* which is beautifully soft and perfumed.

BOULESTIN 1925

PLUM PUDDING

This is the recipe for the English 'pouding' in the old French book: take one pound of raisins and currants mixed, six eggs, a port glassful of rum, a quarter of a pound of suet (chopped), the same quantity of butter, one pound of flour, two glasses of milk, two ounces of sugar, the finely chopped peel of half a lemon, nutmeg, a little salt; also, to improve it, a few blanched almonds and small pieces of candied peel such as lemon, orange, lime, angelica and mixed spices. Mix with breadcrumbs so that it is a fairly stiff mixture. Sew it in a cloth and either boil it or steam it. It is usually served in slices well moistened with rum which you will set alight: '*le mets en devient plus délicat, outre le plaisir que ce feu de joie répand parmi les convives.*'

The sauce is made as follows: put in a bowl a small quantity of fine caster sugar, a tablespoonful of rum and butter just melted; beat well, adding more rum and more butter. All this to be done quickly, and when finished, should have the consistency of *sauce mayonnaise* — which seems to be a version of the famous 'brandy butter.'

BOULESTIN 1928

Fotiades 1961

CHOCOLATE SOUFFLÉ

Beat 4 egg yolks with ½ cup of sugar until the mixture is thick. Dissolve 2 ounces of chocolate in a double boiler with 3 tablespoons of milk. Add this to the egg yolks and sugar. When cool, mix with the beaten egg whites.

Butter a mould, fill it with the mixture and cook for 15 minutes in a medium oven. Before serving, dust the top with icing sugar. Serve with marshmallow sauce.

For the sauce, make a syrup by boiling sugar and water. Beat 2 egg whites until very, very stiff and add the syrup slowly, beating all the time. When the mixture is thick and sticky, flavour with a few drops of vanilla extract. Serves 6.

LADY COLEFAX 1934

GENTLEMAN'S PUDDING

PUDDING
6 oz butter
3 oz caster sugar
6 oz plain flour
3 eggs
3 tbsp raspberry jam
½ tsp bicarbonate of soda
SAUCE
2 egg yolks
1 tbsp sugar
1 glass sherry
jam
cream to serve

Beat the butter and sugar to a cream. Add the flour and eggs, one at a time; beat well, then add the jam and bicarbonate of soda. Butter a pan and steam the mixture for 2 hours.

To make the sauce, whip the egg yolks, sugar and sherry to a froth over hot water, add a little jam, and serve hot around the pudding. Any jam may be used, and cream may also be served.

LADY COLEFAX 1934

Laboureur 1926

PINEAPPLE CREOLE

Cut the top off a large pineapple and carefully lay it aside. Hollow the centre of the fruit, being careful not to break the outer skin. Moisten the interior with rum, sprinkle with caster sugar, and leave in the refrigerator for 1 hour. Cook 1 cup of rice in 2 pints of milk, sweetened, and flavoured with vanilla. When the rice is tender, cool and chill. Shred the pineapple and add it to the cold rice. Fill the shell with the mixture, add rum, and freeze. Replace the top of the fruit. Decorate with grape leaves.

HILDEGARDE VON LOEWENFELDT 1936

BANANA BRAZIL NUT CREAM PIE

Grind enough shelled but not blanched Brazil nuts in a nut grinder to produce 1½ cups of powdered nuts. Add to this 3 tablespoons of granulated sugar. Press this mixture over the bottom and sides of a flan dish. Next make a cream pudding in the following manner:

In the top of a double boiler mix together 3 tablespoons of cornflour with 4 tablespoons of sugar. Add gradually, stirring constantly, 1 cup of scalded milk. Stir while cooking until very thick (about 10 minutes), then thin with ½ cup of cream. When hot again, add the well-beaten yolks of 2 eggs. Cook slowly for 5 minutes longer. Remove from the heat and allow to cool. When cold, flavour with vanilla and fold in ½ cup of whipped cream.

Put a layer of half the cream mixture carefully over the surface of the nut and sugar mixture, then peel and slice 2 ripe bananas and lay them over the surface of the cream mixture. Cover the bananas with the rest of the cream and chill thoroughly for several hours. Just before serving, sprinkle the top with praline powder made by grinding and pounding glacéed Brazil nuts, then sifting them.

JUNE PLATT 1938

FRAISES CARDINAL

First hull some fine ripe strawberries. Powder them with sugar, icing sugar if possible, then sprinkle with lemon juice and place on ice. Pass some raspberries through a fine sieve, sweeten to taste and chill. Place the strawberries in a timbale or pretty crystal bowl, surrounded with crushed ice. Pour over the raspberry purée to mask them. If you have some almonds, scatter a few splinters of the blanched nuts on top.

DORIS LYTTON-TOYE 1947

Tessa Traeger 1977

CRÈME BRÛLÉE

Rinse out a pan with cold water; in it scald ½ pint of milk and ½ pint of evaporated milk with a pinch of salt. Whisk together 2 egg yolks, 2 eggs, one tablespoon of plain flour and 2 tablespoons of sugar. Slowly pour on the hot milk; stir smoothly. Return to the fire, then whisk until the mixture boils once. Remove from the heat and beat in 2 ounces of margarine, a few drops of vanilla and 1 drop of almond essence. Pour into a shallow dish. Make very cold.

Make the caramel about 1 hour or so before dinner otherwise it will lose its toffee-like quality – if it is chilled too much the caramel becomes liquid. In a spotlessly clean heavy pan, dissolve 3 tablespoons of sugar with one tablespoon of water over a low heat. Let it dissolve without stirring. When all the granules have disappeared, turn the heat up, and boil until the sugar becomes golden brown. Immediately spoon the caramel gently over the now cold *crème*; it hardens at once.

DORIS LYTTON-TOYE 1949

PETITS POTS DE CRÈME

Measure out enough milk to almost fill the number of ramekin dishes (1 per person) required. Allow an egg yolk to each pot of milk. Scald the milk with a vanilla pod or a few drops of essence. Infuse for 10 minutes. Whisk the egg yolks with sugar to taste; remove the vanilla pod and pour the milk on to the yolks, stirring. Strain and fill the pots, removing carefully any froth that rises to the top. Stand the pots in a *bain marie* of warm water and set in a very moderate oven. Cover with a tin whilst cooking. When they are just firm, in about 35-40 minutes, take them out of the water immediately. They should have a varnished appearance when properly done and are heavenly to eat when they are slightly chilled.

DORIS LYTTON-TOYE 1950

CASTLE PUDDINGS

Cream well 4 ounces of margarine in a warmed bowl; add 4 ounces of caster sugar and beat until white. Then add 2 eggs, one by one. Sieve 3½ ounces of plain flour and add to the creamed butter, sugar and eggs with ¾ ounce of ground almonds and a little grated lemon rind. Butter some castle pudding moulds; three-quarters fill them with the mixture. Shake down well. Bake in a moderate oven, Gas Regulo 4-5, 360°F, for 15 minutes until risen and firm. Turn out, dust with icing sugar. Serve butterscotch sauce separately.

To make the butterscotch sauce, put 6 ounces of demerara sugar in a strong pan with 2 ounces of margarine and set on a warm place on the stove until the sugar is properly melted (about 15 minutes) or the sauce will be gritty. Pour in ¼ pint of cream or evaporated milk and boil, stirring, till it becomes thick and coffee-coloured. Put in a hot sauceboat, for it hardens quickly. If it must wait, stand the pan over hot water.

DORIS LYTTON-TOYE 1951

Edward McKnight-Kauffer 1925

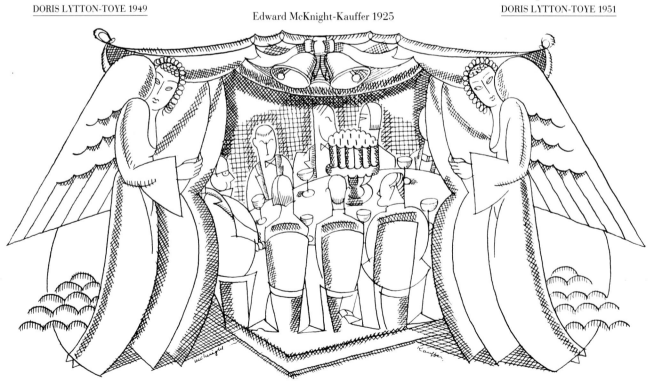

ENGLISH TRIFLE

1 sponge cake, slightly dry
raspberry jam
bananas, sliced
fresh peaches, sliced
maraschino liqueur
sherry
egg custard
whipped cream
angelica and glacé cherries to decorate

There should be a gentle English rain of sherry and maraschino on each and every layer of this trifle, especially the sponge cake. Line a huge crystal dish with sponge cake, spread thinly with raspberry jam, cover with a layer of sliced bananas and then a layer of peaches. Start again with sponge, repeat the fruit layers, and end with sponge. It never stops raining. Cover with the custard and put in a not too cold part of the refrigerator to mellow until the following day. Before serving, cover with huge blobs of cream, leaving space for the custard to show, and decorate with the angelica and cherries. Please don't use crystallized violets.

MRS ROLAND PENROSE 1952

HOLYROOD PUDDING

Into 1 pint of boiling milk stir 2 ounces of semolina, the same of sugar and the same of ratafia biscuits (or water biscuits) crushed to a fine crumb. Boil for 5 minutes, remove from the heat and stir in 3 egg yolks. Fold in the 3 whites, beaten stiff, turn into a greased pudding basin and steam for about 1 hour. Serve hot with almond sauce.

In a saucepan put 1 well-beaten egg with 1 tablespoon of sugar, 1 teacup of milk, 1 ounce of ground almonds and 1 tablespoon of sherry, or failing that, of orange flower water. Whip over a slow heat until thick, but do not boil.

LILY MACLEOD 1953

LEMON AND WHITE WINE CREAM

12 egg yolks
juice of 4 lemons
4 oz caster sugar
½ pt white wine

Beat the egg yolks. Place in the top of a double saucepan with the lemon juice, sugar and wine. Whisk over a moderate heat without stopping while the mixture thickens – this happens quite quickly. The cream must not boil so lift the top of the saucepan out of the water occasionally while you continue to whisk. Serve immediately. Enough for 6.

MAPIE DE TOULOUSE-LAUTREC 1961

FLAN DE LA DUCHESSE

2 pts milk
10 oz vanilla-flavoured caster sugar
1¼ lb macaroons
4 tbsp Cointreau
10 eggs
½ lb plain flour
½ lb butter
cream to serve

Boil the milk with the sugar and set aside to cool. Crush the macaroons into fine crumbs then put them into a bowl, pour the Cointreau over them and mix together thoroughly. Separate the yolks and whites of the eggs, putting each yolk into a container of its own.

Stir the milk little by little into the flour, then, when the mixture is perfectly smooth, put it into a saucepan and stir continuously over low heat for 10-15 minutes. Take the pan off the stove, stir in the butter, beat the mixture well, then add the yolks one by one, beating for 2-3 minutes between each addition. Add the macaroons and Cointreau and mix thoroughly. Whisk the egg whites until they are very firm, then fold them into the mixture lightly with an upward movement.

Roger de LaVererie 1929

Rinse two 7-inch diameter Charlotte moulds in cold water but do not dry them. Pour in the mixture, set the moulds in a baking tin of water and put in a medium oven for 45-60 minutes. Leave the flans to cool completely before unmoulding them and serve surrounded with cream.

FRANCINE 1961

COLD LEMON SOUFFLÉ

2 lemons
5 eggs
5 oz caster sugar

Squeeze the lemons and separate the yolks and whites of the eggs. Beat the yolks thoroughly with the sugar then stir in the lemon juice. Put this into the top of a double saucepan and stir while it thickens but do not let it boil. Take the pan off the stove.

Whisk the egg whites till very firm and fold them into the mixture. Turn into a fruit dish and set in the refrigerator to chill. Enough for 4.

MAPIE DE TOULOUSE-LAUTREC 1961

ORANGE ICE CREAM

3 oranges
4 eggs
8 egg yolks
10 oz caster sugar
1½ pts milk
1 pt double cream
8 tbsp Cointreau

Finely grate the rind of the oranges and put it into a basin with the juice of 1 orange, the eggs, egg yolks and sugar; whip until frothy. Bring the milk to the boil, then stir continuously while you add it, little by little, to the egg mixture. Put into the top of a double saucepan over low heat and continue to stir while the mixture thickens; do not boil. Cool. Whip the cream, then mix it into the egg mixture; add the Cointreau, mix again thoroughly and freeze. Serves 8.

MAPIE DE TOULOUSE-LAUTREC 1961

RASPBERRY BAVARIAN CREAM

1 × 10 oz packet frozen raspberries
juice of 1 lemon
2 tbsp gelatine
4 tbsp milk
2-4 tbsp sugar
2 egg yolks
½ pt double cream
1 cup crushed ice

Defrost the raspberries in a bowl with the lemon juice. Drain ¼ pint of the juices into a saucepan; heat to simmering point. Pour the hot juice into a blender. Add the gelatine and milk, cover and blend at high speed for 1 minute. Add the sugar, raspberries and egg yolks. Then blend at high speed for 5 seconds. Add the cream and crushed ice and blend until smooth. Pour into a mould and chill until set. Serves 4 to 6.

ROBERT CARRIER 1966

Tessa Traeger 1982

WHISKY BANANAS

9 bananas, peeled
3 tbsp butter
4½ tbsp sugar
4½ tbsp whisky

Sauté the whole bananas in butter with the sugar sprinkled thickly over them. Turn carefully. When the sugar begins to caramelize and the bananas are well cooked, heat the whisky in a saucepan. Set it alight and pour it over the bananas. Serve at once.

VERONICA MACLEAN 1969

GREEN GRAPES CARAMEL

3 lb green grapes
¼ pt water
½ lb sugar
a little green Chartreuse liqueur
single cream to serve

Fill 6 goblet-shaped glasses with carefully peeled and seeded white grapes. If you plunge the grapes into boiling water for a few seconds first, this makes the peeling process much quicker.

To make a caramel put the water and sugar into a heavy pan and shake or swirl it over a gentle heat until the sugar is quite dissolved, then turn up the heat and allow the sugar to boil, and boil on for about 3-4 minutes or until it turns a light nut brown. Remove from the heat and pour on to a metal tray or enamel plate or plates, as the caramel should be only ⅛ inch thick. When when cold and hard, break it up into small pieces with a hammer or mallet and sprinkle fairly thickly on top of the grapes. Add a few drops of the green Chartreuse liqueur and chill until it is time to serve. Serve the cream separately.

Variation: Oranges, carefully peeled so as to leave no pith and sliced in thin circles, can be used for this dish instead of grapes. The liqueur should be Grand Marnier or orange Curaçao.

VERONICA MACLEAN 1970

REGENCY PUDDING

CARAMEL
3 oz granulated sugar or pounded sugar lumps
2 tbsp water
a pan of cold water
LEMON CREAM
5 eggs
3 oz butter
3 oz sugar
juice and grated zest of 1 lemon
CARAMEL SAUCE
1 egg
¼ pt cream, warmed

Line a 2½-pint metal mould with caramel: boil the sugar and water in the mould over a moderate heat, swirling the syrup round until it finally goes golden, then toffee brown and begins to caramelize. When it does this, dip the mould at once into a pan of cold water for 2-3 seconds to cool it slightly, and then tilt the mould in all directions to film the sides with caramel. When the caramel has ceased to run, turn the mould over a plate.

For the lemon cream, separate the eggs and beat the yolks and other ingredients lightly over moderate heat until they become like thick cream. This is best done in a basin over a *bain marie*. Take away from the heat and allow to cool. Beat the 5 egg whites to a stiff froth and add to the yolk mixture when cool. Pour the lemon cream into the caramelized mould, cover with a plate and steam in a large saucepan of hot water, for about 45 minutes. The water round the mould must not boil, nor should it go higher than 210°F. Turn the pudding out on to a hot serving dish and pour hot caramel sauce round it. Serve whipped cream separately.

To make caramel sauce, beat the egg lightly, turn it into the warmed cream, and then into the now empty caramel mould. Continue beating while you reheat the mould. There will be plenty of caramel left in it to flavour the sauce.

VERONICA MACLEAN 1970

RØDGRØD MED FLØDE

1 lb 10 oz red currants
1 lb 10 oz raspberries
2½ pts water
vanilla pod
2 tbsp caster sugar
3 oz potato flour
blanched almonds
double cream to serve

Simmer the fruit and water with the vanilla pod, skimming the pan carefully and thoroughly so the juice is clear. Take off ¼ pint of the juice and put aside to cool. Sieve the remainder of the fruit through a fine sieve. Sweeten to taste and return the purée to the heat. When the purée boils, stir in the potato flour, dissolved in the reserved fruit juice, and immediately remove the pan from the heat. Continue stirring until the purée is thick and clear, then pour it into a dish. When it is almost set, decorate it with blanched almonds. Serve with whipped double cream.

VERONICA MACLEAN 1970

18TH CENTURY APPLE CREAM FLAN

6 oz shortcrust pastry, made with 4 oz plain
flour, 2 oz fat
4 large cooking apples
2 oz butter
2 tbsp caster sugar
grated rind of 1 small lemon
3 digestive biscuits, crushed into crumbs
¼ whole nutmeg, grated
2 tbsp brandy
3 egg yolks
2½ fl oz double cream

Preheat the oven to Gas Mark 4, 350°F. Roll out the pastry and line a lightly greased, 8-inch flan tin. Prick the base all over with a fork, and bake it for 20 minutes. Peel, core and slice the apples, then put them in a saucepan with 2 tablespoons of water and cook quickly until they are soft. Drain and empty the apples into a large mixing bowl and beat to a pulp, preferably using an electric hand-whisk.

While the apple pulp is still hot, beat in the butter and enough caster sugar to sweeten. Stir in the lemon rind, the biscuit crumbs, nutmeg and brandy. Mix thoroughly and leave to cool.

Meanwhile, whisk the egg yolks and then lightly whip the cream to thicken it very slightly (but not much). Stir the egg yolks into the cooled apple mixture then stir in the cream. Turn into the half-cooked pastry case and bake at Gas Mark 4, 350°F for 30 minutes. The flan can be served warm or chilled. Serves 6.

DELIA SMITH 1977

Lester Bookbinder 1966

BUTTERED APPLES

Bread fried in butter with cooked apples is one of the best-ever combinations. I like this dish even more than Apple Charlotte since it is less well known, and looks prettier. Serve it on a large platter.

1½ lb cooking apples
4 oz butter
3-4 tbsp sugar
5-6 slices dry white bread
½ pt double cream, whipped

Peel the apples and slice thickly. Melt 1 ounce of butter in a sauté pan and cook as many of the sliced apples as will fit comfortably in one layer. Add 1 tablespoon of sugar and fry gently, lifting and turning now and then, until soft. Then lift them out with a slotted spatula and keep warm while you cook a second batch of apples, adding more butter and sugar. While the apples are cooking, remove the crusts from the bread, and cut each slice into a round, allowing one for each person. When all the apples are done, add more butter to the pan and fry the rounds of bread, turning often, until golden on both sides. Lay them on a flat dish and spoon the sliced apples carefully on to each one. Pour over any remaining juice, and top each pile with a dollop of whipped cream. Serve as soon as possible; if preparing it slightly in advance, add the cold cream at the very last. Serves 5 to 6.

ARABELLA BOXER 1979

BAKED JAM ROLYPOLY

½ lb self-raising flour
4 oz shredded suet
4 tbsp jam, preferably raspberry or plum
cream or custard sauce to serve

Sift the flour and mix with the suet. Add just enough cold water to form a dough. Roll out on a floured sheet of greaseproof paper into a rectangle about 8 inches by

Denton Welch 1945

6 inches. Warm the jam slightly, and spread over the suet, up to 1 inch from the edges. Roll up gently using the paper to lift it with. Pinch the edges together. Lay the roll, paper and all, on a greased baking sheet and bake for 45 minutes at Gas Mark 4, 350°F. Lift off the paper on to a flat dish and serve hot, with cream or custard sauce. Serves 4 to 5.

ARABELLA BOXER 1979

EVE'S PUDDING

2 large Bramley apples
1½ oz granulated sugar
3 oz butter
3 oz caster sugar
4 oz self-raising flour
2 eggs
cream to serve

Peel and slice the apples and stew gently in a covered pan with just enough water to cover the bottom, and the granulated sugar. When soft, turn into a buttered 1½-pint soufflé dish. Blend the butter and caster sugar in a food processor. Add the flour and blend again briefly. Beat the eggs and pour through the lid while processing. Stop immediately all is amalgamated evenly. Spoon over the apples, being careful to cover them completely. (If making the sponge mixture by hand, cream the butter and sugar, then add the sifted flour and beaten eggs alternately, beating constantly.)

Bake for 30 minutes at Gas Mark 4, 350°F, until golden brown and puffy. Serve as soon as possible after baking, with a jug of thick cream.
Variation: Although it is not traditional, a most delicious variation is to add ½ pound of blackberries, either fresh or frozen (thawed), to the apples when stewing. Serves 5.

ARABELLA BOXER 1979

QUEEN OF PUDDINGS

½ pt milk
2 strips lemon peel
1 oz butter
4 oz caster sugar
2 oz soft white breadcrumbs
3 eggs, separated
3 tbsp raspberry jam
cream to serve

Put the milk in a pan with the lemon peel and bring slowly to the boil. Remove from the heat, cover the pan and leave for 10 minutes. Return to the heat, discard the lemon peel, and add the butter and 1 ounce of caster sugar. Stir until the butter and sugar have melted. Remove from the heat and stir in the breadcrumbs. Leave to cool for 10 minutes, then stir in the lightly beaten egg yolks. Pour into a well-buttered pudding dish and bake for 30 minutes at Gas Mark 3, 325°F. Take out of the oven and leave to cool slightly, turning the oven down to Gas Mark ½, 250°F. Warm the jam and spread it over the pudding. Whip the egg whites until stiff, and fold in the remaining 3 ounces of caster sugar to make a meringue. Spoon this over the jam, covering the pudding completely. Return to the cooler oven and bake for 30 minutes, or until the top of the meringue is firm and lightly coloured. This pudding can be served immediately, or kept warm for some time; it is also good cold. Serve with cream. Serves 4 to 5.

ARABELLA BOXER 1979

COLD MANGO MOUSSE WITH PASSION FRUIT

3 limes
3 tbsp caster sugar
5 tbsp water
1½ packets gelatine
2 large ripe mangoes
5 passion fruit
2 oz *fromage blanc*
½ lb green grapes, or 1 mango, or 4 kiwi fruit

Pare the rind of the limes and put it in a small pan with the sugar and water. Bring to the boil and cook gently until the sugar has melted, then turn off the heat, cover the pan, and stand for 10 minutes. Then lift out the rind with a slotted spoon and reheat the syrup. When almost boiling, remove from the heat and shake in the gelatine. Leave to dissolve, then stir in.

Cut the mangoes in pieces and put in the food processor. Cut the passion fruit in half, scoop out the insides, and add to the mangoes. Squeeze the juice of the limes and add. Process briefly, then add the *fromage blanc* and process again, until smoothly blended. Pour in the gelatine through a strainer, process, then pour into small moulds and chill for several hours, or overnight.

Turn out on individual plates to serve, with a garnish of green grapes, peeled, seeded and sliced. Alternatively, decorate with small slices of fresh mango, or semi-circular slices of kiwi fruit.

I like the black seeds of the passion fruit showing through the translucent mousse, but if you do not like them, you can pass the fruit purée through a coarse sieve after processing, before adding the *fromage blanc*. Serves 4 to 6.
ARABELLA BOXER 1985

GINGER APPLE CRUMBLE

2 lb cooking apples, peeled and sliced
4 tbsp granulated sugar
2 tbsp lemon juice
2 tbsp water
custard sauce or whipped cream to serve
CRUMBLE
4 oz plain flour, sifted
1 tbsp ground ginger
2 oz butter, cut in small pieces
2 oz light brown sugar

Pile the apples in a buttered baking dish, sprinkle with sugar, and add lemon juice and water. Sift the flour with the ginger into a bowl. Rub in the butter, as if making pastry, and mix in the sugar. Spread over the apples, level off with the back of a spoon, and bake for about 40 minutes at Gas Mark 4, 350°F, until the top is lightly coloured. Serve warm, about 1 hour after cooking, with custard sauce or whipped cream. Serves 4 to 6.
ARABELLA BOXER 1985

CAPPUCCINO ICE

This is a low-fat version of a delicious ice cream I ate often on holiday in Rhode Island, USA.

2 eggs
2 egg yolks
2 tbsp caster sugar
2 tsp instant coffee granules
¼ pt double cream
½ pt strong black coffee, freshly made and chilled
¼ pt mild yoghurt
1½ oz bitter chocolate

Beat the eggs and yolks with the sugar and coffee granules. Heat the cream until almost boiling, then pour on to the eggs, beating continuously. Stir over hot water for 6-8 minutes, until slightly thickened, then cool quickly by standing in a sink half full of cold water. Stir often while it cools to prevent a skin forming. When it has reached room temperature, blend in a food processor with the liquid coffee and yoghurt. Freeze in an ice cream making machine. Meanwhile, cut the chocolate into small chips and shavings, using a small sharp knife. When the coffee ice is half frozen, stir in the chocolate chips and continue as before. Serves 4 to 5.

Note: For a richer ice, more like the original, use an extra ¼ pint of double cream and omit yoghurt. Increase the coffee granules to 4 teaspoons.
ARABELLA BOXER 1987

Pierre Brissaud 1930

Tessa Traeger 1977

CAKES, BISCUITS AND BREADS

Exiles, foreigners and novelists speak nostalgically of the delights of an English tea party – the firelit room, the gleam of silver, hot buttered toast, scones and strawberry jam. Afternoon tea is a peculiarly British habit and especially adapted to the climate, with toasted tea buns by the fireside in winter, cucumber sandwiches and Earl Grey tea on the lawn in summer.

'Tea always seems to produce sociability, cheerfulness and vivacity. There is an air of comfort and home which hovers over the tea table, one which the more formal dinner table can never present,' wrote Boulestin. 'What more welcome and cheering sight can meet our eye on the return from a long journey or a distant excursion, or from a strongly contested battle on the croquet lawn, than the hissing, steaming urn, the array of cups and saucers, the sociable genial air, which the tea table invariably presents.' Although Boulestin was frequently critical of the British attitude to food – 'the idea, unfortunately prevalent in England, that you can cook by the clock and thermometer is utterly ridiculous' – tea was the one meal that he really appreciated.

An anonymous writer in 1920 considered

Above: John Minton 1947
Opposite: Daniel Jouanneau 1979

there was more to tea than the food: 'Of all hours of the day perhaps teatime is the most fraught with pleasurable impressions and charming intimacies. It comes at such a cosy pause in the energies of life. Socially, as every woman knows, the tea hour is invaluable. But it is only the woman of taste who realizes what scope and possibilities lie in the tea table for expressing her own delicate personality, for gently making evident any aesthetic, original or discriminating qualities she may possess.'

What to eat at teatime? Cecil Beaton had a point when he remarked, 'It is astonishing how limited one's choice of food is made for one. Why, for instance, only hot cross buns, if one likes their spiciness, at Easter? Why only wedding cake, if one likes its richness and china exterior, at wedding nuptials?' Is it because they are occasional treats that they seem so special?

Certainly teatime is special; whether it's nursery tea (gingerbread and flapjacks), fireside tea (singin' hinny and hot buttered scones) or family tea (lemon sponge and chocolate chip cookies), even the adjectives that go with it are so pleasing . . . fragrant, warming, refreshing tea.

PAIN DE GÊNES

This excellent cake will be useful either for tea or served with a *crème*. Peel half a pound of almonds (and five or six bitter ones), pound them well; add four eggs, one at a time, two tablespoonsful of ground rice, a piece of butter the size of an egg (it is advisable to cut it in small pieces) and about three tablespoonsful of caster sugar. Mix well together, then add a sherry glassful of *Kirschwasser* and mix well again. Prepare a tin lined with buttered paper – the flat kind for open tarts being the best shape – put in your batter and cook it in a hot oven for about twenty-five minutes; let it get cold before you take it out of the tin.

BOULESTIN 1924

WEDDING CAKE

3 lb butter

3 lb sugar

¾ oz mace

1 tsp grated nutmeg

1 oz allspice

½ oz ground cinnamon

½ oz ginger

9 eggs

3 lb plain flour

1 lb finely chopped almonds

2 lb mixed peel

3 lb currants

1 lb raisins

1 large cup brandy

1 small cup old ale

lemon juice

ALMOND PASTE

12 oz ground almonds

12 oz very fine caster sugar

1-2 egg yolks

12 oz icing sugar

ROYAL ICING

2 lb icing sugar

1 dessertspoon or more of lemon juice

2-3 egg whites (or more if required)

Grease the baking tins. Line on both the sides and at the bottom with 4 layers of greased paper. Make a dough of flour

Denton Welch 1946

and water and spread thinly on the paper and cover again with two or three layers of greased paper. This is essential to prevent burning. Stand the tins on another baking tin.

Cream the butter, sugar and spices; add the eggs one by one, and 1 cup of flour with each. Beat well each time. Beat for at least 30 minutes before adding the almonds and fruit. Add the brandy and ale and lemon juice last. Stir well. Place in the tins and smooth the top of the mixture with a little milk. Bake for 4 hours in a moderate oven. Stand for 45 minutes before turning out. Leave at least 2 days before icing.

To make the almond paste, work all the ingredients together. Spread on the cake. This should be done at least 12 hours before the royal icing is put on.

To make royal icing, sieve the icing sugar, add the lemon juice and the unbeaten egg whites. Work in the sugar and beat for at least 20 minutes with a wooden spoon. It will not be a good white unless beaten very hard. When sufficiently soft to spread, apply with a broad-bladed knife dipped occasionally in cold water. Before spreading, a drop of blue may be stirred in to ensure a shiny whiteness. When spread on the cake, leave for 24 hours to harden. The cake can be decorated with the same mixture forced through a bag. Makes 1 large cake or 2 small ones to be set in tiers.

1933

WALNUT MOCHA CAKE

Cream ½ cup of butter with 1 cup of sugar. Add the well beaten yolks of 2 eggs and ½ cup of milk. Add 1½ cups of plain flour with 2 teaspoons of baking powder and a pinch of salt. Mix well and add a teaspoon of vanilla and 1 cup of broken and lightly floured walnuts. Fold in carefully the stiffly beaten whites of 2 eggs and pour into a well-buttered loaf tin. Bake the cake in a moderate oven for about 40 minutes or until a fork inserted comes out clean.

Ice when cold with frosting made by creaming ¼ cup of butter and gradually adding 1 cup of icing sugar and ¼ cup of cocoa mixed together. Cream well, then soften with hot, very strong, black coffee and vanilla mixed together. If it should get too thin, thicken with more sugar and cocoa. Spread unevenly on the cake and decorate with walnut halves.

JUNE PLATT 1935

WHITE PLUM CAKE

Blanch ½ pound of almonds; reserve 12 of them for decorating the cake and shred the rest with a sharp knife. Scald ½ pound of sultanas and soak them until plump; then dry well. Cream 6 ounces of butter with 1 cup of granulated sugar, add the beaten yolks of 4 eggs and beat well. Sift 2 cups of plain flour with 1 teaspoon of baking powder, ½ teaspoon of grated nutmeg and ¼ teaspoon of salt. Put 1 teaspoon of vanilla and ½ teaspoon of lemon extract in ¼ cup of cold water. Add it alternately with the flour to the butter and egg mixture. When well mixed, add the sultanas and shredded almonds, which have been lightly floured, and 1 cup of shredded coconut. Beat the egg whites until stiff, then fold into the cake mixture. Pour into a well-greased and lined oblong tin and bake in a moderate oven for about 1 hour. Decorate with the reserved almonds.

JUNE PLATT 1935

PLUMKAGER

Plumkager, in spite of its name, has no plums in it, but takes its name from the fact that it is a favourite accompaniment to fresh and preserved plums.

Blend 1⅓ cups of sugar with 1 cup of butter, mix until smooth, and add 5 eggs, one at a time, stirring vigorously. Then add 3 cups of plain flour, sifted with a scant teaspoon of baking powder and, lastly, stir in ¼ cup of currants (softened in water) and 1 teaspoon of grated lemon peel. Bake in an oblong tin in a moderate oven for 1¼ hours. When cold, slice and serve.

ELIZABETH BAAGOE 1935

A BABY'S FIRST BIRTHDAY CAKE

First grate the rind of 1 lemon. Next squeeze and strain the juice of 1½ lemons. Add the rind to the juice and add ½ cup of cold water. Now separate the whites from 6 cold eggs. Beat the yolks until light and creamy. Add ¾ cup of granulated sugar and continue beating until very light. Now take another beater and beat the whites to which you have added a pinch of salt, until quite stiff. Fold in ¾ cup of granulated sugar, add the lemon juice and water and beat with the rotary beater for 5 minutes. Fold the whites and yolks together, then fold in lightly 1½ cups of sifted cake flour. Pour into a large ungreased round cake tin. Bake in a slow oven (about Gas Mark 2, 300°F) for 50 or 60 minutes. When cooked, invert the cake tin on to a cake rack so that air may pass under it while cooling.

Ice with twice-cooked icing tinted a very pale pink. Boil 1½ cups of granulated sugar moistened with ½ cup of water, until it forms a soft ball in cold water. In the meantime, beat the whites of 2 eggs until stiff but not dry. Add the cooked syrup slowly to the whites, beating with a rotary beater, then add ⅛ tea-

Norman Eales 1965

spoon of cream of tartar, 1 teaspoon of vanilla and a drop or two of red colouring and beat with a spoon until smooth and thick. Put the bowl over boiling water and stir until the spoon makes a grating noise on the bottom of the bowl. Remove from the heat and pour it on to the sponge cake, letting it run over the sides and smoothing it on with a silver knife. When it has dried enough to form a light crust, decorate it with one pink candle in the centre, in a little blue rose.

Put a delicate border of white ornamental icing round the top edge and a heavier one round the bottom. Polka dot the top of the cake with tiny pink rosebuds, and the sides with forget-me-nots, made by squeezing 5 little dots of pale blue icing out in a circle touching each other just slightly, leaving a little hole in the centre into which a dot of yellow colouring can be dropped.

JUNE PLATT 1936

HONEY CAKE

2 eggs
2 heaped tbsp granulated sugar
6 tbsp warm liquid honey (or melted thick
honey)
½ tsp ground cinnamon
6 oz self-raising flour
1 oz raisins
1-2 oz chopped nuts

Beat the eggs and sugar over a pan of hot water for about 5 minutes. Mix in the honey and cinnamon. Add the flour, then the raisins and nuts. Put the mixture into a well-greased tin and bake in a moderately hot oven (Gas Mark 5, 375°F) for 1 hour. Leave for a while to cool then turn out.

If you prefer to make small cakes they take about 30 minutes to bake. They really should be eaten within a day or two as they do not keep moist as long as a larger cake does.

LILLA GIBSON TAYLOR 1944

LEMON SPONGE

Cream 2 ounces of butter or margarine; then cream into it 4 ounces of sugar. Beat in 1 egg and 4 ounces of plain flour, previously sieved with 1 teaspoon of baking powder. Add orange or lemon rind, a little vanilla and a little milk to mix to a dropping consistency. Bake in a greased and floured tin in a moderate oven for about 25 minutes. Allow a longer time for baking in a high tin.

To make the lemon glacé icing, over a low flame, dissolve 4 ounces of sugar in 3 dessertspoons of water. When it is clear, allow just to boil up in the pan. Pour into a basin, add ½ coffee-spoon of tartaric acid, and beat till it turns white. Pour quickly over the cake (enough for an ordinary-sized sandwich cake).

DORIS LYTTON-TOYE 1946

June Platt 1935

CHOCOLATE ALMOND CAKE

3 eggs
5 oz margarine
5 oz caster sugar
2 oz chocolate, melted
½ tsp ground cinnamon
5 oz ground almonds (unblanched)
a little jam
ICING
1 tbsp black coffee
2 tbsp water
4 oz sugar
3 oz chocolate
1 heaped tsp margarine

Separate the egg yolks from the whites. Cream together the margarine and sugar, then gradually add the egg yolks, melted chocolate and cinnamon. Finally fold in the stiffly beaten egg whites and ground almonds. Pour into a greased and floured cake tin (rectangular, if possible) and bake in a moderate oven (Gas Regulo 4, 350°F) for about 1 hour. Remove from the oven and leave to cool. Melt a little jam in a saucepan and spread over the top and sides of the cake.

To make the icing, put the coffee and water in a saucepan and heat gently. Stir in the sugar and chocolate, add the margarine and blend well over a low flame. Remove from the heat, stir briskly and spread over the cake.

PETER PIRBRIGHT AND GRETEL BEER 1949

NUSSTORTE

Separate the yolks and whites of 3 eggs. Keep 1 yolk for the cream. Sift together 5 ounces of self-raising flour and 1 teaspoon of baking powder. Cream 4 ounces of margarine with 4 ounces of sugar until light and fluffy. Add the 2 egg yolks and continue stirring. Whisk the egg whites until stiff and gently fold them into the creamed mixture, then gradually sprinkle in the flour and baking powder, 1 dessertspoon of cocoa powder and 1 heaped tablespoon of ground nuts. Bake in a greased and floured cake tin in a moderate oven (Gas Regulo 4, 350°F) for about 45 minutes. A knitting needle inserted in the cake should come out clean. It is most important that you should resist the temptation to open the oven door for the first 20 minutes after putting in the cake. When the cake is baked, take it out of the tin and place it upside down on a rack. Cover with a cloth and leave to cool.

To prepare the cream, put ½ cup of milk and 1 egg yolk in a bowl and beat over steam until thick. Remove from the fire and continue whisking until cool. Cream 2 ounces of margarine with 2 ounces of sugar and gradually, by the spoonful, add the egg-milk cream. When well blended, fold in 2 heaped tablespoons of ground nuts and stir in 1 teaspoon of rum. Cut the cake into 3 layers, spread the bottom layer with jam, and the second one with the cream. Warm a little jam in a saucepan and spread over the top and sides of the cake. Leave to dry for a few minutes.

Beat the lumps out of ½ cup of icing sugar and gradually work in a little lemon juice, until the mixture is of a thick spreading consistency. Spread over the top and sides of the cake and decorate with halved nuts and glacé cherries. The icing will take a little time to harden, so be careful not to touch the gâteau for at least 3 minutes.

PETER PIRBRIGHT AND GRETEL BEER 1949

PUNCH GÂTEAU

3 eggs
6 oz sugar
3 oz self-raising flour
1 dessertspoon cocoa
½ cup orange juice
½ cup rum
a little jam
ICING
¾ cup icing sugar
pink culinary colouring

Separate the egg yolks and whites. Beat together the yolks and 4 ounces of the sugar until creamy and pale yellow in colour. Fold in the stiffly beaten egg whites and finally the flour. Put aside 2 dessertspoons of this mixture. Bake the remainder in a greased and floured cake tin at Gas Regulo 5, 375°F, for about 25-30 minutes. Divide the cake mixture which has been put aside into two equal parts. Mix one half with the cocoa and bake both the mixtures in greased and floured patty tins at Gas Regulo 6, 400°F. When baked, turn the cake on to a wire rack and remove the two small 'cakes' from the patty tins. Cut the small cakes into cubes and arrange in a pie dish. Dissolve the remaining sugar in the orange juice and bring to the boil. Add the rum and quickly pour over the cake cubes. Cover with a plate (which should be slightly smaller than the pie dish) and weigh down. Leave overnight.

Cut the cake in half and arrange the 'punch' mixture on one half. Cover with the cake top. Spread a little warmed jam over the gâteau. Cover with pink icing.

Sift the icing sugar and blend to a smooth paste with a little cold water. Add one drop of pink colouring.

PETER PIRBRIGHT AND GRETEL BEER 1949

BISKOTTEN-TORTE

5 oz ground walnuts
½ cup hot milk
5 oz butter
5 oz sugar
5 egg yolks
36 finger biscuits
a little cold milk
a few drops of rum
whipped cream, grated nuts and grated chocolate to decorate

Place the ground nuts in a bowl, pour over the hot milk and leave for 30 minutes. Cream the butter and sugar; gradually add the egg yolks and nuts. In a well-buttered cake tin, arrange alternate layers of finger biscuits (previously dipped in milk to which a few drops of rum have been added), and the nut cream, starting and finishing with a layer of finger biscuits. Cover with a well-buttered plate. Place a weight on top and put in a refrigerator or cool place. Leave for at least 4 hours before turning out. Decorate with whipped cream and sprinkle the top with grated nuts and chocolate.

PETER PIRBRIGHT AND GRETEL BEER 1950

FROTHY ORANGE CAKE

1 large orange
1 tbsp cream
5 tbsp milk
2 oz butter
2 oz caster sugar
2 oz flour
4 eggs

Grate the rind of the orange on the finest grater and put it into a small bowl with the cream. Heat up the milk just short of boiling. Melt the butter in a saucepan over a very low heat and, directly it has melted, add the sugar and stir with a wooden spoon for 1-2 minutes. Stir in the flour, the cream and rind and the milk, stirring continuously while the mixture thickens. Take the saucepan off the stove and let it cool while you prepare the eggs.

Separate the yolks and whites and whip the whites till very stiff. Beat the yolks, one at a time, into the cooled mixture, then fold in the whites lightly with an upward movement.

Grease a Charlotte mould, turn the mixture into it, and put it in a *bain marie*. Set in a slow oven for 30 minutes. Let the cake get tepid before you unmould it and serve as it is or leave to get cold. Enough for 4.

MAPIE DE TOULOUSE-LAUTREC 1961

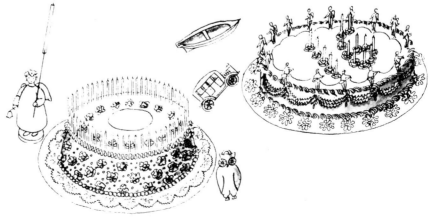

June Platt 1936

SACHER TORTE

5 oz vanilla chocolate, grated
1 tbsp water
5 oz butter
6 eggs
5 oz caster sugar
5 oz plain flour, sifted
apricot glaze
chocolate icing

Put the chocolate and water to melt in a warm oven. Stir well and add the butter. Beat all together until well combined. Separate the yolks and whites of the eggs. Add the yolks of the eggs and the sugar to the chocolate mixture, and beat until frothy. Then add alternately the flour and stiffened, beaten egg whites (folding in with a metal spoon). Place in a sandwich tin, and bake at Gas Mark 5, 375°F. When cooked, spread the cake with the apricot glaze, and ice with chocolate icing.

NELL HEATON 1952

GÂTEAU BASQUE

1 lb plain flour
½ oz yeast
½ lb butter
½ lb caster sugar
3 egg yolks
1 liqueur glass brandy
juice of ½ lemon
FILLING
½ lb caster sugar
3 egg yolks
5 tbsp plain flour
1 pt milk

Make the dough the day before it is needed. Sieve the flour into a bowl and mix in the yeast. Make a well in the middle and put in the butter, softened but not melted, the sugar, egg yolks, brandy and lemon juice. Mix thoroughly with your hands, and work the dough until it no longer sticks to your fingers.

To make the filling, put the sugar, egg yolks and flour into a bowl and stir (do not whisk) until thoroughly mixed. Bring the milk to the boil and add, little by little, the sugar, egg and flour mixture. Bring to the boil, stirring all the time to prevent sticking. Then turn the mixture out and leave to cool.

Line a flan tin with buttered grease-proof paper, then divide the dough into 2 equal parts and roll each one into a circle sufficiently large to overlap the tin all round. Put one piece of dough into the tin, and if it tears (it is very fragile) press the torn edges together with the tips of your fingers. Put the filling into the case, cover with the other piece of dough and seal by rolling the pieces together with your fingers. Cook for 30 minutes in a hot oven, but if the tart is colouring too quickly, lower the heat.

MAPIE DE TOULOUSE-LAUTREC 1961

CROQUEMBOUCHE

Translated, this eye-taking confection is simply choux pastry profiteroles filled with cream and coated with caramel.

CHOUX PASTRY
4 oz butter
salt
6 oz plain flour, sifted
5 eggs
1 egg yolk
PASTRY CREAM
4 eggs
6 tbsp plain flour
6 tbsp caster sugar
1 heaped tbsp powdered gelatine
½ pt milk
¼ pt whipped cream flavoured with rum or vanilla
CARAMEL SYRUP
12 oz granulated sugar
1 coffee-spoon cream of tartar

Put ½ pint of water into a heavy saucepan with the butter and salt and bring slowly to the boil, stirring all the time. Add the sifted flour, lower the heat and stir on until the mixture leaves the sides of the pan. Take the pan off the stove, stir on for 1-2 minutes while it cools slightly, then add the whole eggs one by one, beating for 2-3 minutes between each addition. Finally, beat in the yolk. Using a plain tube in a forcing bag, pipe the mixture on to a greased baking sheet in equal-sized rounds not larger than ¾ inch in diameter – you should have about 64 profiteroles. Bake in a fairly hot oven for 30 minutes and then in lower heat until the profiteroles are golden brown and firm (about 10 minutes). Cool, then fill with pastry cream piped through a hole in the base.

For the pastry cream, separate the yolks and whites of the eggs and set 2 of the whites aside (the remaining 2 whites can be used for meringue). Put the egg yolks, flour and sugar into a basin and whisk until the mixture is frothy. Stir in the gelatine. Bring the milk to the boil, let it cool for 1-2 minutes, then stir it gradually into the mixture. Put this back into the milk pan and heat up to just short of boiling, stirring all the time. Remove the pan from the stove and let the mixture get quite cold. Beat the 2 egg whites very stiff, fold them into the cream, then fold this into the cold egg mixture.

To make the caramel syrup, put both ingredients into a heavy pan with ½ pint of cold water, bring very slowly to the boil then boil on until the syrup is deep gold. Take the pan off the stove and set it over ice to prevent the caramel darkening. Dip the tops of the profiteroles in the caramel and leave to set.

Arrange the profiteroles, after they have set, in a mound or in separate dishes as you prefer.

CHRIS HASKETT-SMITH 1961

Tessa Traeger 1976

LEMON FOUR-QUARTERS

4 oz plain flour

1 tsp baking powder

2 lemons

4 oz butter

4 oz caster sugar

2 eggs

1 tsp hot water

6 oz icing sugar

Mix together the flour and the baking powder. Squeeze the lemons. Put the butter in a warm place to soften. When soft, cream the butter with the caster sugar until perfectly smooth, then add 1 egg and beat the mixture for several minutes. Add the second egg and beat for several minutes more. Stir in 1 tablespoon of lemon juice then sieve in the flour and mix.

Turn the mixture into a greased cake tin and bake in a fairly hot oven for about 30 minutes. Leave the cake in the tin until cold. While it is cooling, stir the remaining lemon juice and 1 teaspoon of hot water into the icing sugar, and beat until it is smooth. Turn out the cake and ice it. Enough for 4.

MAPIE DE TOULOUSE-LAUTREC 1961

SCOTCH COFFEE CAKE

1½ oz caster sugar

4 eggs

2 tbsp whisky

4 oz plain flour

2 tbsp instant coffee

2 oz butter, melted

2 oz chopped walnuts

ICING

2 oz butter

14 oz icing sugar

1 small egg, beaten with 1 tbsp whisky

walnut halves to decorate

Put the sugar, eggs and whisky into a basin over a pan of hot water, whisk until thick and light. Remove the basin from the pan and continue whisking for 2 minutes. Sieve the flour and coffee

'Black coffee can be used instead of milk for mixing fruit cakes. It improves the flavour and darkens the cake.'

PAMELA PAIN

together and fold into the mixture with the melted butter and walnuts. Turn into 2 greased 7-inch sandwich tins. Bake for 20-25 minutes at Gas Regulo 4, 350°F. Turn out and leave till cool.

To ice, cream the butter and gradually beat in the icing sugar with the egg beaten with the whisky. Sandwich the cakes together with part of the icing, spread the rest on top and decorate with walnut halves in a ring.

ELIZABETH MITCHELL 1965

WALNUT AND LEMON MERINGUE CAKE

4 egg whites

9 oz caster sugar

5 oz walnuts

½ pt thick cream

4 heaped tbsp lemon curd

Set the oven at Gas Mark 5, 375°F. Line the bottoms of 2 sandwich tins with rounds of greaseproof paper. Brush the paper and sides of the tins with a little oil or melted lard. Whisk the egg whites until stiff, then add half the sugar. Beat again until stiff. Beat in the rest of the sugar and keep whisking until the meringue is so stiff that it will not flow at all, but holds its shape rigidly. Chop 4 ounces of the nuts roughly, and stir into the mixture. Divide between the 2 sandwich tins, smoothing the tops slightly. Bake for 40 minutes. Turn the cakes out on a wire rack, and peel off the paper. Whip the cream and mix half of it with the lemon curd. Sandwich the cakes with this. Use the rest of the whipped cream and nuts for decoration.

PRUE LEITH 1977

FRUIT CAKE

This is an old Scottish recipe; the cakes can be iced if wished, but I like them as they stand. They can be cut in half for packing into small hampers, or left whole. Wrap tightly in foil after cooling.

½ lb butter
½ lb soft brown sugar
2 tbsp treacle
4 medium eggs
12 oz flour, sifted
1 tsp baking powder
1½ tsp ground cloves
1½ tsp ground cinnamon
1½ tsp ground nutmeg
4 oz ground almonds
½ lb currants
½ lb raisins
½ lb sultanas
⅛ pt milk
juice of 1 orange

Cream the butter, either in a food processor or by hand, and beat in the sugar. Stir in the treacle, after warming it very slightly to thin it. Break in the eggs one at a time, folding in a spoonful of the sifted flour after each egg to prevent it separating. When all the eggs are incorporated, stir the baking powder and the spices into the remaining flour and fold into the mixture. Stir in the ground almonds, currants, raisins and sultanas. Lastly, stir in the milk and orange juice.

Have two bread tins, measuring roughly 8 by 4 inches, buttered and lined with buttered greaseproof paper. Divide the mixture between them and bake for 2½ hours at Gas Mark 3, 325°F. After 1 hour, lay a piece of foil loosely over the tins to prevent the cakes getting burnt.

ARABELLA BOXER 1981

VANILLA RINGS

Knead together (do not stir) 2 cups of plain flour with 1 egg and 1 cup of softened butter. To this, add 1 cup of sugar and ½ teaspoon of vanilla essence, and set the dough aside in the refrigerator for an hour. Use no more flour, but form tiny rings of the batter, either with your fingers or by forcing through a mincing machine, using the largest appliance on the machine. Sprinkle the tops with chopped almonds and bake in a moderate oven until light brown.

ELIZABETH BAAGOE 1935

BANANA WAFFLES

Sift 2 cups of plain flour with 3 teaspoons of baking powder and 1 teaspoon of salt. Melt 6 tablespoons of butter. Separate the yolks of 2 eggs. Beat the whites stiff, then beat the yolks well with the same beater. Add 1¼ cups of milk to the yolks, beat well, then add the flour all at once. Remove any lumps with a beater. Add the melted butter, stir, then fold in the egg whites. At the last minute, thinly slice a small banana, sprinkle with caster sugar and add to the mixture. Bake at Gas Regulo 5, 375°F.

JUNE PLATT 1938

LEMON WAFERS

4 oz lard and margarine, mixed
3 oz sugar
½ lb flour (4 oz plain, 4 oz self-raising)
a pinch of salt
milk to mix
½ tsp lemon juice

Cream the fat and sugar. Sift the flour with a pinch of salt and add to the fat and sugar alternately with some milk, keeping the mixture fairly dry. Add the lemon juice. Roll out very thinly and cut in small rounds. Bake in a medium oven till golden.

PAMELA PAIN 1942

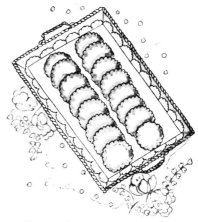

Above and opposite: June Platt 1935

CIDER BISCUITS

2 oz margarine or butter
4 oz plain flour
1 egg
2 tsp cider
2 tbsp jam

Rub the fat into the flour till it is the consistency of breadcrumbs. Mix in the egg, cider and jam, and knead well. Roll out thinly, cut into rounds, and bake in a moderate oven for about 15 minutes.

The flavour may be varied by adding lemon essence or grated rind of lemon or orange. Another method is to use a sprinkling of rolled oats for decorating.

NELL HEATON 1944

GINGERBREAD

½ lb plain flour
6 tbsp treacle
1 tsp ground ginger
1 tsp bicarbonate of soda
1 small cup tepid water
1 oz sultanas

Mix the flour and slightly warmed treacle in a basin. Stir the ginger and bicarbonate of soda into the water; mix well with the flour and treacle; add the sultanas. Pour into a greased tin and bake in a moderate oven for about 45 minutes. Cut into small squares.

LILLA GIBSON TAYLOR 1944

FLAPJACKS

4 oz margarine
3 heaped tbsp granulated sugar
3 tbsp syrup or treacle, warmed
½ lb rolled oats or flaked barley

Melt the margarine and mix well with the sugar in a saucepan; add syrup or treacle and then the oats or barley. Spread the mixture ½-inch thick in a shallow tin and bake until brown in a moderate oven for about 30 minutes. Cut into slices in the tin.

LILLA GIBSON TAYLOR 1944

COFFEE CRUMBLE

Mix and sift 2 cups of plain flour, 3 teaspoons of baking powder and ½ teaspoon of salt. Add 2 ounces of sugar. With 2 knives cut in 2 ounces of margarine till fine as meal. Beat 1 egg into 1 cup of milk, and stir into the flour mixture till you have a soft dough. Spread this in a greased shallow pan, ½-inch thick.

Cream 3 tablespoons of margarine till soft. In a separate bowl, mix 1½ ounces of plain flour, 2 ounces of sugar and 1 teaspoon of powdered cinnamon. Blend these mixtures together and sprinkle evenly over the dough. Bake in a hot oven for about 30 minutes. When cold, cut in fingers. To be eaten fresh.

DORIS LYTTON-TOYE 1946

JUMBLES

Warm 2 ounces of golden syrup, 2 ounces of demerara sugar and ½ teaspoon of powdered ginger in a pan until just melted. Sift in 2 ounces of plain flour, then stir in ½ teaspoon of lemon juice. Grease a baking sheet and drop teaspoons of the mixture thereupon, far apart. Cook in a moderate oven for about 15 minutes. Lift out separately and press round a rolling pin. Store in an airtight tin.

DORIS LYTTON-TOYE 1948

Norman Eales 1965

ALMOND MACAROONS

2 egg whites
2½ oz sugar
2½ oz almonds, shelled, blanched and peeled
lemon juice

Whisk the egg whites until stiff, then fold in the sugar and almonds which have been cut into thin strips. Place the bowl over steam and stir briskly until the mixture is of a thick and rather stiff consistency. Remove from the fire and continue stirring until cool. Add a few drops of lemon juice. Scoop out small balls with a teaspoon and bake on a well-greased and floured baking sheet until they are golden brown (Gas Regulo ½, 250°F).

PETER PIRBRIGHT AND GRETEL BEER 1949

184

NUT PASTRIES

white water icing to decorate
PASTRY
4 oz margarine
6 oz self-raising flour
2 oz sugar
FILLING
2 oz ground nuts
2 oz sugar
½ tbsp grated orange or lemon rind
1 tbsp biscuit or cake crumbs
a little milk
a few drops of rum

Rub the margarine into the flour, add the sugar and knead to a dough, adding a little water if necessary. Cover with a cloth and leave for 30 minutes. Roll out thinly, cut into rounds and line the greased and floured tartlet tins with this pastry. Bake 'blind' on Gas Regulo 5, 375°F.

For the filling, blend together all the ingredients to a smooth paste: fill the tartlets with this mixture and cover with thin white water icing.

PETER PIRBRIGHT AND GRETEL BEER 1949

BANANA BRAN COOKIES

Cream ⅝ cup of butter with 1 cup of light brown sugar and ½ cup of granulated sugar. Add a well-beaten egg and 2 well-mashed bananas. Mix in ½ cup of bran and 1 teaspoon of vanilla. Next sift 1½ cups of plain flour with 2 teaspoons of baking powder and a pinch of salt. Add to the first mixture. Stir well, then drop the mixture from a teaspoon on to well-buttered cookie tins and bake for 10 minutes in a moderately hot oven (Gas Regulo 6, 400°F).

BERYL GOULD-MARKS 1954

CHOCOLATE CHIP COOKIES

I like these made very thin and lacy, with bits of good plain chocolate instead of chocolate chips and without nuts.

3 oz unsalted butter
3 oz caster sugar, sifted
2 oz light brown sugar
1 egg, beaten
6 oz self-raising flour, sifted
pinch of salt
2 oz plain chocolate or chocolate chips
2 oz chopped pecans or walnuts (optional)

Cream the butter, add the sifted sugar and brown sugar, and cream again. Stir in the beaten egg, then the sifted flour and a pinch of salt. If using plain chocolate, chop it in a blender or food processor; it can be done by hand but tends to fly over the room. Stir the little bits of chocolate (or the chocolate chips) into the mixture, with the chopped pecans or walnuts, if using.

Using 2 teaspoons, drop tiny mounds of the dough – about ½ teaspoon only – on to oiled baking sheets. Leave 1 inch between them, as they spread on baking. Bake near the top of the oven, at Gas Mark 5, 375°F, for 12-15 minutes, or until golden brown. Take them out of the oven and allow to cool for a moment or two only before lifting off the tin. If left until completely cool they will break. Lay them on a wire rack. If they have run together, they will break apart quite easily as they cool. Store in the refrigerator if not to be eaten immediately, or freeze. Makes about 40 cookies.

ARABELLA BOXER 1982

GINGER THINS

These are exquisite biscuits for eating either at teatime or with a dessert. They are delicious with cold apple purée, ice cream, or fruit fools.

4 oz flour, sifted
¾ tsp ground ginger
4 oz butter, cut in pieces
4 oz light brown sugar
1 heaped tbsp golden syrup
1 heaped tbsp treacle
2 tbsp cream

Sift the flour with the ginger and rub in the butter. Add the sugar and rub all together lightly. Warm the syrup and treacle (use double quantities of one if this is simpler), and stir in the cream. Mix with the dry ingredients, beating well with a wooden spoon until well mixed. Drop in small teaspoonful on to a greased baking sheet, leaving about 2 inches between them. Bake for about 8 minutes at Gas Mark 4, 350°F, until cooked in the centre and lightly coloured – but not burnt – round the edges.

Remove the biscuits from the oven and leave to cool for 2-3 minutes before lifting with a palette knife on to a flat surface. They will become crisp on cooling. If used for serving with dessert, you may prefer to make larger biscuits, using a heaped teaspoon of dough, and leaving more space between them. As they cool, lay them over a greased rolling pin so that they harden in a curved shape, like *tuiles d'amandes*.

Note: They are best eaten on the day they are made, but the dough can be made in advance, and kept in the refrigerator or the freezer. It must be brought back to room temperature before use.

ARABELLA BOXER 1985

HOT BUTTERED SCONES

Wash and dry well ½ cup of currants. Mix and sift together 2 cups of plain flour with 4 level teaspoons of baking powder, ¾ teaspoon of salt and 8 teaspoons of granulated sugar. Work into this 4 tablespoons of salted butter. Add the currants and then mix to a dough with about ⅔ cup of milk. Divide into 6 parts, toss each piece on to a lightly floured board and pat into a circle 4 inches wide and ½ inch thick. Bake on a hot griddle which has been very well buttered. When delicately brown on one side, turn with a pancake turner. When cooked through, split and toast under a hot flame, spread with creamed butter and serve on a napkin.

JUNE PLATT 1935

SINGIN' HINNY

Our nurse used to make this and serve it hot, split and buttered.

6 oz plain flour
1 oz ground rice
a pinch of salt
1 oz sugar
1 heaped tsp baking powder
1 oz currants
1 oz lard
milk to mix

Switch on an electric hotplate or gridiron full for 3 minutes, then turn to low. Sieve the dry ingredients, add the currants and rub in the lard. Mix to a soft but not sticky dough with the milk. Roll out very lightly to ¼-inch thickness, cut into a round and then into quarters. Cook till brown on one side, then turn, and cook the other side (about 20 minutes altogether).

PAMELA PAIN 1942

John Minton 1946

BLINI

1 lb plain flour
1 oz fresh yeast
1½ pts milk
3 eggs
salt
butter to grease

Sift the flour. Dissolve the yeast in about ½ pint tepid milk in a bowl, then add just enough flour to make a very thick batter. Cover the bowl with a cloth and leave in a warm place for about 2 hours.

Take the chill off the remaining milk and beat about half of it into the batter, together with the yolks of the eggs, then add enough flour to make the mixture about the consistency of pancake batter, then add a little more milk and then more flour until one or the other is used up while the batter remains at the right pancake consistency. Set this aside for about 1½ hours. Whisk the egg whites stiff, beat the batter again thoroughly, then fold in the egg whites and add salt to taste. Grease, sparingly, the smallest frying pan you've got with butter and drop in just enough batter to cover the bottom with a wafer-like layer. Cook until brown underneath, then turn and brown the other side.

Serve with caviar in a bowl set on crushed ice (or with smoked salmon or trout), sieved yolks and chopped whites of hard-boiled eggs, chopped parsley and onion, slices of lemon and a bowl of sour double cream. Serves 10 to 12.

CHRIS HASKETT-SMITH 1961

BRIOCHE

To make the batter for the *brioche*, use, say, one pound of flour and pass it through a fine sieve, take a quarter of it and make a heap on the board. Melt, in the middle, a small quantity of yeast with lukewarm water; mix it gradually with the flour, adding water if necessary, so as to make a fairly firm mixture. Put it aside in a bowl, and keep it fairly warm.

Work the rest of the pound of flour with a pinch of salt, two of sugar, a quarter of a pound of butter (well worked) and six eggs. Mix and beat this well for about twenty minutes on the board. Flatten it, add the yeast and flour mixture previously put aside, and put the whole thing away in a bowl sprinkled with flour; keep it at the same slightly warm temperature for six or seven hours; it should rise to double its original size. Then put it once more on the board, work it a little while, let it rest a few minutes, and bake your *brioche* in a very hot oven, the crown shape being the best for your purpose.

BOULESTIN 1924

IRISH BREAD

1 lb self-raising flour
14 oz wholemeal flour
2 oz rolled or medium oats
2 tsp bicarbonate of soda
1 tsp cream of tartar
2 tsp salt
½ pt whey or sour milk

Sieve the dry ingredients and mix well together, then add the liquid and stir quickly with a knife. Gather together into a lump and knead slightly; flour well and either cut in half or shape into a long roll and place on a floured baking sheet. Bake for 45 minutes in a moderately hot oven (Gas Regulo 6, 400°F).

PAMELA PAIN 1942

SAFFRON BREAD

1 lb white bread flour
1½ tsp salt
½ oz fresh yeast
4 tbsp tepid water
¼ pt milk
2 packets saffron
2 eggs

Put the flour in a warm bowl with the salt. Put the yeast in a cup with the water and leave it in a warm place for 10 minutes. Heat the milk with the saffron to boiling point, then leave to cool until lukewarm. Beat the eggs. Make a well in the flour, pour in the yeast mixture, cover with flour, then add the saffron milk and the beaten eggs. Mix well with a wooden spoon, adding a little extra milk or water if needed. Turn out and knead for about 5 minutes. Return to the bowl, cover with a cloth and leave for 1 hour to rise.

Punch down, turn out and knead it again for 4-5 minutes. Turn into a buttered loaf tin and leave to rise again for 45 minutes. For a shiny crust, brush with a beaten egg yolk, but this is purely optional. Bake for 30 minutes at Gas Mark 5, 375°F. It emerges a beautiful golden yellow, and is delicious with *soupe au pistou*, or mixed vegetable dishes, hot or cold. Serves 6 to 8.

ARABELLA BOXER 1975

COUNTRY LOAF

Take 4 pounds of coarse ground whole-wheat flour, 5 dessertspoons of dark brown sugar and 2 dessertspoons of salt and mix them in a large bowl. Crumble 2 good knobs of fresh yeast into a pint mug with 1 dessertspoon of dark brown sugar, add warm water and stir until both are dissolved. Pour the solution into the dry mixture and add 1 more pint of warm water and stir until you have a good dough that does not stick to the bowl. The amount of water needed varies with the flour used and more may

Norman Parkinson 1965

be required. When the dough makes a good ball, break it in two and put each half in a well-buttered bread tin. Leave to rise under a cloth in a warm place out of all draught. When the loaves have risen under the cloth (30-45 minutes), put them into an oven preheated to Gas Mark 5, 375°F, and bake for about 1 hour 15 minutes. A meat skewer pushed into the loaf should come out clean when the bread is done. When the loaves are taken from the oven they should be put upside down on a rack for 10 minutes or so, after which time the tins should lift off without difficulty. The loaves should be left to cool for at least 2 hours before any attempt is made to slice them.

ANTHONY WEST 1973

John Minton

POTATO BREAD

This is probably my favourite of all the home-made breads. I find it equally good eaten fresh, or toasted the following day.

½ oz fresh yeast
2 tbsp sugar
5 tbsp warm water
4 fl oz milk
3 oz butter
1½ tsp sea salt
1 egg, beaten
3 oz freshly mashed potato
12 oz unbleached white flour

Crumble the yeast into a cup with 1 teaspoon of sugar and all the warm water. Put in a warm place for 10 minutes. Heat the milk until lukewarm, then add the butter cut in small bits, off the heat. Pour the yeast into a large bowl, adding the milk and half-melted butter. Stir in the remaining sugar with the salt and beaten egg. Then add the warm mashed potato, beating well. Add the flour, a cup at a time. When it all clings together, turn out on a floured surface and knead for 4-5 minutes, adding the remaining flour as needed. When it is smooth, put it back in the clean bowl which you have rubbed with butter. Leave in a warm place, covered, for about 1½ hours, or until doubled in size.

Punch down, turn out and knead again briefly. Then lay in a buttered loaf tin, cover again, and leave for about 45 minutes, or until the dough has risen to fill the tin. Then bake for 45 minutes at Gas Mark 5, 375°F. Cool on a wire rack before eating.
Note: This bread makes a good base for poached or fried eggs, and is as good with sweet things like jam and marmalade as it is with cheese.

ARABELLA BOXER 1988

MUFFIN BREAD

This is a perfect teatime food; much simpler to make than muffins, it is absolutely delicious toasted, either alone, or as a base for poached eggs, or for eggs Benedict.

½ oz fresh yeast
½ tbsp sugar
4 tbsp warm water
14 oz unbleached white bread flour
1 tsp sea salt
⅛ tsp baking powder
8 fl oz milk

Prove the yeast in a cup with the sugar and warm water. Put half the flour in a large warm bowl with the salt and baking powder. Heat the milk until it is very warm, about 120°F, as if making yoghurt. Pour on to the flour and mix, adding the yeast mixture. Then stir in the remaining flour until the right consistency is reached (you may not need to use all the flour). When you have a soft dough, form into a loaf shape and turn into a buttered loaf tin roughly 9 by 4 inches. Leave to rise for 45 minutes in a warm place, then bake for 45 minutes at Gas Mark 6, 400°F. Cool on a rack. Eat fresh the same day, or toasted the following day.

ARABELLA BOXER 1982

CORN BREAD

4 oz cornmeal (polenta)
4 oz plain flour
4 tsp baking powder
1 tsp salt
2 tsp sugar
1 large egg
8 fl oz milk
2 oz butter, melted

Sift all the dry ingredients into a large bowl. Beat the egg with the milk and melted butter, and stir into the dry ingredients. Beat quickly and lightly and pour into a shallow well-buttered tin, about 8 inches square by 1½ inches deep. Bake for 35 minutes at Gas Mark 6, 400°F, until puffed up and golden brown. Serve while still warm, if possible, cut into squares. Makes 9 squares. *Note:* Any left uneaten makes an excellent stuffing for a roast chicken, turkey, or game bird.

ARABELLA BOXER 1987

Tessa Traeger 1984

INDEX

aïoli, 117
almond macaroons, 184
anchovy:
 ansjovisoga, 70
 Janssons frestelse, 70
apple:
 buttered apples, 171
 and celery salad, 124
 cheese and apple tart, 47
 and chestnut salad, 132
 ginger apple crumble, 172
 soup, 12
artichokes:
 artichauts à la barigoule, 140
 with green mayonnaise, 140
 à la polita, 140
asparagus, 140
 tips à la française, 143
aubergine:
 aubergines sautées, 143
 moussaka, 90
 salad, 132

banana:
 banana bran cookies, 185
 banana Brazil nut cream pie, 164
 bananes créole, 162
 waffles, 183
 whisky bananas, 169
beans:
 bean shoot salad, 135
 Boston baked, 144
 cassoulet, 86
 Chinese green, 143
 fèves maître d'hôtel, 143
 gratin de haricots verts, 143
 haricots mangetout, 144
 haricots rouges bourguignonne, 144
 Hopping John, 144
 Mexican, 145
 purée de haricots blancs, 144
 string bean salad, 128
beef:
 boeuf en daube froid, 74
 boeuf stroganoff, 77
 braised, with glazed vegetables, 79
 curried, 75
 grilled steak with roquefort butter, 77
 langue de boeuf, 92
 olives, 80
 poached sirloin steak, 79
 ragoût de boeuf, 74
 roast wing rib, 75
 shepherd's pie, 78
 souvlakia, 77
 steak with coriander, 78

steak, kidney and mushroom pudding, 44
steak and kidney stew, 79
stew, 74
beetroot:
 Harvard beets, 146
 salad, 126
blini, 186
bouillabaisse, 16
bread, 186-8
bream in aspic, 52
brioche, 186
Brussels sprouts:
 appetizer, 146
 chestnut purée with, 151
 choux de Bruxelles à l'italienne, 146

cabbage:
 choux à la crème, 146
 red cabbage, 146
 Savoy cabbage, 146
cake:
 see also torte
 baby's first birthday, 177
 chocolate almond, 178
 frothy orange, 179
 fruit, 183
 honey, 178
 lemon four-quarters, 182
 pain de Gênes, 176
 plumkager, 177
 punch gâteau, 179
 Scotch coffee, 182
 walnut and lemon meringue, 182
 walnut mocha, 176
 wedding, 176
 white plum, 176
carp, stuffed, 52
carrot:
 carrot, fennel and celery salad, 136
 carrottes Vichy, 148
 flan, 42
 ring mould, 148
cassoulet, 86
castle puddings, 166
cauliflower:
 beignets de choufleur, 149
 with cream sauce and buttered crumbs, 149
 curried, 149
 salad, 130
celery, braised, 151
cheese:
 aigrettes, 34
 and apple tart, 47
 d'Artois, 35
 cheese, potato and onion pie, 36

Chippenham cheese savoury, 33
 custard, 36
 dreams, 36
 fondues, 33, 34
 French macaroni cheese, 35
 freshly herbed cream cheese, 35
 fromage à la truffe, 34
 gaufrettes fromagées, 34
 macaroni cheese, 36
 mozzarella allo spiedo, 34
 omelette au fromage, 29
 salad, iced, 132
 soufflé, 30
 straws, 36
 Welsh rarebit, 35
chestnut purée with Brussels sprouts, 151
chicken:
 with chervil sauce, 100
 coq au vin, 96
 flambé, 99
 liver pâté, 40
 okra gumbo, 98
 paprika (gulyas), 74
 pie Massachusetts, 44
 with piquant tunny fish sauce, 99
 poulet Bamako, 100
 poulet bonne femme, 98
 poulet portugaise, 98
 Strabane groundnut and chicken casserole, 99
 truffled chicken mousse, 99
chicory:
 braised, with mushroom sauce, 151
 gratin of endives au jambon, 151
chocolate chip cookies, 185
chocolate soufflé, 164
Christmas poultry, 101-2
cider biscuits, 183
cod:
 baked, 57
 brochettes of cod and sole with mustard sauce, 56
 brown nut fish, 56
 chowder, 56
 fillets de cabillaud marinée, 56
coffee crumble, 184
coq au vin, 96
corn batter cakes, 152
corn bread, 188
Cornish pasties, 48
courgette, 152
couscous, vegetable, 158
crab:
 jambalaya, 68
 Maryland crab soup, 17
 mousse, 68

crayfish, feuilleté of, 49
crème brûlée, 166
crème, petits pots de, 166
crêpes:
 à l'anis, 163
 Suzette, 162
croque monsieur, 33
croquembouche, 180
crumbles, 172, 184
cucumber:
 concombres farcis, 152
 pea and cucumber soup, 13
 Siamese cucumber and prawns, 67
curried dishes, 32, 63, 75, 149
custard sauce, creamy, 120

duck:
 braised, 103
 canard au raisins, 103
 Canton steamed duck and parsnip, 102
 roast, with sauce rouennaise, 102

eggs:
 in aspic, 26
 curried, 32
 egg croquettes, 32
 egg sauce, 114
 île flottante, 162
 oeufs à la diable, 26
 oeufs à l'estragon, 32
 oeufs à l'indienne, 28
 oeufs au caviar, 32
 oeufs Bercy, 26
 oeufs Elizabeth, 28
 omelette Arnold Bennett, 26
 omelette aux coquilles St Jacques, 32
 omelettes to order, 29
 pipérade, 26
 poached, à la bourguignonne, 28
 scrambled, with anchovies, 26
 soufflés, 30
Eve's pudding, 171

fennel:
 braised, 153
 fennel, onion or leeks, with cheese, 153
fish, 52-70
 see also bream, cod etc.
fish soups, 15-17
flan:
 carrot 42
 18th century apple cream, 170
 flan de la duchesse, 167
flapjacks, 184

flounders in red wine. 62
fondues. 33, 34

game. 104-8
  pudding. 48
  small game pies. 47
  stuffings for. 121
  terrine. 40
gaufrettes fromagées. 34
gazpacho. 18
gentleman's pudding. 164
ginger apple crumble. 172
ginger thins. 185
gingerbread. 183
goose. Christmas. 102
goulash (gulyas). 74
grapefruit, orange and avocado
  salad. 130
green grapes caramel. 169
grouse. roast. 104
guacamole. 143
guinea fowl with morels sauce. 105

haddock:
  creamed finnan haddies. 70
  fish pie. 57
  kedgeree. 64
  New England fish chowder. 15
  omelette Arnold Bennett. 26
  salad. 132
halibut:
  soufflé. 58
  strachur. 58
ham:
  boiled. baked with brown sugar
    and cloves. 81
  gratins. 81. 151
  ham loaf. 80
  potted. 81
hare:
  in cream sauce. 108
  jugged. 107
hash. red flannel. 74
herrings:
  baked. with apples and
    potatoes. 59
  soused. 59
Holyrood pudding. 167

ice cream:
  cappuccino. 172
  orange. 169
  sweet sauces for. 120

kebabs. turbot. 63
kedgeree. 64
kidney:
  kidneys sautéd in white wine. 92
  pancakes. 91
  rognoncini trifolati. 92
  steak and kidney stew. 79
  steak. kidney and mushroom
    pudding. 44
kipper mousse. 70
kohlrabi. 130

lamb:
  a modified cassoulet. 86

côtelettes d'agneau au four. 85
épaule de mouton aux navets.
  85
Lancashire hot-pot. 85
navarin printanier. 84
roast rack of lamb with garlic
  sauce. 86
selle d'agneau farcie. 85
souvlakia. 77
tagine. 86
Trader Vic's Indonesian lamb.
  86
langue de boeuf à la romaine. 92
leeks:
  fennel. onion or leeks with
    cheese. 153
  poireaux au gratin. 153
  quiche aux poireaux. 47
lemon:
  four-quarters. 182
  soufflé. cold. 167
  sponge. 178
  wafers. 183
  and white wine cream. 167
lentil soup with duck skin. 23
lettuce:
  laitues au four. 153
liver:
  blender liver terrine. 41
  calves' liver in cream. 91
  chicken liver pâté. 40
lobster:
  Fitz's lobster risotto. 65
  homard au champagne. 64
  homard frappé. 65
  Thermidor. 64

macaroni cheese. 35. 36
macaroni salad Lucullus. 130
macaroons. almond. 184
mango mousse. cold. with passion
  fruit. 172
marrow:
  in cream sauce. 153
  gratinée. 153
  vegetable marrow soup. 12
mayonnaise. 118
meat. 74-93
  salad. 133
mousse:
  crab. 68
  kipper. 70
  mango. cold. with passion fruit.
    172
  truffled chicken. 99
mushroom:
  fresh pasta with game sauce and
    wild mushrooms. 106
  Ivanhoe mushrooms. 154
  mushrooms à la grecque. 154
  omelette aux champignons. 29
  pudding. 154
  sauce. 114
  soup. 12
  steak. kidney and mushroom
    pudding. 44
  and sweet pepper salad. 135
mussels:

au gratin. 67
moules marinière. 66
Sheffield Island bisque. 66
soupe aux moules. 17

nut pastries. 185

omelettes. 26. 29. 32
onion:
  baked onions. 154
  fennel. onion or leeks with
    cheese. 153
  French onion soup. 14
osso buco. Marina's 92
oxtail:
  braised. 93
  oxtail ragout. 91
oyster:
  cream sauce. 114
  huîtres au gratin. 67
  salad. 132

parsley sauce. 113
parsnip:
  with Canton steamed duck. 102
  fritters. 154
partridge:
  perdreaux poêlés. 104
pasta. fresh. with game sauce and
  wild mushrooms. 106
pâtés. 40
pear:
  poires au caramel. 162
peas:
  à la française. 156
  pea soups. 12. 13. 22
  petits pois au lard. 156
  purée St Germain. 156
pepper-pot. 74
peppers:
  green peppers. 156
  pipérade. 26
  stuffed green peppers. 156
pheasants in cream. 104
pie:
  American chicken. 42
  cheese. potato and onion. 36
  chicken and ham. 45
  chicken pie Massachusetts. 44
  Cornish pasties. 48
  feuilleté of crayfish. 49
  fish. 57
  individual pork. 49
  shepherd's. 78
  small game. 47
  squab. 42
pigeons. braised. 104
pineapple créole. 164
pipérade. 26
plum pudding. 163
plum sauce. 117
poisson farci au vin blanc. 52
pork:
  cold crown roast of pork. 82
  côtes de porc with rosemary. 83
  à la flamande. 82
  individual pork pie. 49
  loin of pork with prunes. 83

pork chops with cheese. 83
roast loin of pork with wine
  and herbs. 83
potato:
  bread. 188
  cheese. potato and onion pie.
    36
  pommes de terre château. 157
  pommes frites paysan. 156
  provincial potatoes. 157
  puffkins. 157
  salads. 129
  salade lorraine. 125
  soup. 20
  sweet potatoes. 157
  watercress and potato soup. 12
poultry. 96-103
  stuffings for. 121
prawn:
  bisque. 17
  grilled Dublin prawns. 68
  rice with prawns and cream
    sauce. 68
  Siamese cucumber and prawns.
    67
  soup. 16
prunes:
  loin of pork with prunes. 83
  pruneaux au whisky. 162
pudding:
  baked jam rolypoly. 171
  castle puddings. 166
  Eve's. 171
  game. 48
  gentleman's. 164
  Holyrood. 167
  plum. 163
  queen of puddings. 171
  Regency. 169
  steak. kidney and mushroom.
    44
pumpkin soup. American. 12
purés:
  chestnut. with Brussels sprouts.
    151
  mixed root vegetable. 158
  purée de navets. 158
  purée St Germain. 156
  watercress. 158

queen of puddings. 171
quiche:
  quiche aux poireaux. 47
  quiche lorraine. 45

rabbit. 107
  pâté vendéen. 40
ragoût de veau. 88
ragoût landais. 158
raspberry:
  Bavarian cream. 169
  rodgrød med fløde. 170
red cabbage. 146
red currant:
  rodgrød me fløde. 170
red mullet:
  rougets grillés. 60
  rougets provençale 59

Regency pudding, 169
rehbraten, 108
rice with prawns and cream sauce,
    68
ris de veau au citron vert, 92
risotto, Fitz's lobster, 65
Rutilio's rognoncini trifolati, 92

salad:
    apple and chestnut, 132
    aubergine, 132
    bean shoot, 135
    beetroot, 126
    Burmese, 133
    carrot, fennel and celery, 136
    cauliflower, 130
    celeriac, 126
    celery, with mustard dressing,
        126
    cooked mixed vegetable, 136
    cowslip, 130
    cucumber, tomato and radish,
        128
    dandelion, 130
    grapefruit, orange and avocado,
        130
    green walnut, 130
    haddock, 132
    iced cheese, 132
    jellied spinach, 126
    Jerusalem artichoke and
        watercress, 135
    kohlrabi, 130
    lamb's lettuce and tomato, 136
    macaroni salad Lucullus, 130
    meat, 133
    mushroom and sweet pepper,
        135
    orange, lettuce and pepper, 136
    oyster, 132
    Palm Beach, 126
    potato, 129
    rice, 135
    Romaine salad, with hard-boiled
        egg dressing, 128
    salade algérienne, 124
    salade Alonzo, 126
    salade aux fines herbes, 129
    salade Carmen, 125
    salade de coeurs de laitues aux
        pointes d'asperges, 125
    salade de concombres aux oeufs
        durs, 124
    salade Defour, 126
    salade au lard, 125
    salade lorraine, 125
    salade parisienne, 126
    salade rhénane, 124
    string bean, 128
    sunshine, 130
    tomato, avocado and
        mozzarella, 136
    tomato and cabbage slaw, 133
    tuna and flageolet, 135
    Waldorf, 133
    watercress, 130
    wilted, 126
    winter, 132

world's best, 126
young raw, 130
salmis of game with celery and
    tarragon, 105
salmon:
    brandade de saumon, 53
    galantine de saumon, 53
    kedgeree, 64
sauce:
    aïoli, 117
    creamy custard, 120
    Cumberland, 117
    egg, 114
    foamy yellow, 118
    mushroom, 114
    mustard and dill, 118
    Norwegian, 113
    oyster cream, 114
    parsley, 113
    plum, 117
    rainbow sauces of Toulouse-
        Lautrec, 115
    rich tomato, 117
    sauce bâtarde, 113
    sauce béchamel, 112
    sauce bordelaise, 112
    sauce espagnole, 112
    sauce flamande, 112
    sauce hollandaise, 112
    sauce mousseline, 112
    Signor Parmigiani's spaghetti,
        114
    simple white, 113
    sweet sauce for ice cream,
        120
scallops:
    coquilles St Jacques, 69
    fried, with tartar sauce, 69
    omelette aux coquilles St
        Jacques, 32
    steamed, 70
scones, hot buttered, 186
shepherd's pie, 78
shrimps:
    broiled, 67
    kedgeree, 64
    shrimp soup, 16
Singin' Hinny, 186
sole:
    brochettes of cod and sole with
        mustard sauce, 56
    filets de sole à l'indienne, 62
    filets de sole Dorothée, 60
    paupiettes de sole Elisabeth, 60
    in red wine, 62
    sole bretonne, 60
    sole meunière à l'orange, 62
    sole Monica, 60
sorrel and spinach soup, 13
soufflé, 30
    of cauliflower à la baronne, 149
    cheese, 30
    chocolate, 164
    cold lemon, 167
    halibut, 58
    vanilla, 30
soup:
    American pumpkin, 12

apple, 12
beef broth with cabbage toasts
    and cheese, 20
blender spinach, 13
la bouillabaisse, 16
chestnut, 22
crème sénégale, 22
fish, 15, 16
French onion, 14
gazpacho, 18
lentil, with duck skin, 23
Maryland crab, 17
mushroom, 12
pea, 12, 13, 22
petite marmite, 20
potage de garbanzos, 20
potage rubis, 18
potato, 20
prawn, 16, 17
purée de Ciboure, 20
ribollita, 22
shrimp, 16
soupe de chasse, 20
soupe aux moules, 17
soupe au poisson, 15
spinach, 13
Spitalfield, 19
tomato, 12, 19
vegetable marrow, 12
vichyssoise, 18
watercress and potato, 12
souvlakia, 77
spinach:
    blender spinach soup, 13
    florentine d'épinards, 157
    jellied spinach salad, 126
    pudding, 157
    sorrel and spinach soup, 13
squab:
    pie, 42
    roasted squab with garlic, 106
stew:
    beef, 74
    oxtail ragout, 91
    ragoût de veau, 88
    steak and kidney, 79
strawberries:
    fraises cardinal, 164
stuffings, 121
sweet sauces, 120
sweetbreads:
    ris de veau au citron vert, 92

terrines, 40, 41
thousand island dressing, 117
tomato:
    bisque of tomato and green pea,
        12
    and cabbage slaw, 133
    fried tomatoes, in cream, 157
    rich tomato sauce, 117
    soups, 12, 19
    stuffed tomatoes, 157
    tomato, avocado and mozzarella
        salad, 136
    tomatoes mignonne, 158
tongue:
    langue de boeuf à la romaine, 92

torte:
    biskotten-torte, 179
    nusstorte, 178
    sacher torte, 180
trifle, English, 167
trout:
    fillets in oatmeal, 54
    finger trout meunière, 54
    in red wine, 54
    truites au chablis, 54
truffled chicken mousse, 99
tuna and flageolet salad, 135
tunny fish sauce, chicken with, 99
turbot:
    kebabs, 63
    turbot aux champignons, 63
turkey, 101
    croquettes de dinde, 102
turnips:
    épaule de mouton aux navets,
        85
    purée de navets, 158

vanilla:
    rings, 183
    soufflé, 30
veal:
    aubergine moussaka, 90
    braised veal chops en gelée, 89
    chuletas de ternera a la
        Catalonia, 90
    cotelettes à la milanaise, 89
    côtes de veau paillard, 88
    cutlets in papillotes, 107
    escalopes de veau, 88, 89
    grenadin de veau Elizabeth, 89
    ragoût de veau, 88
    ris de veau au citron vert, 92
    roast veal, 90
    roti de veau braisé, 88
    souvlakia, 77
    veau au citron, 88
    vitello tonnato, 90
vegetables, 140-59
    cooked mixed vegetable salad,
        136
    terrine of vegetables, 41
venison casserole, 108
vichyssoise, 18
vol-au-vents financière, 42

wafers, lemon, 183
waffles, banana, 183
walnut salad, green, 130
watercress:
    and potato soup, 12
    purée of watercress, 158
    salad, 130

zucchini:
    fritti, 152
    ripieni, 152